California's K–12 Public Schools

How Are They Doing?

Stephen J. Carroll, Cathy Krop, Jeremy Arkes,
Peter A. Morrison, Ann Flanagan

Supported by the William and Flora Hewlett Foundation

RAND EDUCATION

The research described in this report was conducted by RAND Education for the William and Flora Hewlett Foundation.

Library of Congress Cataloging-in-Publication Data

California's K–12 public schools : how are they doing? / Stephen J. Carroll ... [et al.].
p. cm.
"MG-186."
Includes bibliographical references.
ISBN 0-8330-3716-1 (pbk. : alk. paper)
1. Public schools—California. 2. Education—California—Evaluation. 3. Educational equalization—California. 4. Education and state—California. I. Carroll, Stephen J., 1940–

LA243.C34 2005
371.01'09794—dc22

2004025761

Published 2005 by the RAND Corporation
1776 Main Street, P.O. Box 2138, Santa Monica, CA 90407-2138
1200 South Hayes Street, Arlington, VA 22202-5050
201 North Craig Street, Suite 202, Pittsburgh, PA 15213-1516
RAND URL: http://www.rand.org/
To order RAND documents or to obtain additional information, contact
Distribution Services: Telephone: (310) 451-7002;
Fax: (310) 451-6915; Email: order@rand.org

Foreword

Jorge Ruiz-de-Velasco and Marshall S. Smith
The William and Flora Hewlett Foundation

This RAND report carefully documents how California's public schools have declined in quality along many important dimensions since the 1970s. Moreover, the investigators report a growing, if somewhat vague, awareness among Californians that the quality of our public schools has slipped both relative to the past, as well as to schools in other states. Yet, despite this growing awareness, it is fair to say that there has been little sense of urgency among voters about the condition of our schools. Even as an enormous revenue shortfall in the spring and summer of 2003 forced state and local districts to make large cuts in school budgets, media and public attention to the problems facing our schools has been scant or localized. The danger now, as in previous budget crises, is that leaders will look for short-term solutions in the hope that the economy turns around quickly enough to keep them from having to make hard reform choices.

Why the complacency at the state level about the quality of our schools? We believe the problem is two fold. First, although the state collects a great deal of data about student performance and the distribution of resources to schools, these data are difficult and costly for reporters and even professional policy analysts to obtain and synthesize. Consequently, journalists and others rely on local reports about individual schools or groups of schools or even about individual students to tell the story. The result is that attentive citizens get a glimpse of heroic teachers and stalwart students struggling to teach and learn in decrepit schools that lack books, certified teachers, or functioning bathrooms. The take-away has often been a recognition that things in some schools are pretty bad, but no real sense of the scope of the crisis across the state in general. In this context, it has been easy for voters and leaders to minimize the situation and to seek only short-term solutions, or to target only the offending schools for improvement.

A second explanation for public complacency involves the old rule that a problem with no apparent solution (or consensus about a solution) is generally not defined as a problem. Instead it comes to be accepted as "just the way things are." In the case of schools there has been little attention paid to the yawning gap between our high curriculum standards and the inadequate resources we provide to schools, in part because state leaders have been divided about the scope of the problem or about the proper solution when the problem is acknowledged. In this ambiguous context only stakeholders (teachers and sometimes parents) get involved in the political fray while the confused public tunes out.

In response, the William and Flora Hewlett Foundation launched a multi-year effort, begun in 2002, to address the two problems we have just outlined. This study is the most recent product in an effort to gather, analyze, and broadly disseminate information about the status of public education across the state. Our hope is that studies like this will provide important context for all those individual investigations of local schools by giving Californians and our policy leaders reliable information about the scope of the challenges facing our teachers and students in virtually every California school district.

We hope that these studies will do more than just define the challenges we face, but will also underscore lessons learned and point the way to solutions and policy options that would have wide appeal to voters and school stakeholders across the state. Indeed some of those solutions have been suggested in the following pages. The report, for example, concludes that California students rank among the lowest in the nation in student achievement, and that this is consistently true across all racial and ethnic groups. One source of this problem is that California's accountability system provides school leaders with an end-of-the-year snapshot of how the school performed, but does not provide data in a time and manner that could be used by teachers and principals for continuous improvement. By contrast, states with similar demographics, like Texas, have made more robust progress on student achievement because their accountability systems provide multiple opportunities for teachers to assess student progress on meeting state standards and, potentially, to make mid-course corrections. Our accountability system needs to move in this direction before we can hope to begin closing the achievement gap with other states.

The RAND report also suggests that the time is right for Californians to rethink Proposition 98, which was intended to establish a minimum funding formula for schools, but which has come to function more as a funding ceiling than a floor. Despite the good intentions behind Proposition 98, the RAND report documents continuing inequalities in the resources—both capital and human—available to schools in poor communities with large concentrations of African-American and Latino students. The inequalities represent a moral—and arguably a state constitutional—problem. The issues are simple to understand. Is it fair that schools with our highest poverty students also have the poorest resources? Should schools that do not have sufficient resources to succeed be held accountable for goals that require success? Shouldn't all students have a fair chance to succeed? These questions are currently before the California courts in *Williams v. State of California*, and it is important that state leaders step up to the plate and find a fair and equitable solution to the legal complaint out of court.

Moreover, the poor performance and often shaky financial condition of schools in even well off communities calls into question the fundamental adequacy of our school finance system across the board. To be fair, over the last seven years the state has attempted to address these problems by decreasing class size, providing money for teacher training, and holding schools accountable for student achievement. The result is that test scores have increased. But even with the gains, in the latest national assessments every group of our students (whites, Asian, Hispanic, and African American) fall below the national average for similar groups in other states. A different approach is needed. Coming up with more effective solutions will be the central charge of the new bipartisan California State Quality of Education Commission. It is our hope that this and other studies will help the fledgling Commission square our school accountability system with a new finance system that together provide the incentives and resources schools really need to help all California students meet the state performance standards.

Preface

As recently as the 1970s, California's public schools were considered to be among the nation's best. Today, however, there is widespread recognition that the schools are no longer top performers. As a consequence, many Californians share a growing sense of alarm about the ineffectiveness of their public education system and the generation of children whose educational needs are not being met.

Researchers at the RAND Corporation examined California's system of kindergarten through grade 12 (K–12) public schools on several dimensions, including student achievement and other student outcomes that schools may influence, as well as school finances, teachers, and facilities. Their goal was to describe the state of California's K–12 public schools, not to pinpoint why schools are in the shape they are or to advocate solutions (except where one seemed obvious from their findings). This descriptive report should be of interest to policymakers at the state and federal levels and to educators, especially in California. Parents may also benefit from the information it provides.

This research was conducted within RAND Education, a division of the RAND Corporation, with support from the William and Flora Hewlett Foundation. The statements made and views expressed are solely the responsibility of the authors.

Contents

Figures

Tables

Summary

As recently as the 1970s, California's public schools were reputed to be excellent. Today, that reputation no longer stands. Instead, there is widespread concern that California's schools have slipped in quality over the years and that they are no longer performing as well as they did previously or as well as schools in other states.

The primary objective of our study was to look closely at California's public system of kindergarten through twelfth grade (K–12) schools in order to provide an accurate, comprehensive picture of the system as it is today. We describe in this report the student population and the schools' resources, including their financial resources, teachers, and facilities. We also describe the schools' outcomes, initially focusing on student academic achievement as measured by standardized tests, and then turning to other outcomes that may be influenced by schools and are not adequately captured in test scores. These include both educational attainment measures—high school graduation and continuation on to college—and a variety of non-academic measures—teenage pregnancy, substance abuse, and juvenile delinquency—on the grounds that the purpose of schooling goes beyond academic achievement to include students' broader preparation for adult success and citizenship.

In looking at the student population, the resources, and the various outcomes, we also analyzed trends and compared California with other states and to the nation as a whole as much as the data would allow. In some cases, the data allowed us to focus broadly on the schools since the 1970s; in other cases, however, the available data limited our analyses. For example, we were able to analyze academic achievement trends only for students through eighth grade and only since 1990, because there are no appropriate data on academic achievement for high school students or for years prior to 1990.

Where the data would allow, we also compared trends and patterns in California to trends and patterns in the four states that are comparable to California in that they had the largest populations of 5–18 year olds (presumably K–12 students) in the nation in 2000. After California, which ranks first in number of school-age children, these four other "most populous" states are Texas, New York, Florida, and Illinois.

K–12 Reforms in California

To place the study in context, we discuss various educational reforms that California has considered and either adopted or rejected. These reforms include school finance reform, class size reduction, charter schools, voucher programs, and California's standards and assessment system. The discussion is intended to provide information on what California has or has not done to reform its K–12 public schools and to serve as a backdrop for the trends reported.

California was the first state to implement comprehensive school finance reform. When it did so, nearly 30 years ago, spending per pupil became significantly more equal across California school districts. However, this reform may also have contributed to lower levels of spending on average, which led to larger class sizes in California's K–12 public schools.

In 1992, California became the second state to enact charter school legislation. As of the 2002–2003 school year, the state's 452 charter schools served about 2.5 percent of all public school students. In fact, California ranks fifth among all states for the highest percentage of public school students enrolled in charter schools.

Two efforts to provide vouchers for private schools, ballot initiatives in the 1993 and 2000 elections, failed. Neither was able to capture more than one-third of the votes in California.

In 1996, California enacted a popular voluntary program to reduce class sizes for grades K–3 and 9. Although this program clearly succeeded in reducing class sizes in grades K–3, the reductions came at substantial expense, and the evidence is mixed on whether the program has improved students' academic achievement. An unintended consequence of this effort was that the state hired many teachers lacking certification in order to meet the requirements for smaller class sizes. In addition, other programs were cut to pay for the additional teachers and to provide the extra classrooms needed. And classes in the nontargeted grades remained large. Finally, despite the class size reduction program, in 2001 California still had the second highest ratio of pupils to teachers in the nation.

California legislated an accountability system in the Public School Accountability Act (PSAA) of 1999. California now tests students in more grades than most states do, but other states test in more subjects and have more-varied types of questions.

California Demographics

California is among the most racially and ethnically diverse states, and racial/ethnic diversity is especially evident among California's youth. Moreover, the racial/ethnic distribution of the state's youth population is rapidly changing. The available data identify K–12 public school enrollments by race/ethnicity for four groups. They show that enrollments are presently 45 percent Hispanic, 34 percent Anglo (non-Hispanic white), 12 percent Asian and other (with "other" being mostly Filipino but also including "Asian and Pacific Islander" and a small number of American Indian), and 8 percent black. The earliest comparable data show that in 1987–1988 (15 years earlier), these percentages were 30 percent Hispanic, 50 percent Anglo, 11 percent Asian and other, and 9 percent black. It is likely that by 2012–2013, the majority of California public school children will be Hispanic.

Furthermore, nearly one in every ten Californians is a recent immigrant—i.e., a foreign-born person who entered the United

States within the past ten years. By comparison, not even one in 20 persons nationally is a recent immigrant. Consequently, California has an abundance of English learners and linguistically isolated households, both of which are disparities that heighten educational costs for affected school districts—English learners by imposing specialized and/or higher per capita staffing needs, and linguistic isolation by hampering two-way communication between schools and parents.

California has within its borders 12.8 percent of the nation's school-age population but only 11.8 percent of the nation's adult population—i.e., potential taxpayers. This means that California taxpayers shoulder disproportionate responsibility for persons of school age.

About one of every five children in California lives in a family whose income is below federally established poverty thresholds. Of the children in California who live in single-mother families, 39.7 percent live in poverty; the corresponding proportion for children living in married-couple families is 12.9. Furthermore, California, at 29.6 percent, trails the nation in the percentage of children living in high-poverty neighborhoods and currently displays a worsening trend.

Child poverty is most prevalent in a handful of counties in California's Central Valley (e.g., Tulare, Fresno, and Madera counties). The level of child poverty places several of these counties among the poorest tenth of the nation's 3,142 counties. Moreover, the continuing geographic redistribution of population within the state will amplify public school enrollment growth in these counties and in counties around Los Angeles. Inevitably, schools in these areas will be particularly strained by enrollment pressure, staffing needs, and the crowding of existing facilities.

School Funding

California has fundamentally transformed its system of public school finance. In 1970, public education in California was primarily locally financed. School districts set their own local property tax rates, subject to the approval of the voters. Districts raised more than half of their total revenues by taxing local property. Now, however, the state controls the vast majority of school district revenues. The school districts currently have few options for raising their own funds. Further, a growing share of education dollars is being distributed as categorical, or restricted, aid, as opposed to "revenue limit," or general purpose, aid. These trends have raised concerns about a decline in local discretion.

Proposition 13, passed by California voters in 1978 (combined with Proposition 98, approved by California voters in 1988), has had significant consequences for K–12 public education funding. In general, K–12 real revenues and expenditures per pupil grew fairly rapidly in California and the United States until the early 1980s, and California's per-pupil spending largely tracked that of the United States. But California fell well behind the other states in the late 1980s. Beginning in the mid-1990s, California steadily added to its education funding, as did other states, with an estimated real growth of 27 percent between 1994–1995 and 2001–2002. However, after several years of more positive finances, California's schools are again confronting the challenges that go with severe budget constraints.

Figure S.1 shows California per-pupil expenditures relative to the national average. As can be seen, spending per pupil went from about $400 above the national average in 1969–1970 to more than $600 below the national average in 1999–2000. Despite recent funding increases for K–12 education, California schools have continued a decade-long pattern of spending well below the national average per student.

California has a relatively high capacity to fund its schools (as measured by per capita personal income) compared with its "effort." Figure S.2 shows public school spending as a percentage of personal income. In the early to mid-1970s, California spent about the same share of its personal income on public education as the rest of the country did, about 4.5 percent. However, in the late 1970s, the share of personal income that Californians devoted to their public schools

Figure S.1
California's K–12 Public School Per-Pupil Spending Relative to the National Average, 1969–1970 to 1999–2000

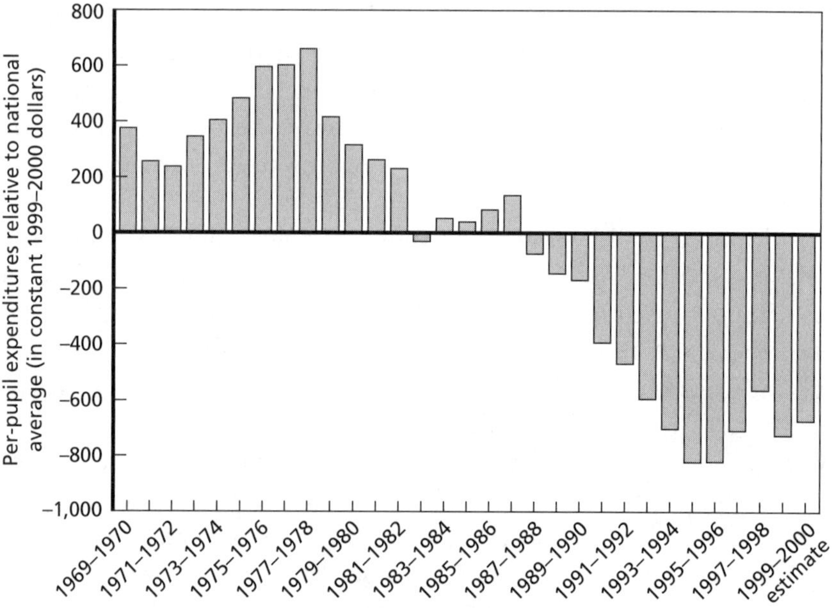

SOURCE: U.S. Department of Education, NCES, Digest of Education Statistics, various years.

RAND *MG186-S.1*

fell to about 1.2 percentage points below the national average and remained well below the national average through 2000.

How does California spend its school budget? Education, especially K–12 education, is labor intensive. About 85 percent of all K–12 expenditures are devoted to personnel salaries and benefits, and close to 40 percent of all expenditures are devoted to teacher salaries and benefits.

Compared to other states, California saw relatively large dollar growth in its school districts' spending on instructional items other than teacher salaries—such as supplies, materials, and contractual services for regular, special, and vocational programs—and on school administration over the 1990s. California per-pupil spending on

Figure S.2
K–12 Public School Spending as a Percentage of Personal Income, California and the United States, 1970 to 2000

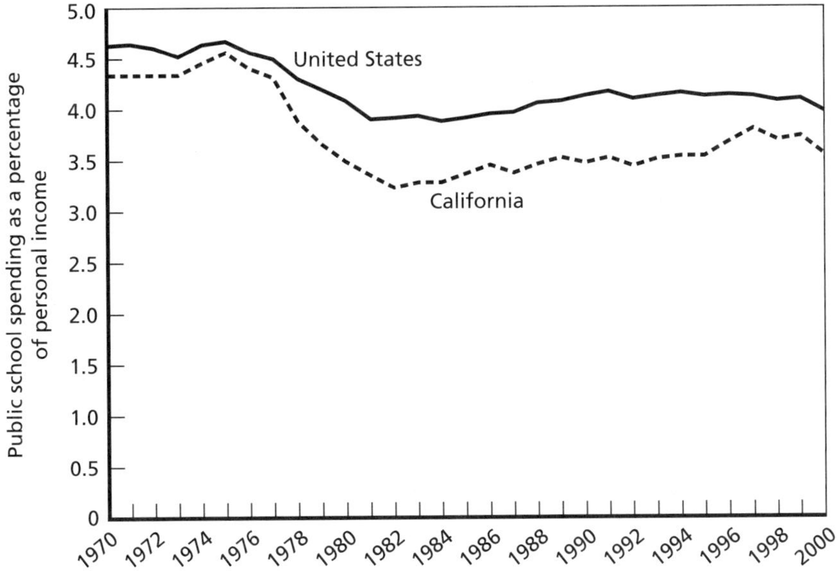

SOURCE: U.S. Bureau of Labor Statistics, and U.S. Department of Education, NCES, Digest of Education Statistics, various years.
RAND *MG186-S.2*

pupil support and general administration has fallen by relatively large dollar amounts compared with spending in other states and represents a relatively small share of total spending.

Teachers

In 1999–2000, California employed 287,000 K–12 teachers, who were paid an average salary of $47,680. Real annual teacher salaries in California in 2000–2001 were on average about the same as they were in 1969–1970, and salaries had remained relatively flat over time. California's average annual teacher salaries have consistently placed California's teachers in the top ten in the nation over time in terms of absolute salaries. If the dollars are adjusted to reflect purchasing power, however, California's teacher salaries are actually lower than the national average. The adjusted average annual salary of $38,845 places California last among the five most populous states and 32nd nationwide.

Figure S.3 displays the pupil-teacher ratios in California and the United States for the past 30 years. Until 1979, these state and national ratios largely tracked each other. In the late 1970s, however, California's pupil-teacher ratio grew, and it remained well above the national average through the 1980s and the early and mid-1990s. In the 1996–1997 school year, California's pupil-teacher ratio began to fall as a reflection of Senate Bill 1777, which was passed in July 1996 to promote class size reduction and provided $650 per student for each K–3 classroom with 20 or fewer students.[1]

Currently, California continues to have the second highest ratio of students per teacher of any state, about 20.9 students to one teacher. The current U.S. average is 16.1.

As a group, California's public K–12 teachers are formally trained, state-certified professionals. However, by 1999–2000, newly employed teachers made up a substantial portion of the teacher workforce—about 15 percent—and the majority of these new teachers were not formally trained and state-certified. In particular, the 1990s saw a growth in those coming into teaching by way of pre-internships, internships, and emergency permits. As a result, the gap between the demand for teachers and the supply of fully credentialed teachers widened over the 1990s.

Teacher qualification requirements are generally lower in California than in other states. For example, 82 percent of school districts in the United States require full standard state certification in the subject to be taught, compared with 46 percent of districts in California. Teachers in California who have not completed all requirements for a credential are concentrated in urban schools, the lowest performing schools, and schools with high percentages of low-income and minority students.

---

[1] The incentive was later increased to $800 per student.

Figure S.3
Pupil-Teacher Ratios in K–12 Public Schools, California and the United States, Fall 1969 to Fall 1999

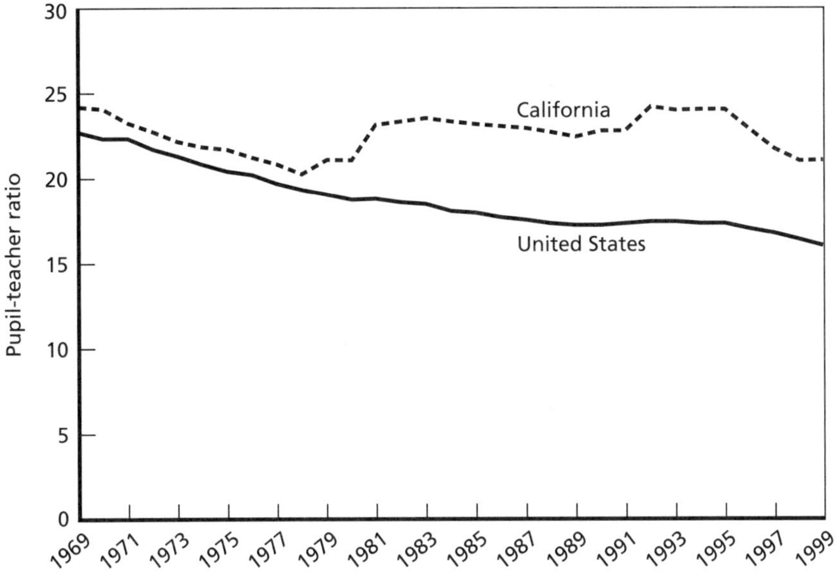

SOURCE: U.S. Department of Education, NCES, Digest of Education Statistics, various years.
RAND *MG186-S.3*

School Facilities

Concerns about K–12 public school facilities in California mirror those at the national level. A national study conducted in 1995 suggested that school facilities had reached the breaking point and that many schools in California were in especially bad condition. Per-pupil construction expenditures in California fell behind those of the United States—ranging from about $5 per pupil below in 1997 to about $235 per pupil below in 1995. Figure S.4 shows the differences in per-pupil construction expenditures between California and the United States when the annual differences between 1991–1992 and 1999–2000 are added up. Adding these differences together shows

Figure S.4
Cumulative Differences in Per-Pupil Construction Expenditures Between 1991–1992 and 1999–2000, California and the United States

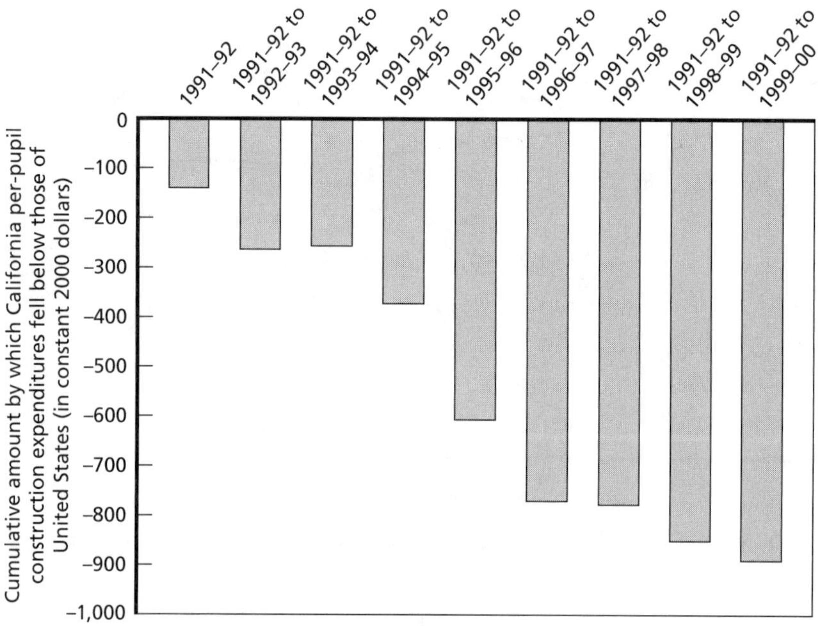

SOURCE: U.S. Census Bureau, Public Education Finances, various years.
RAND *MG186-S.4*

that cumulative California per-pupil spending on construction came to about $890 less per pupil than the national average over that period.

California has made progress in addressing K–12 facility needs, largely due to voter approval of several large state general obligation bonds and a variety of legislative changes that have enabled districts to approve local general obligation bonds. In 2002 alone, voters approved the issuance of over $11 billion in state bonds and close to $10 billion in local bonds. The recent passage of Proposition 39 suggests that progress will continue to be made in addressing the state's facility needs.

However, even with this progress, California still lags the nation and the other large industrial states in terms of the adequacy of the school buildings' environmental and other features, and per-pupil construction expenditures. These inadequacies are concentrated in central cities serving high minority and low-income populations, as well as in rural areas. The court decisions that lessened the financial disparities between low- and high-income districts have pertained primarily to the state's role in providing for instruction, not buildings. The past 25 years have seen a general increase in the state's involvement in facilities-related matters; but districts still contribute to facilities costs, and the extent to which state funding will address the differences between districts is not yet clear.

Student Academic Achievement

A variety of standardized tests have been administered in California. The longest running statewide testing program was the California Assessment Program (CAP), which began in 1973 and ended in 1992. The most recent assessment program, Standardized Testing and Reporting (STAR), continues to collect standardized test score data.

The raw data from California's CAP test are no longer available, making it impossible to track student performance from the beginning of statewide testing in California. A California Department of Education publication in 1986 provided some historical data on student performance in California relative to that in the nation, but these comparative analyses of early California state test scores rely on a set of outdated national norms from several different publishers and are therefore unreliable.

The only assessment that allows for reliable comparative analyses of student academic achievement among states is the National Assessment of Educational Progress (NAEP), a national test administered in all states. Figure S.5 shows the ranking of states by average performance on NAEP tests between 1990 and 2003 (the NAEP scores have been converted to standard deviation units). The data

Figure S.5
Average State Performance on NAEP Reading and Mathematics, Grades 4 and 8, 1990–2003

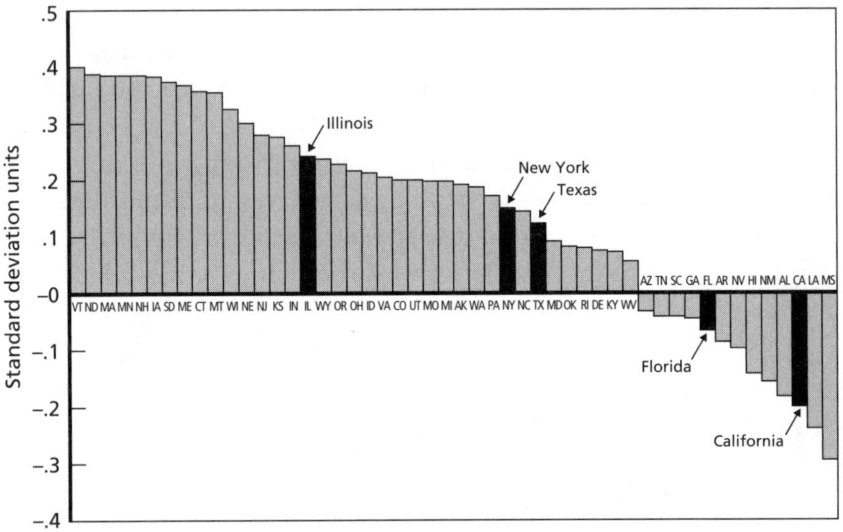

RAND *MG186-S.5*

show that California performs at the bottom end of the distribution of states, just above Louisiana and Mississippi. Also depicted in the figure are the average NAEP scores for the four other most populous states. As can be seen, California falls well below these states in student performance.

Our analyses of NAEP scores show the following:

- California NAEP scores are significantly lower than the average scores in the nation and are the lowest scores of the five most populous states.
- California's low NAEP scores cannot be accounted for by the state's high percentage of minority students. When students' family backgrounds are controlled for, California's scores are the lowest in the nation (–0.18 standard deviations below the mean). This suggests that California's low scores must be in

some part a result of the schools, rather than simply a result of family characteristics in the state.

California is making gains in NAEP scores. California's scores on the 2002 reading test and the 2003 mathematics and reading tests show some relative progress. California's rank using the average score across the 2002 and 2003 NAEP is 45th out of 50 states. California's rank over the period 1990 to 2002 was 48th out of 50 states. This increase in relative standing can be attributed to the large gains made on the 2003 grade 4mathematics NAEP. Between 1996 and 2003, California gains in grade 4 mathematics scores were larger than the gains made in the nation and by any of the four other most populous states. While this is promising, California is still the lowest scoring of the five most populous states.

Other Indicators of Student Progress

Academic achievement is only one measure of how well schools are serving California's young people. Schools can influence (with health education, counseling, and after-school programs, for example) educational attainment outcomes such as high school graduation and college continuation, as well as behavioral outcomes, such as teenage pregnancy, substance abuse, and juvenile delinquency.

Relative to other states, California has a low rate of students continuing on to college, but California's trends for high school graduation are favorable compared to those of other states.

The average pregnancy rate for 15–17 year olds is higher in California (9.5 percent per year) than in any state except the District of Columbia. However, the teenage pregnancy rate is declining faster in California than in most states, even when racial/ethnic differences are adjusted for.

California teenagers compare favorably to teenagers in other states with respect to cigarette and alcohol use and property crime arrests. And when the racial/ethnic composition of the states is adjusted for, California keeps its strong marks, retaining its low rates of cigarette and alcohol use and property crime arrests, and it ranks well with respect to arrests for violent crimes as well.

Conclusions

Californians were once proud of their state's public K–12 education system, but there have been signs in the last few decades that the system has slipped badly relative to its own past performance and that of other states' school systems. We found reason to be concerned about California's public K–12 schools. The results are not uniformly discouraging; California's schools compare favorably to those in other states in some respects. But overall, the comparisons are unfavorable to California more often than not. And in many instances, the results support the impression that California's relative standing in the nation has declined over the last three decades, and especially since the finance reform legislation in the 1970s.

California's demography presents extraordinary challenges to public education and it may be the case that these challenges cannot be effectively met unless the state's K–12 system is funded at relatively high levels. However, California school districts have experienced comparatively low levels of funding compared to funding in most other states. California's schools have been further stressed by extreme fluctuations in real spending per pupil. These relatively low funding levels in California's K–12 schools reflect comparatively low effort relative to the state's capacity.

The comparatively low funding afforded K–12 public education in California can be seen in the resources the schools are able to make available to their students. A substantial portion of the state's teachers are not fully qualified and state certified. California continues to have the second highest pupil-teacher ratio of any state. And despite substantial progress in dealing with school facilities over the past 10 years, California continues to lag the nation in addressing K–12 facility needs.

The combination of a student population with relatively great needs, relatively low funding levels, and relatively inadequate resources may have contributed to California's comparatively low levels of student academic achievement. California NAEP scores are at the bottom of the distribution of participating states; California's minorities' scores are particularly low. There is, however, a bright spot: California is making statistically significant annual gains in mathematics scores.

California students' nonacademic outcomes present a mixed picture. California lags other states in terms of high school graduation rates but is catching up. California generally lags other states in college continuation and is falling further behind. Teenage pregnancy rates are much higher in California than in most other states, but they are rapidly decreasing. And California is roughly similar to other states in the rates of substance abuse and teenage crime arrests.

Acknowledgments

We are grateful to the William and Flora Hewlett Foundation, and particularly to Marshall Smith, for supporting this work.

We are greatly indebted to RAND Education colleagues Brian Gill, Cassandra Guarino, Sue Bodilly, and Sheila Kirby, who carefully reviewed earlier drafts of this report and whose comprehensive and constructive criticism improved the final product immensely. We also thank RAND Research Communicator Shelley Wiseman, who worked closely with the authors. Finally, we are grateful to Mary Wrazen in RAND's Publications Department and to Christopher Dirks for improving the presentation of the material in this report.

CHAPTER ONE

Background, Scope, and Organization

Californians were once proud of their state's public kindergarten through twelfth grade (K–12) education system, but in the last few decades they have seen signs that the system may be slipping relative to other states' systems and to its own past performance. Both policymakers and the general public have voiced serious concerns about the condition and performance of California's schools.

In 1999, the California legislature evidenced the extent of these concerns when it passed California Senate Concurrent Resolution 29,[1] which established a joint committee to develop a "Master Plan for Education for California." The resulting Plan, published in 2003,[2] addresses all levels of education in California: preschool, K–12, adult, and postsecondary. However, the committee was clearly primarily concerned with the performance of the state's K–12 system. The Introduction to the Master Plan observes: "The sobering reality of California's education system is that too few schools can now provide the conditions in which the state can fairly ask students to learn to the highest standards, let alone prepare themselves to meet their future learning needs."[3] The Introduction then goes on to list facts about the educational performance of the California system, most of

[1] Senate Concurrent Resolution No. 29, Statutes and Amendments to the Codes, Chapter 43, filed with Secretary of State, May 27, 1999.

[2] See http://www.sen.ca.gov/masterplan.

[3] http://www.sen.ca.gov/ftp/sen/committee/joint/master_plan/_home/020909_final_master_plan_documents/020909_final_mp_intro.pdf, p. 1.

which pertain more specifically to the effectiveness of the K–12 system. It concludes: "These data are indicative of the huge gap that exists between what many Californians need from their educational system and what they are actually receiving."[4]

California policymakers and educators are also increasingly concerned about the state of California's public schools in light of federal legislation called the No Child Left Behind Act of 2001 (NCLB). NCLB emphasizes accountability based on student test results, establishes minimum standards for teacher quality, and imposes sanctions on states and districts that fail to comply with NCLB requirements.

This Study

The study presented in this report describes California's current K–12 public education system. Our objective is to provide information to those concerned with the system. We focus broadly on California schools, grades K–12, analyzing trends within California and comparing California's system with those of other states. We use data from the 1970s onward when they are available, and from more recent years when the data available do not go back that far (e.g., the data on racial/ethnic makeup enrollments only go back to 1987). Thus, for example, we analyze achievement trends only for K–8 students and only from 1990 on, because no appropriate data on achievement exists for high school students, and the data on achievement for K–8 students goes back no further than 1990.

We generally compare California to the nation as a whole and, when the available data are sufficient, we compare California with the four other states that had the largest populations of 5–18 year olds (presumably, students in grades K–12) in 2000. The five states with the largest numbers of school-age children, which we refer to throughout this report as the "most populous" states, are, in order: California, Texas, New York, Florida, and Illinois. In some cases,

[4] http://www.sen.ca.gov/ftp/sen/committee/joint/master_plan/_home/020909_final_master_plan_documents/020909_final_mp_intro.pdf, p. 3.

however, depending on the topic and the data available, we also make comparisons with additional states.

California's distinctive demographic situation presents extraordinary challenges to the state's public education system. Accordingly, we begin with a description of California's student population, extending our view as far back historically as the data permit—to provide racial/ethnic and language breakdowns, as well as levels of immigration and within-state mobility.

We then describe the inputs, or resources, the state has made available to meet students' educational needs. We consider a variety of finance issues: expenditures per pupil, sources of school funding, and the distribution of expenditures among major expenditure categories. We also consider two other major categories of resources—teachers and facilities. We describe California's teaching force, including indicators of teacher qualifications; we also consider nonteaching professional staff—librarians, counselors, etc. With respect to facilities, we explore the status of California's K–12 facilities and capital funding, as far as the available data allowed.

Next, we turn to students' academic achievement. We examine achievement in California as measured by the National Assessment of Educational Progress (NAEP), broken down by both subject area and student characteristics (e.g., race/ethnicity).

To account for the fact that the purposes of schooling go beyond educational achievement to include children's broader preparation for adult success and citizenship, we then examine other important indicators of students' progress that may be influenced by schools. These include both educational attainment measures—the percentage of high school seniors who graduate and the percentage of high school seniors who go on to attend college—and nonacademic measures—substance abuse, teenage pregnancy, and the incidence of school and adolescent crimes. In all of these analyses, we attempt to put California's current K–12 system into perspective. We compare it with the systems of all other states and, in particular, with the systems of the four other most populous states, along each of the dimensions listed above. And, to the extent the available data allow, we examine changes over time in California, again along each of the dimensions listed above.

K–12 Reforms in California

To place the study in context, we review the various educational reforms that California has considered and either adopted or rejected: school finance reform, class size reduction, charter schools, voucher programs, and California's standards and assessment system. This discussion is intended to inform the reader about what California has and has not done to reform its schools and to provide context for the trends reported here.

School Finance Reform

School finance reform in California began in 1971, when the constitutionality of California's school finance system was challenged in the *Serrano v. Priest* case. The California Supreme Court agreed with the Serrano plaintiffs that the large differences in school spending per pupil across districts based on differences in per-pupil property values violated the equal protection clause of the Fourteenth Amendment. In a series of related decisions, the California legislature limited both how much school district revenues related to property wealth could vary from district to district and how much money school districts would be allowed to raise. Low-wealth districts were allowed to increase per-pupil spending at a greater rate than were high-wealth districts, thereby allowing the former to "catch up" to the state average over time.

In 1978, California's Proposition 13 limited property tax rates to 1 percent and capped annual increases in the property taxes levied on a given property.[5] In response, the California legislature passed Assembly Bill (AB) 8, under which the state took control of school district funding. In the following academic year, the percentage of

[5] Properties were reassessed at market value when they changed hands.

school funding coming from the state government increased from 32 to 62 percent; in 1979–1980, it increased to 71 percent. (See Figure 3.1 in Chapter Three.)

After these developments in California, litigation challenging the constitutionality of local funding for public schools arose in 42 other states. By 1999, the school finance systems in 19 of the 42 states were overturned (Evans, Murray, and Schwab, 2001). Many of these states' legislatures followed with equalization efforts, which often included a shift in spending from local sources to the state.

Evidence suggests that the state has equalized resources across school districts so that students in low-wealth districts are at less of a disadvantage in terms of spending per pupil than they were before. At the same time, research suggests that the new laws have had unintended consequences. First of all, because resources were being equalized across districts, California voters had less incentive to spend as much on public schools, which contributed to a significant decline in school spending relative to that in other states. And this decline in spending likely led to the greater class sizes and, perhaps, the poor achievement levels for students in California compared to students across the nation.

Class Size Reduction

In 1994, in response to the poor performance of California's students, the California Department of Education convened a task force to suggest reforms. Among the suggestions was a reduction in class sizes, which at the time averaged 29 students per class for elementary students. This was the largest pupil-teacher ratio in the country (Bohrnstedt and Stecher, 2002a).

In July 1996, the California legislature passed and Governor Pete Wilson signed Senate Bill (SB) 1777, which provided $650 per student for each K–3 classroom with 20 or fewer students. The incentive was later increased to $800 per student. The legislation also allotted money to build 8,000 additional classrooms as part of a one-time provision. The program cost the state about $1 billion the first year and now costs about $1.6 billion per year (Bohrnstedt and Stecher,

2002a). A less extensive program, established in 1998, offered $135 per ninth grader in courses averaging 20 or fewer students.

According to Bohrnstedt and Stecher (2002b), at least 27 states have laws that make reduced class sizes mandatory or voluntary (typically through incentives). Of these, 13 states had passed legislation to reduce class sizes before California did, and eight had mandatory stipulations. California's CSR program was voluntary, but the monetary incentives were initially strong enough to be nearly as effective as a mandate.

Bohrnstedt and Stecher (2002a) found that the implementation of California's CSR program was fairly rapid except in low-income schools, for which the supply of qualified teachers and available classrooms was inadequate. By the 2000–2001 school year, over 95 percent of K–3 teachers taught in reduced-size classes.

California's CSR program did have several significant unintended effects. First of all, it created a windfall for schools with fewer minorities and lower percentages of low-income students. The windfall gains to these schools created more inequality in school funding, counteracting to some extent the redistributive efforts of the state's school finance reform. Second, teacher quality, as measured by teacher experience and credentials, decreased, and the gap in the percentage of teachers who were credentialed between low-income and high-income schools grew larger over a few years (Bohrnstedt and Stecher, 2002a). Third, many schools transferred classroom space and money from other programs to help meet the CSR criteria (Bohrnstedt and Stecher, 2002a). Resources and classroom space were reported as having been cut in, among others areas, special education, music and arts, athletics, childcare programs, teacher professional development, libraries, and even facility maintenance.

Overall, California's CSR program was one of the largest in the nation in terms of how many schools and classrooms were affected. However, California's class size reduction efforts were intended to make up for the fact that California had the largest classes in the country.

Charter Schools

In 1992, California became the second state to enact charter school legislation.[6] As of the 2002–2003 school year, in which 89 charter schools opened, there were 452 charter schools in the state. These schools served about 2.5 percent of all public school students in 2002–2003, making California fifth among all states for the highest percentage of public school students enrolled in charter schools.

California's law states that priority for awarding charters is given to schools that would serve low-achieving students. Because minority students' families tend to have lower incomes than do white students' families and low-achieving students tend to be from low-income backgrounds, there were fears that charter schools would enroll disproportionate numbers of minority students. However, when we control for racial/ethnic heterogeneity across districts, charter schools have a higher percentage of blacks, lower percentages of Hispanics and Asians, and about the same percentage of whites as do conventional public schools. Evidence on whether student achievement is higher in charter schools was mixed and depended on the type of charter school.

Vouchers and Open Enrollment

Two efforts to provide vouchers for private schools have failed among California voters, and no state has implemented a comprehensive voucher program. Proposition 174, a voucher initiative in 1993, would have paid $2,600 of private school tuition for California students. It lost by a 2-to-1 margin. Proposition 38, on the ballot in California's 2000 election, would have offered every school-age child in the state a voucher worth a maximum of $4,000—one-half of the national average spending per pupil in public schools, and one-half of California's spending per public school pupil. The vouchers would have been redeemable at any private school. The proposal received the support of only 29 percent of the voters.

---

[6] Charter schools are public schools that are sponsored and funded by the local or state public school system but are designed, organized, and operated by people or organizations distinct from the sponsoring and funding school system.

High-Stakes Testing and Accountability Systems

In the 1990s, states began to attach "high stakes" to the standardized tests they administered to students—that is, test scores would be the basis for whether students, teachers, and/or schools were rewarded or sanctioned. With the Improving America's Schools Act (IASA) of 1994, states were required to test students at least once in three different grade ranges: 3–5, 6–9, and 10–12. Mandates for testing were strengthened with the NCLB Act, which requires that by the 2005–2006 school year, states must administer annual tests in reading and mathematics, aligned with their academic standards, in grades 3–8 and one high school grade. The states must also include testing in science by 2007–2008 for at least one grade in each of the elementary, middle, and high school levels.

As of 2001, most states had an accountability system that included goals for performance standards, measures of progress, targets for performance, and incentives for meeting the targets (Hamilton and Koretz, 2002). NLCB put these practices into law by mandating that each state develop a statewide accountability system for all its public schools that requires those schools to meet certain standards for student performance in reading and mathematics.

California legislated an accountability system when it passed the Public School Accountability Act (PSSA) of 1999. Under the PSAA, each school gets an Academic Performance Index (API) score that is supposed to be based on results from the Standardized Testing and Reporting (STAR) program, attendance rates, graduation rates, and test results from other statewide tests where applicable. In practice, the API has been based solely on STAR results. Schools are judged on their growth from one year to the next for the school as a whole and for significantly large racial/ethnic and socioeconomic groups.

The PSAA includes both rewards and sanctions. Under the Governor's Performance Award (GPA) program, schools that meet the API level or growth criteria receive monetary and nonmonetary awards. For the first round of awards, for growth from 1999 to 2000, $227 million was allocated to the program, which translates to an average of $68 per student.[7] Schools that improve by more than twice their targeted improvement become eligible for teacher bonuses.

The PSAA also includes the Immediate Intervention/Underperforming Schools Program (II/USP). Schools in the bottom half of the API distribution and not meeting the API growth targets are subject to an intervention program that involves experienced external evaluators planning how to improve student performance. Schools are given $50,000 to undertake this process. If a school fails to meet the goals the following year, further sanctions may be imposed through local interventions, such as personnel reassignments. Failure to meet the goals for a second year may result in sanctions, which may include school closure, imposed by the state superintendent.

Report Overview

Chapter Two describes the demographics of California's K–12 public school student population. The next three chapters then describe the resources for the public school system: Chapter Three examines the financial resources made available to the school system by the state, Chapter Four describes the teachers, and Chapter Five discusses school facilities. Chapters Six and Seven assess the outcomes of the system, Chapter Six focusing on student academic achievement, and Chapter Seven looking at other indicators of student progress. Chapter Eight summarizes and draws together our findings. Two appendices provide auxiliary information on the data and methods of analysis used.

---

[7] See http://www.ose.ca.gov/governor/performance/.

CHAPTER TWO

Demographic Overview of California's K–12 Public School Student Population

Among the demographic characteristics that distinguish California from other states are its racial/ethnic diversity and abundance of English learners, the relatively young age of its population, its prevalence of child poverty, and the fact that the its neediest school-age population is concentrated in just a few counties. Some of these characteristics are problems in and of themselves for California's children—child poverty, for example—but they all also cause secondary problems in that they isolate children linguistically, hamper their access to computers and the Internet (computer literacy is widely recognized as essential for future members of the workforce), and affect educational outcomes, such as school enrollment.

California's distinctive demographic profile is expected to continue imposing extraordinary demands on the state's public elementary and secondary education system. This chapter discusses the state's demographic characteristics and the challenges they pose.

Historical Perspectives

California's demographic distinctiveness derives from historical growth patterns extending back many decades. Public school enrollment mushroomed in the aftermath of the baby boom "echo," taking annual increases, which had averaged 0.9 percent during the early 1980s, to levels of 3.5 to 3.8 percent in the early 1990s.

An increasing share of these growing enrollments was made up of children of immigrants. In 1970, only 11 percent of all births in California were to mothers born outside the United States; by 1995, however, that percentage had risen to 44 percent, as reflected in the kindergarteners of 2001.

California has long been a destination for migrants seeking opportunities beyond their regions of birth. Newcomers to California once originated in Texas, Arkansas, and other states; but recent decades have witnessed many newcomers from Latin America, Asia, and other continents. By 1990, half of all Southeast Asian refugees who had come to America had made California their home. By 2000, two-fifths of the nation's 1.1 million Vietnamese-Americans were Californians. Included in this influx are many who settled initially in other states, later wending their way to California.

Over the decades, kinship ties have reinforced and perpetuated the state's ongoing attractiveness to people from foreign originations. Future growth is likely to be continued by these firmly anchored social mechanisms.

Racial/Ethnic Diversity and Fluency in English

According to Census 2000, recent immigrants (i.e., foreign-born persons who have entered the United States within the past ten years) number fewer than one in every 20 persons in the United States today. However, this ratio is nearly one in every ten persons in California. California is among the most racially/ethnically diverse states, with a "majority minority" population that is expected to increase in the future (see Figure 2.1).

Racial/ethnic diversity is greater among California's youth, especially in the public schools, than among the general population. On a statewide basis, K–12 public school enrollments in 2002–2003 were 45 percent Hispanic, 34 percent Anglo (non-Hispanic white), 11

Figure 2.1
California's Population, by Race/Ethnicity

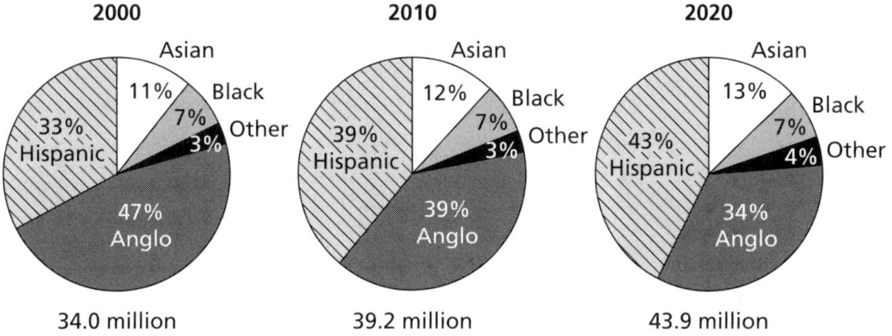

SOURCE: State of California, Dept. of Finance, 2004.

NOTE: Percentages may not total 100% due to rounding. The Other category combines persons classified as "Pacific Islander," "American Indian," and "Multirace."

RAND *MG186-2.1*

percent Asian, 8 percent black, and 2 percent other (see Figure 2.2).[1] Sixteen years earlier (1986–1987), they were 30 percent Hispanic, 50 percent Anglo, 11 percent Asian and other, and 9 percent black.

By 2012–2013, the majority of students in California's public schools will be Hispanic according to official state projections. Figure 2.3 shows the numerical shift for the two most numerous groups—Hispanics and Anglos.

Blurring these group distinctions are the growing numbers of California children classified as multiracial on Census 2000. They now exceed 7 percent of all California children, well above the 4 percent at the national level.

---

[1] The classifications shown in Figure 2.2 (and notes thereto) are the only racial/ethnic classifications available; the state does not publish more-detailed data for enrollments. Data for these classifications are available since 1986–1987. Earlier data distinguish only between "white and black" or "white and non-white," depending on the year. The current "Hispanic" and "non-Hispanic white" categories are not directly comparable with earlier categories, such as "Persons of Spanish language or Spanish surname."

Figure 2.2
Student Population Enrolled in California's K–12 Public Schools, by Race/Ethnicity

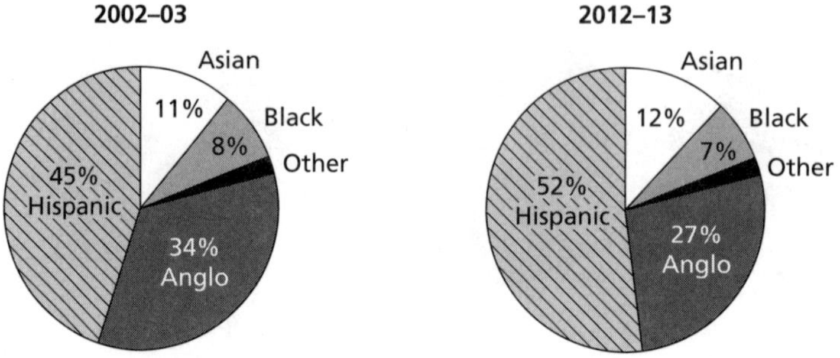

SOURCE: State of California, Dept. of Finance, 2003b.
NOTES: Percentages may not total 100% due to rounding. The 0.8 percent of students categorized as "Multiple or No Response" are allocated to the known race/ethnicity groups (see Source for details). The Other category includes students classified as "Pacific Islander" or "American Indian."
RAND *MG186-2.2*

An important correlate of California's ethnic diversity is that some of the population is in the process of learning English or becoming more fluent. As an immigrant "entry port," California has an abundance of "English learners" and linguistically isolated households.[2] California ranks nationally as the state with the highest percentage of children with limited English fluency. Fully 5.8 percent of all California children ages 5–17 have difficulty speaking English, versus 2.5 percent nationally.[3] Within this age group, 13.4 percent are linguistically isolated (versus 5.1 percent nationally). Both these disparities heighten educational costs for affected school districts: English learners impose specialized and/or higher per capita staffing needs, and linguistic isolation hampers two-way communication between schools and parents.

---

[2] Children of ages 5–17 are classified as being linguistically isolated if they reside in a household in which no one age 14 and over speaks English "very well."

[3] "Difficulty" is defined on Census 2000 as speaking English "less than very well."

Figure 2.3
California K–12 Public School Enrollment, 2003 Series

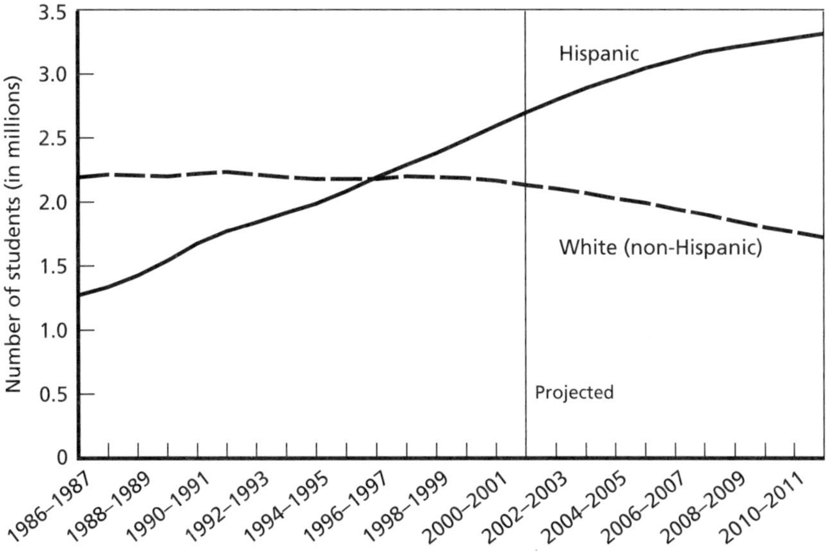

SOURCE: State of California, Dept. of Finance, 2003a.

NOTE: From 1998–1999 onward, multiple race and nonresponses were allocated to known categories (see Source for details).

RAND *MG186-2.3*

Age Composition

The age structure of California's population differs from that of the national population: The share of the population that is under age 18 is 27.3 percent for California and only 25.7 percent for the nation. Consequently, California has within its borders 12.8 percent of the nation's school-age population but only 11.8 percent of the nation's adult population, which means that the number of potential taxpayers (i.e., adults) in California available to shoulder the financial responsibility for persons of school age is relatively small. Put another way, California's youth-to-adult dependency ratio is 9 percent higher than that of the nation as a whole.[4]

Child Poverty

About one in every five California children lives in poverty—i.e., in a family whose income is below federally established poverty thresholds (which vary according to a family's size and the ages of its members). For California children in single-mother families, the proportion living in poverty is 39.7 percent, which is marginally lower than the corresponding 40.6 percent for the nation (see Table 2.1). For those living in married-couple families (by far the most common type), the proportion of children living in poverty is noticeably higher for California than for the nation: 12.9 percent compared with 8.4 percent. Overall, California's poor children are just as numerous in married-couple families as in single-parent families.

Table 2.1
Number and Percentage of Related Children Under Age 18 in Poverty in 2000, by Family Type, California and the United States

	California		United States	
Family Type	Number in Poverty	Percentage of All Children	Number in Poverty	Percentage of All Children
Related children under 18	1,705,797	19.0	11,386,031	16.1
In married-couple families	844,893	12.9	4,255,820	8.4
In single-mother families	711,818	39.7	6,281,647	40.6
In single-father families	149,046	23.9	848,564	20.8

SOURCE: Census 2000.
NOTE: "Related children" are all household members, regardless of marital status, who are related to householder; householder's spouse and foster children are excluded.

---

[4] The youth-to-adult dependency ratio compares the number of persons in the population under age 18 to the number 18 and older. In 2000, this ratio was 0.376 for California and 0.346 for the United States.

California trails the nation and displays a worsening trend on two key indicators of child poverty: the percentage of children living below the poverty line (19.5 percent in 2000) and the percentage of children living in high-poverty neighborhoods (29.6 percent in 2000)—see Figure 2.4. Each California percentage is higher than the corresponding national level and has risen since 1990, contrary to the national trend.

The evidence showing that child poverty limits educational attainment is abundant.[5] The indirect public costs of child poverty (to schools, health clinics, etc.) are tied to the uneven prevalence of children in poverty across the state. Child poverty is most prevalent in a

Figure 2.4
Selected Key Indicators of Child Well-Being, California and the United States, 1990–2000

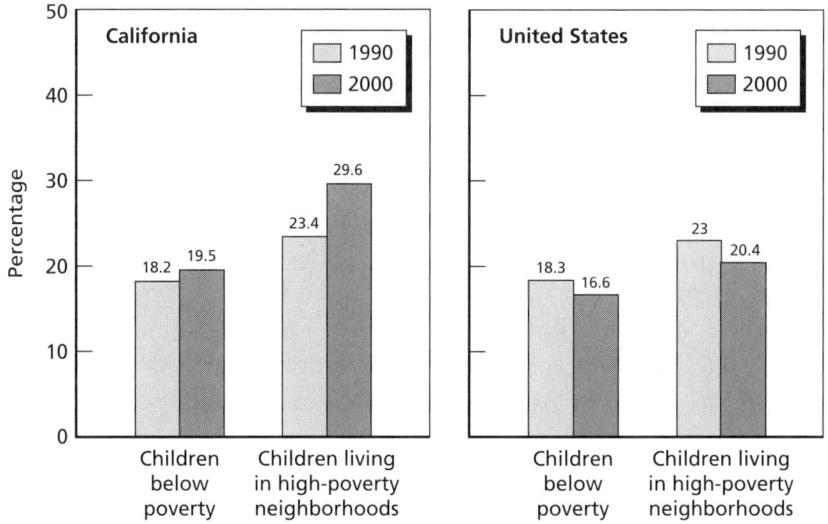

SOURCE: Census 1990 and 2000.

RAND *MG186-2.4*

---

[5] For a review of evidence, see U.S. Department of Education, National Center for Education Statistics, 2003.

handful of Central Valley counties (Tulare, Fresno, Madera, and Merced), and the levels of child poverty in Tulare and Fresno counties put them among the poorest tenth of the nation's 3,142 counties.

Geographic Redistribution

As California's population grows, its continuing redistribution will amplify public school enrollment growth in particular clusters of counties—for example, the Central Valley and the counties surrounding Los Angeles County will experience particularly high enrollment growth (see Figure 2.5 and Table 2.2).[6] Inevitably, particular school districts in California's most rapidly growing regions, highlighted in Figure 2.5, will be strained by enrollment pressure, staffing needs, and the crowding of existing facilities.

The geographic redistribution of the population is important in another way, as well: Recent immigrants, English learners, and poor families are overly concentrated in certain California counties, adding to the strain on these counties to provide appropriate services. The extent of local variation across the state is apparent in comparisons of the state's 58 counties, 53 congressional districts, dozens of metropolitan areas, and hundreds of incorporated cities on specific indicators of educational outcomes or socio-demographic burdens.[7] The percentage of children with limited English fluency exceeds 20 percent in four counties: Imperial, Monterey, Los Angeles, and Merced. And it exceeds 35 percent in three congressional districts—31 and 34

---

[6] The county-level enrollment projections shown in Figure 2.5 and Table 2.2 were prepared using a cohort survival projection technique, with grade progression ratios representing the proportion of students expected to progress from one grade to the next. The most likely progression model is chosen based on an analysis of historical trends, knowledge of each county's migration trends and demographic characteristics (including the most recent population estimates), and survey results from selected school districts. For further details on methodology, see Source noted on Table 2.2.

[7] An extensive set of geographic rankings is accessible at the Annie E. Casey Foundation's Kids Count Website: http://www.aecf.org/kidscount/ census/.

Figure 2.5
Percent Change in K–12 Enrollment, by County, 2002–2012

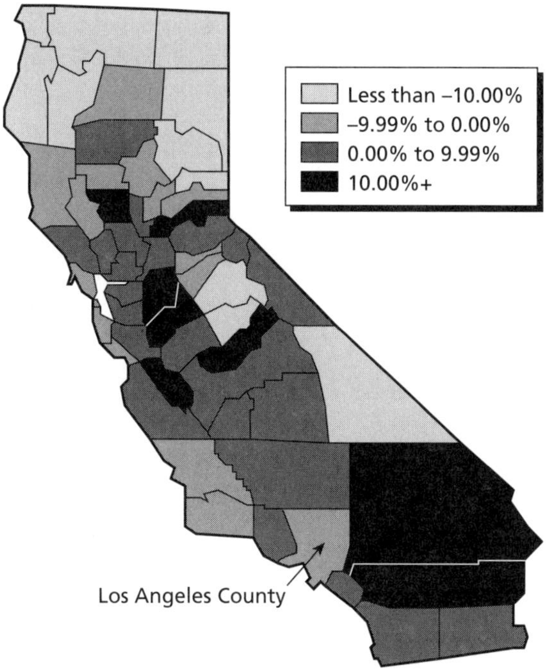

SOURCE: State of California, Dept. of Finance, 2003a.
RAND *MG186-2.5*

(both of which are in Los Angeles County) and 47 (in Orange County)—making these three districts the highest nationwide.

School Enrollment

The universality of school enrollment among school-age children is one measure of child well-being. Indicators more likely than school enrollment to be influenced by the schools themselves—e.g., academic achievement and educational attainment—are discussed in Chapters Six and Seven.

Table 2.2
Projected California Public School K–12 Enrollment, by County and School Year

	2003-04	2004-05	2005-06	2006-07	2007-08	2008-09	2009-10	2010-11	2011-12	2012-13
Alameda	217,839	218,681	220,290	221,602	222,206	222,264	222,436	222,874	223,575	224,515
Alpine	141	147	143	146	148	154	155	158	164	161
Amador	4,906	4,881	4,835	4,834	4,752	4,715	4,696	4,646	4,615	4,633
Butte	33,709	33,323	32,924	32,606	32,216	31,789	31,421	31,097	30,871	30,652
Calaveras	6,821	6,767	6,712	6,619	6,580	6,464	6,421	6,408	6,414	6,449
Colusa	4,402	4,458	4,521	4,594	4,604	4,666	4,716	4,767	4,828	4,876
Contra Costa	162,778	164,684	167,133	169,175	170,722	171,415	172,336	173,333	174,453	175,749
Del Norte	4,817	4,704	4,593	4,459	4,357	4,216	4,108	4,013	3,946	3,875
El Dorado	29,064	29,016	28,966	28,903	28,894	28,842	28,773	28,911	29,218	29,485
Fresno	188,053	189,014	190,024	190,895	192,056	192,738	193,205	194,031	194,986	196,280
Glenn	5,955	5,831	5,738	5,678	5,632	5,586	5,576	5,578	5,604	5,672
Humboldt	20,201	19,870	19,480	19,251	18,930	18,601	18,286	18,024	17,830	17,572
Imperial	34,537	34,768	35,004	35,136	35,200	35,244	35,434	35,650	36,008	36,397
Inyo	3,330	3,267	3,183	3,134	3,034	2,950	2,883	2,815	2,787	2,729
Kern	155,777	157,536	159,536	160,853	162,087	162,864	163,575	164,525	165,715	167,273
Kings	26,172	26,375	26,634	26,770	27,066	27,226	27,300	27,384	27,509	27,699
Lake	10,377	10,265	10,241	10,218	10,177	10,159	10,196	10,267	10,381	10,511
Lassen	6,854	6,800	6,663	6,492	6,424	6,342	6,243	6,176	6,125	6,037
Los Angeles	1,717,596	1,730,719	1,738,157	1,732,446	1,721,904	1,702,746	1,681,020	1,661,332	1,638,242	1,615,011
Madera	27,020	27,529	28,049	28,597	29,002	29,390	29,810	30,255	30,757	31,215
Marin	28,279	28,162	28,198	28,134	27,984	27,734	27,604	27,462	27,431	27,521
Mariposa	2,551	2,502	2,460	2,435	2,388	2,320	2,276	2,252	2,232	2,238
Mendocino	14,656	14,500	14,390	14,277	14,160	14,003	13,946	13,923	13,953	13,999
Merced	54,019	54,590	55,261	55,721	56,182	56,150	56,236	56,407	56,582	56,837
Modoc	2,270	2,233	2,199	2,141	2,070	2,008	1,929	1,853	1,784	1,722
Mono	2,279	2,253	2,249	2,262	2,277	2,268	2,279	2,311	2,346	2,385
Monterey	73,753	74,144	74,632	75,115	75,577	75,868	76,251	76,979	77,687	78,958
Napa	19,669	19,716	19,810	19,937	20,017	20,082	20,141	20,173	20,211	20,341
Nevada	14,176	14,091	14,177	14,282	14,363	14,403	14,424	14,481	14,606	14,744
Orange	518,738	527,172	534,669	538,040	539,544	537,944	535,493	532,548	528,954	525,593
Placer	62,315	64,474	66,719	68,825	71,074	73,057	75,017	76,994	78,820	80,641
Plumas	3,093	3,022	2,963	2,898	2,866	2,837	2,802	2,774	2,765	2,771
Riverside	358,168	370,135	382,181	391,757	401,690	409,618	417,285	424,684	431,038	436,898

Table 2.2 (continued)

	2003-04	2004-05	2005-06	2006-07	2007-08	2008-09	2009-10	2010-11	2011-12	2012-13
Sacramento	236,027	240,297	244,329	247,908	251,029	253,787	255,937	257,861	259,680	261,894
San Benito	12,086	12,511	12,805	13,203	13,523	13,790	14,065	14,326	14,584	14,858
San Bernardino	412,338	419,639	425,395	430,866	435,850	439,609	443,333	447,312	451,475	455,678
San Diego	500,818	504,147	507,179	508,662	508,900	507,600	506,714	505,788	505,198	505,168
San Francisco	58,905	58,248	57,782	56,982	56,309	55,604	54,870	54,031	53,309	52,562
San Joaquin	128,833	131,342	134,255	136,407	138,633	140,417	142,245	144,418	146,558	149,031
San Luis Obispo	36,137	35,861	35,702	35,417	35,028	34,510	34,091	33,867	33,822	33,742
San Mateo	89,123	88,953	88,908	88,517	88,006	87,312	86,660	86,366	86,322	86,601
Santa Barbara	67,410	67,551	67,745	67,600	67,455	66,920	66,412	66,174	66,025	66,042
Santa Clara	248,896	249,570	251,348	252,131	252,622	252,262	251,990	251,502	251,279	251,377
Santa Cruz	39,040	38,708	38,488	38,273	37,883	37,551	37,250	37,070	37,125	37,305
Shasta	29,799	29,432	29,090	28,820	28,518	28,180	28,043	27,978	27,942	27,944
Sierra	674	612	589	541	553	554	563	576	594	613
Siskiyou	6,694	6,568	6,340	6,153	6,021	5,877	5,763	5,678	5,595	5,576
Solano	72,671	72,545	72,802	72,899	72,737	72,564	72,395	72,410	72,641	73,089
Sonoma	72,597	72,342	72,270	72,282	71,952	71,661	71,548	71,681	72,029	72,555
Stanislaus	104,669	106,538	108,177	109,816	111,656	113,076	114,307	115,626	116,917	118,002
Sutter	16,749	16,895	17,006	17,183	17,342	17,446	17,551	17,654	17,804	17,997
Tehama	11,025	11,039	11,150	11,122	11,140	11,085	11,085	11,096	11,073	11,091
Trinity	2,064	1,997	1,955	1,923	1,887	1,817	1,797	1,761	1,728	1,701
Tulare	88,589	89,313	90,482	91,699	92,746	93,477	94,242	95,151	96,120	97,318
Tuolumne	7,567	7,513	7,464	7,399	7,307	7,224	7,136	7,100	7,063	7,023
Ventura	144,983	146,552	148,021	148,961	149,419	149,078	148,911	148,842	148,827	149,235
Yolo	29,673	29,975	30,269	30,558	30,842	31,050	31,281	31,576	31,843	32,120
Yuba	14,511	14,512	14,553	14,544	14,577	14,593	14,648	14,651	14,682	14,648
California	6,246,193	6,308,289	6,366,838	6,398,098	6,418,118	6,413,707	6,407,110	6,405,580	6,402,672	6,404,609

NOTE: Projections exclude California Youth Authority and state special schools.

Proportionally fewer 3–4 year olds are enrolled in school in California (45.8 percent) than are enrolled nationwide (49.3 percent). Among 5–14 year olds, California compares closely with the nation; and among 15–17 year olds, California boasts a slightly higher percentage than the nation as a whole (see Table 2.3).

Access to Computers and the Internet

Because computer literacy has become essential for future members of the workforce, the concern about barriers to children's acquisition of computer literacy has been increasing. For many children, exposure to computers and the Internet may be limited—by hardware shortages or connectivity limits in the classroom and/or by economic factors at home. Furthermore, saying that users are "connected" to the Internet is not equal to saying users are equal—there are many inequities. For example, some children can access the Internet from home, while others can connect only through a classroom or public library; and some children enjoy ultrahigh-speed connections, while others must dial in through antiquated phone lines.

The barriers of concern here are best characterized as several "digital divides," rather than a single one. The indicators presently

Table 2.3
School Enrollment in 2000 for Children Ages 3–17, California and the United States

	Percent Enrolled in School	
Children's Age Group	**California**	**United States**
3–17	90.3	90.8
3–4	45.8	49.3
5–9	96.0	95.9
10–14	98.7	98.9
15–17	95.3	94.9

SOURCE: Census 2000.

available are analytically limited and geographically coarse; data for individual states or regions, for example, are sparse. However, one recent survey found that the proportion of California school-age children that have home Internet access is 48 percent, which puts the state at 35th among all states (Wilhelm et al., 2002; National Telecommunications and Information Administration, 2002). And national data document several points (Wilhelm et al., 2002): Overall, computer and Internet access at home is up sharply in recent years (Figure 2.6), although among children, proportionally fewer blacks and Hispanics use home computers and the Internet than do non-Hispanic whites (Figure 2.7).

Figure 2.6
Computer and Internet Access at Home, United States, 1984–2000

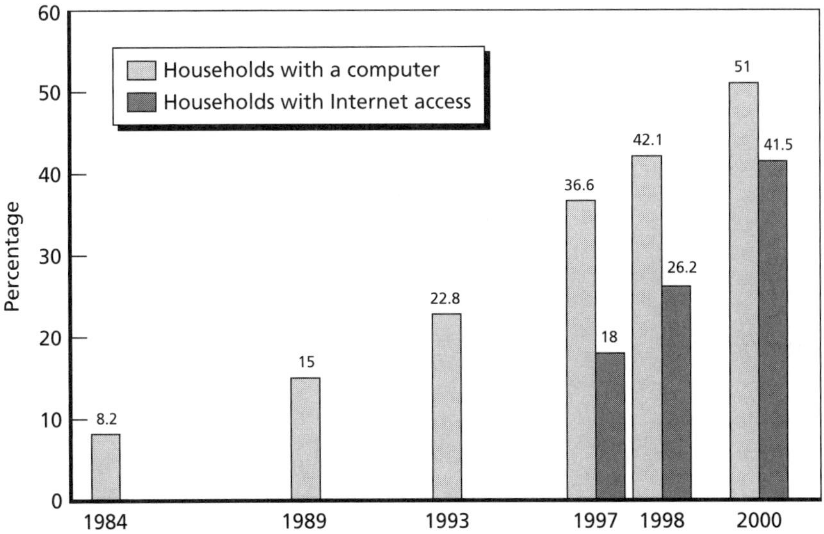

SOURCE: U.S. Census Bureau, 2001.

RAND *MG186-2.6*

Figure 2.7
Home Computer and Internet Use among Children Ages 3–17, by Race/Ethnicity, United States, 2001

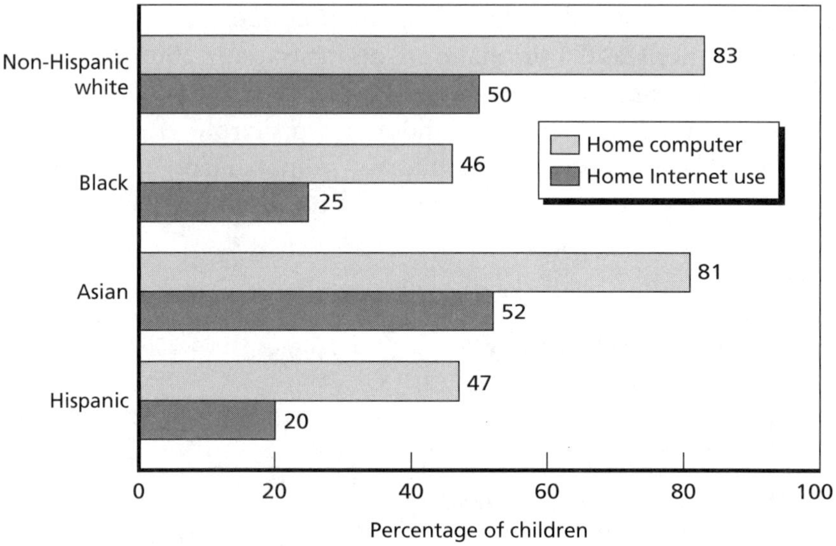

SOURCE: Wilhelm, Carmen, and Reynolds, 2002.
RAND *MG186-2.7*

Conclusions

The educational challenges posed by the demographics of California for school-age children are not altogether different from those found among their counterparts elsewhere in the nation. Extremes within the state, though, are remarkable. Particular subgroups of children (e.g., Hispanics; recent immigrants; children in particular family types, such as single-parent families) and children in certain locales (e.g., California's Central Valley, Imperial County, metropolitan Los Angeles) are far more disadvantaged than their counterparts statewide and nationally. There are wide variations as well across California's 53 congressional districts. Consequently, political pressures for responding to particular needs or shortcomings in specific areas may be emphasized. Several distinctive features of California's demographic profile will shape the state's future educational needs:

- *The relative youth of the population.* California has within its borders 12.8 percent of the nation's school-age population, but only 11.8 percent of the nation's adult population of potential taxpayers, so the state will shoulder disproportionate responsibility for persons of school age.
- *Racial/ethnic diversity and an abundance of English learners and linguistically isolated households.* On a statewide basis, K–12 public school enrollments in 2002–2003 were 45 percent Hispanic, 34 percent Anglo (non-Hispanic white), 12 percent Asian and other (mostly Filipino), and 8 percent black. By 2012–2013, the majority of students in California's public schools will be Hispanic according to official state projections. Many California children ages 5–17 have difficulty speaking English, and many are linguistically isolated. Both these disparities heighten educational costs for affected school districts: English learners by imposing specialized and/or higher per capita staffing needs; linguistic isolation by hampering two-way communication between schools and parents.
- *The continuing geographic redistribution of the population.* Public school enrollment will grow the most in particular clusters of counties, notably within the Central Valley and surrounding the Los Angeles basin. Inevitably, particular school districts will be strained by enrollment pressure, staffing needs, and the crowding of existing facilities.

CHAPTER THREE

California's K–12 Public School Finances

When it comes to funding K–12 public education, the sheer number of students and the diversity of their needs present the people of California with a formidable challenge. To begin, we review some history on the evolution of the current school finance system. We then examine public elementary and secondary school revenues, looking at the sources of those revenues and their size and volatility over time. In addition, we examine the extent to which revenues given to California public schools have restrictions on how they can be used. We then describe public school expenditures—both their size and how they are divided among several large expenditure categories. The last section of the chapter then describes California's capacity to fund its public schools and its effort to do so.

Evolution of the Finance System

California's current school finance system evolved over the last three decades through a combination of court decisions, legislative actions, voter-approved initiatives, and government regulations (EdSource, 2000). The result of all these changes is that California's system of public school finance has been fundamentally transformed.

The transformation began in 1971, when the California Supreme Court ruled in *Serrano v. Priest* that differences in property tax revenue per pupil across districts could not be related to differences in the property wealth of those districts. The court found that California's system of local school finance was unconstitutional and gave the legislature the task of designing a new system. A series of legislative and popular initiatives followed.

Proposition 13, passed by California voters in 1978, helped shape the new system. Proposition 13 took away from school districts and other local governments the power to set their own property tax rates, and limited the sum of all property taxes in any particular locale to 1 percent of assessed property value. In a very short time, California went from a system in which each school district determined its own revenue through local property taxes to a system in which school revenues are controlled at the state level (Sonstelie, Brunner, and Ardon, 2000).

Under Proposition 13, each year the California legislature and governor determine how much state and property tax funding will go to public education.[1] However, the provisions of a 1988 voter-approved constitutional amendment, Proposition 98, set the minimum level of state and property tax revenue guaranteed to K–12 schools[2] each year,[3] thereby guaranteeing schools a minimum percentage of the state's budget. In general, Proposition 98 funding to school districts is either categorical aid, which is funds that may be used only for specific programs and purposes (such as special education or instructional materials), or general purpose funds, which can be spent at a district's discretion.

---

[1] Most school revenues come from state and local property tax revenues. The federal government contributes about 10 percent of total K–12 revenues, and local miscellaneous revenues (including community contributions, interest income, developer fees, and revenues from local parcel tax elections) account for about 7 percent.

[2] Community colleges are also included in Proposition 98 and fall under its funding calculations.

[3] Over time, the state has chosen to supplement the guaranteed minimum Proposition 98 funding. The calculation of the guaranteed minimum amount is largely based on the health of the state's economy. In practice, Proposition 98 has meant that in stable economic years, education is entitled to the same amount allocated the previous year, plus enrollment growth and an inflation adjustment equal to the change in per capita personal income in the state. In difficult economic years, the state can provide a lesser amount, restoring the shortfall in the next year that state revenues grow sufficiently, as defined by Proposition 98. For a more detailed discussion on calculating the Proposition 98 guarantee, see EdSource, 2002c.

Court decisions form the basis for some categorical programs; legislative and gubernatorial actions create others. The state distributes categorical aid in a variety of ways, including across-the-board grants to all schools, reimbursements for specific services, incentives to encourage particular activities, and competitive grants (EdSource, 2001b). Currently, about one-third of Proposition 98 school funding is earmarked by the state for about 70 specific programs and purposes.

The amount of Proposition 98 general purpose funding that a school district receives per student, based on its average daily attendance (ADA), is called its "revenue limit." Each of the nearly 1,000 school districts in California has its own revenue limit, calculated by a lengthy formula that includes its type (elementary, high, or unified), size (small or large), and historical spending patterns. The intent of the system is to ensure that districts of similar type—i.e., large elementary districts—receive approximately equal per-pupil base revenue amounts. Revenue limit income comes from local property taxes, to which state funds are added.[4] Once a district's revenue limit is set for a given year, the district's share of local property tax revenues is used toward the district's revenue limit. The state adds the additional state tax revenue needed to meet the calculated revenue limit. The share of local property tax revenues meets the full revenue limit guarantee in roughly 60 districts,[5] which are called "basic aid" districts. For these, the state contributes an additional $120 per ADA (or

[4] One of the fundamental changes created by Proposition 13 was a shift in the revenue limit calculation (Goldfinger, 1994). Prior to Proposition 13, a district computed its revenue limit and subtracted from it the amount of state aid it would receive; the difference then came from property taxes. When Proposition 13 limited the amount of school districts' property tax revenues, state law was changed to reverse this process. Now the district computes its revenue limit and subtracts its share of the local property tax raised at the one percent maximum rate. The balance is what the district is entitled to in state aid. Because the amount of money raised fluctuates, depending on the state economy, education funding is not stable.

[5] Because local property tax revenues fluctuate from year to year, some districts are basic aid one year but not the next.

$2,400 per district—whichever is greater) to fulfill its constitutional guarantee to provide all public schools with "basic aid."[6]

California K–12 Revenues

Sources of Public K–12 Revenues

Revenue Sources in California. In 2001–2002, California spent over $50 billion in state, local, and federal funds to educate about six million elementary and secondary students. As discussed above, the sources of K–12 funding changed dramatically with the passage of Proposition 13. Figure 3.1 displays the share of total K–12 revenues from state, local, and federal sources over time.

In 1977–1978, the year just before passage of Proposition 13, property tax revenue constituted 59 percent of total revenue; it had consistently been around 60 percent of total revenue over time. One year later, property tax revenue had fallen to 23 percent of revenue, and the gap was filled by state aid. By 1981–1982, property tax revenue and state aid constituted, respectively, 25 percent and 67 percent of total revenue, levels that were sustained until the recession of the early 1990s, when the state share fell somewhat.[7]

In recent years, federal education support has grown gradually but steadily. All federal dollars are "categorical" programs, earmarked for specific purposes.[8] For many years, federal programs provided

---

[6] If the local property tax revenues exceed the revenue limit, the district gets to keep the overage and receives the $120 per ADA constitutionally guaranteed funding. Information about basic aid is available at http://www.edsource.org/edu_fin_basicaid.cfm.

[7] In response to state budgetary problems, the state shifted some additional property tax revenue from cities, counties, and special districts to schools, thereby decreasing the amount of state general funds necessary to fund schools. It also required counties to deposit some property tax revenue that had previously gone to cities, counties, and special districts into an Educational Revenue Augmentation Fund, which was distributed to schools (Sonstelie, Brunner, and Ardon, 2000).

[8] Federal programs for elementary and secondary education have generally provided a variety of services for special needs students, with the bulk of funding targeted for compensatory services to disadvantaged students.

Figure 3.1
Sources of Public K–12 Revenues, California, 1977–1978 to 2001–2002

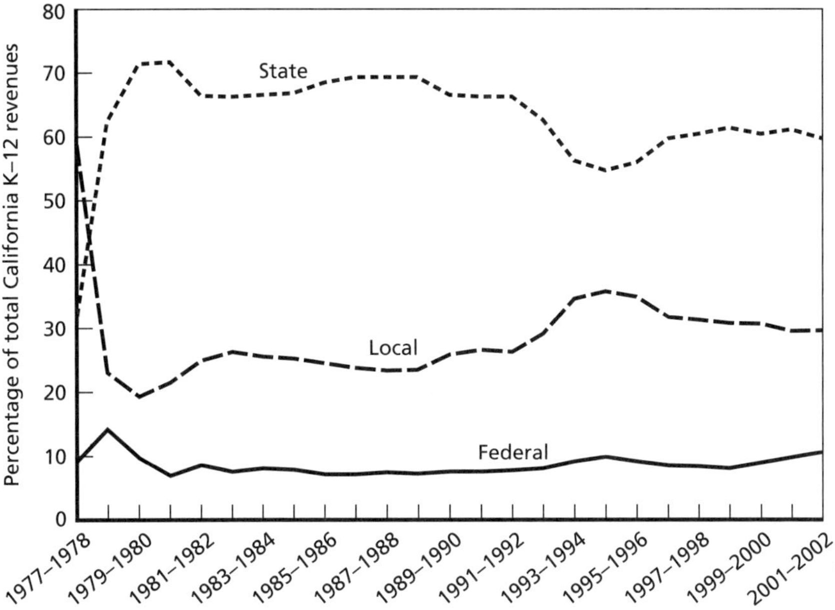

SOURCE: National Education Assoc., Rankings of the States, various years.
RAND *MG186-3.1*

about 8 percent of K–12 funding in California. In 2001–2002, they provided just over 10 percent of total revenues.[9]

Revenue Sources at the National Level. A somewhat different trend in the sources of K–12 revenues is seen at the national level. As Figure 3.2 shows, states have consistently contributed between 45 and 50 percent of total education revenues, while local governments

---

[9] This growth reflects increases in funding for Title 1 programs for disadvantaged students, special education students with disabilities, and smaller class sizes. For 2002–2003, it was estimated that federal revenues would be close to 12 percent of total revenues in California, or about $6.5 billion (EdSource, 2002a). Most of the recent increases in federal K–12 dollars have come as part of the No Child Left Behind Act (NCLB), which came into effect in January 2002.

Figure 3.2
Sources of Public K–12 Revenues, United States, 1977–1978 to 2001–2002

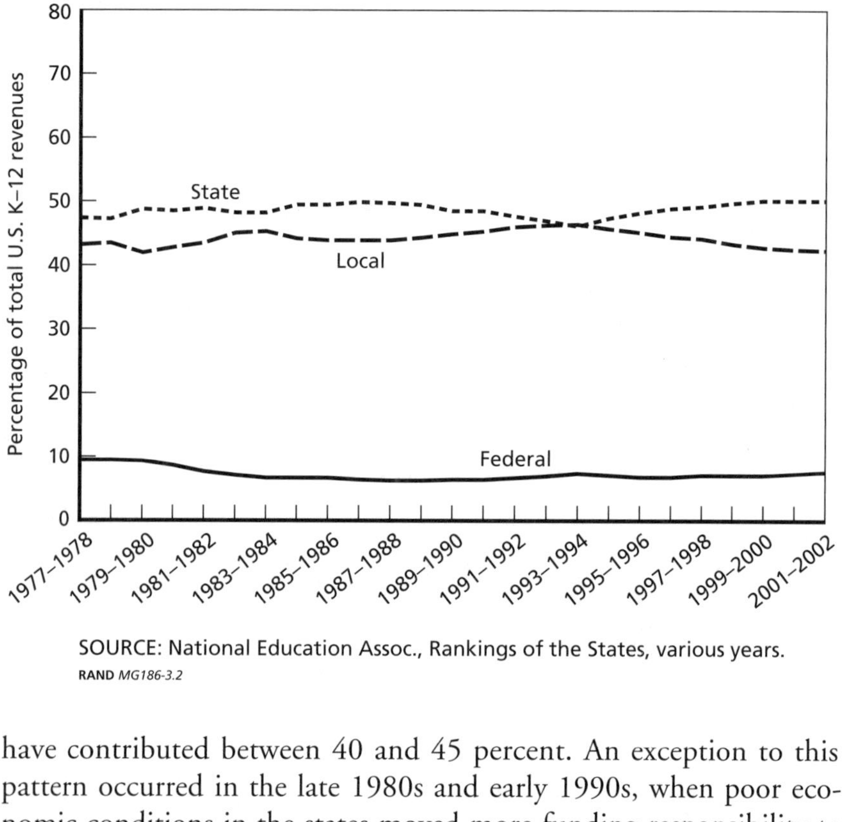

SOURCE: National Education Assoc., Rankings of the States, various years.
RAND *MG186-3.2*

have contributed between 40 and 45 percent. An exception to this pattern occurred in the late 1980s and early 1990s, when poor economic conditions in the states moved more funding responsibility to local governments. There has been a slight trend over time toward states providing more funding. This trend likely stems from efforts in many states to reduce the fiscal disparities among districts and to become more involved in education reform efforts.[10]

Revenue Sources: California Compared to Other States. Today's school finance systems look dramatically different from state to state.

---

[10] A great deal has been written on educational equity-related finance reforms across the states. See, for example, Odden, 1992; Henderson, 1991; and Sonstelie, Brunner, and Ardon, 2000.

The general trend has been toward a larger portion of state funding and control, but the proportions and funding structures vary. Illinois, for example, depends somewhat on state funds but still relies most heavily on local property taxes. A few states, including California, have state-controlled school finance systems (EdSource, 2000). Figure 3.3 shows the total revenues and the shares of revenues from federal, state, and local sources for California and the four other most populous states. This figure illustrates the sheer magnitude of California's public education system in terms of revenues. California's public elementary and secondary revenues are about $15 billion higher than those in any of the four other largest states, and at 61 percent, the state share of total funding in California is considerably larger.

Figure 3.3
Public K–12 Revenues from Federal, State, and Local Sources, Five Most Populous States, 2000–2001

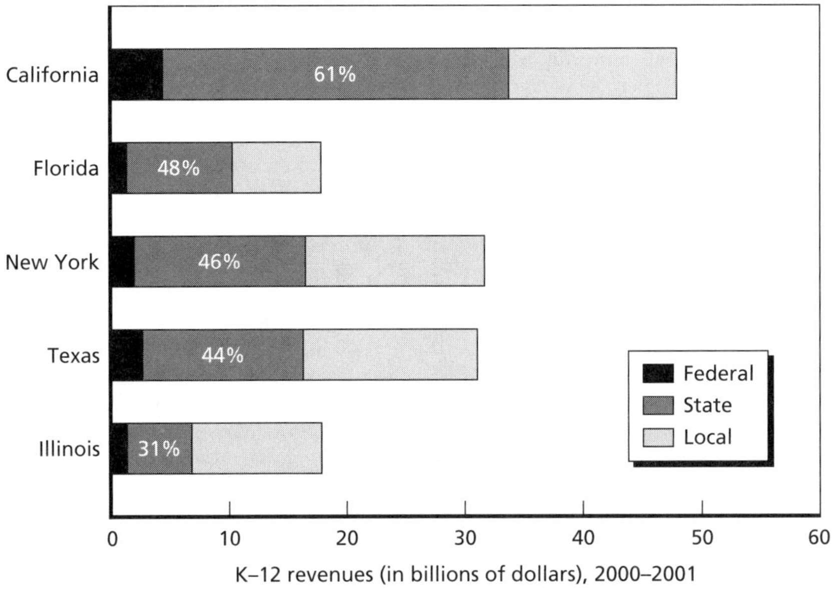

SOURCE: National Education Assoc., Rankings of the States, various years.

RAND *MG186-3.3*

Per-Pupil K–12 Revenues

Per-Pupil Revenues: California Compared to the Nation. Figure 3.4 shows total K–12 revenues per pupil[11] from 1978–1979 through 2002–2003 for California and through 2001–2002 for the United States.[12] Between the late 1970s and the late 1980s, K–12 real (adjusted for inflation) revenues per pupil generally grew fairly rapidly in both California and the United States (except for a notable dip in California following passage of Proposition 13). California per-pupil revenues were consistently above the national average prior to 1978–1979 and passage of Proposition 13 (Sonstelie, Brunner, and Ardon, 2000).[13] After that, on average, they remained below the national average by about $200.

Numerous circumstances propelled per-pupil revenue increases across the United States between 1950 and 1990. School finance liti-

---

[11] Throughout this section of our revenue discussion, we use average daily attendance (ADA) as the student count with which we divide revenues to come up with per-pupil revenue figures. ADA is what the states generally use to allocate monies. Enrollment measures the number of pupils registered to attend school at a given point in time, whereas ADA measures the number of pupils attending school each day averaged over the course of the year. The difference in the two measures is largely due to absences. In the context of national comparisons, however, another matter arises (Legislative Analyst's Office, 2001a). Until 1998–1999, California was unique among the states in including excused absences in its ADA counts. As a result, for data collected prior to 1998–1999, California's ADA totals are relatively higher than other states' ADA totals. For example, the National Education Association (NEA) reports that California's operating expenditures per fall enrollment in 1997–1998 were $5,580, ranking the state at 31st in the nation. However, NEA reports that in the same year, California expenditures, measured by ADA, were $5,627, ranking it at 40th in the nation. We use ADA in this section on revenue because enrollment numbers are not available for all years in the NEA data. Most states report revenues divided by ADA (rather than by enrollment) because that is what is used for allocation purposes. In addition, researchers most commonly use revenues divided by ADA. At the same time, however, it is important to note that the use of ADA before 1998–1999 in comparisons between California and other states likely overestimates differences in revenues per student.

[12] The national average may serve as a proxy for addressing basic K–12 program needs. At the same time, the level of spending necessary for California to provide quality K–12 programs depends on many variables and may be higher or lower than the national average.

[13] Sonstelie, Brunner, and Ardon (2000) show real spending per pupil as being anywhere from about $100 to about $800 above the U.S. average between 1969–1970 and 1977–1978. In addition, the gap between real spending per pupil in California and the United States grew over time, being at its largest just prior to passage of Proposition 13.

Figure 3.4
Revenues per Pupil, California, 1977–1978 to 2002–2003 (est.), and the United States, 1977–1978 to 2001–2002

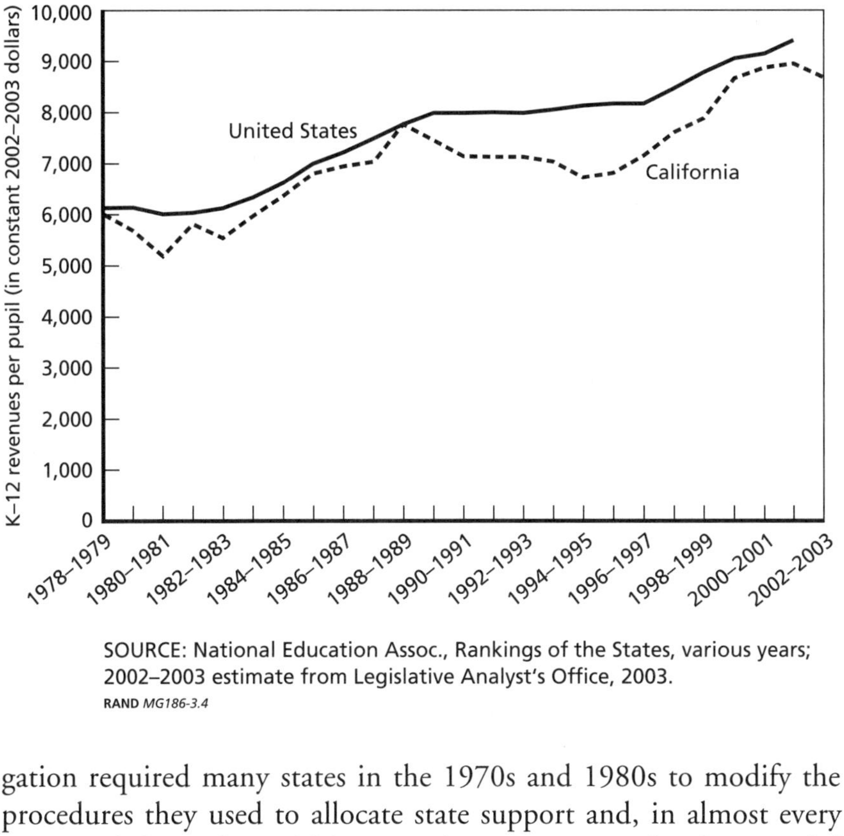

SOURCE: National Education Assoc., Rankings of the States, various years; 2002–2003 estimate from Legislative Analyst's Office, 2003.
RAND *MG186-3.4*

gation required many states in the 1970s and 1980s to modify the procedures they used to allocate state support and, in almost every instance, led to substantial increases in state support that far exceeded any associated reductions in local support (or resulted in higher levels of local support). Desegregation litigation, while focused on certain school districts, produced dramatic increases in state and local spending. The expansion of services over this period included the provision of new programs for students who might not have received them previously, such as assistance for physically or mentally handicapped students, for students with limited English proficiency, and for students at risk of failure. Over this same period, many states were reducing class sizes, extending the length of the school day or the school year, or broadening course offerings (Augenblick, 2001).

After decades of increase (with one plateau in the late 1970s), per-pupil revenues across the United States leveled off beginning in 1989–1990, partly because the states' shares of education funding leveled off. Beginning in the 1970s, the overall trend was for states to assume a greater share of education funding, but this trend did not continue once the states' shares peaked at about 50 percent in the mid-1980s. If we look at trends in the competition for state revenues, we find that education's share of state budgets decreased between fiscal years 1987 and 1994, while Medicaid, which provides medical care for the poor, and corrections, which builds and operates prisons, increased their shares (U.S. General Accounting Office, 1995a).

The early to mid-1990s saw flat per-pupil revenues at the national level and decreases in per-pupil revenues in California. Part of this was caused by an economic downturn that hit many states in the early 1990s and a recession that was particularly long and pronounced in California. It has also been argued that the slowdown in growth stemmed from a combination of tax and spending limitations, as well as a focus in the states on pursuing a "standards-based" approach to education reform that tied added revenues from the state to increased performance (Augenblick, 2001). The late 1990s and early 2000s again saw increases in revenues per pupil across the United States and sharp increases in revenues per pupil in California. The strong economic condition in many states, including California, at that time was a partial cause for these increases.

Proposition 98's formulas and requirements for setting minimum guaranteed K–12 funding were based on the assumption that the growth of the state's General Fund would be relatively stable from one year to the next. Policymakers did not anticipate precipitous drops in state tax revenues followed by more normal rates of growth, as was seen to some extent in the late 1980s and early 1990s and, possibly to a greater extent, in the early 2000s (EdSource, 2002c). A deep and extended recession in California resulted in declines in real (adjusted for inflation) per-pupil funding in the late 1980s and early 1990s and put California's K–12 funding well below both the national average and the funding in other large states. When California started its strong recovery in the mid-1990s, Proposition 98 ensured that a substantial portion of the growth would go to schools. In ensuing years, the legislature and governor approved an allocation that was higher than the minimum required amount. California state leaders steadily added to education funding from the mid-1990s through 2001. The California Legislative Analyst's Office (LAO) calculates that from 1994–1995 to 2001–2002, the state increased its support of K–12 education by 27 percent in inflation-adjusted dollars.

Now, however, local schools in California are once again confronting the challenges that go with severe budget constraints, and given the extent of the constraints, they may possibly be facing new challenges as well.[14] The LAO projects that it will take the state at least five years to bounce back from its current budget shortfall (EdSource, 2002c). While Proposition 98 to some degree protects total state funding for schools, the economic situation will put pressure on local school districts as they attempt to maintain salary commitments made to employees during better times, cover their basic operational expenses, and provide the extra support that both educators and students need to meet higher, standards-based achievement expectations.[15]

Per-Pupil Revenues: California Compared to Other States. Figure 3.5 shows per-pupil revenues in each state in 2001–2002, the school year in which California ranked 27th in the nation in per-pupil revenues. In comparison to the four other largest states, Cali-

---

[14] Recent state budget gaps have been addressed by K–12 funding actions that include deferring some K–12 expenditures, borrowing from future state receipts to provide more money in a given year, and instituting mid-year cuts. For more information on the K–12 budget for the 2001–2002 and 2002–2003 school years, see EdSource, 2002a, and Legislative Analyst's Office, 2003.

[15] The federal NCLB initiative imposes some of these expectations but also provides additional funding to schools.

Figure 3.5
Public K–12 Revenue per Pupil, by State, 2001–2002

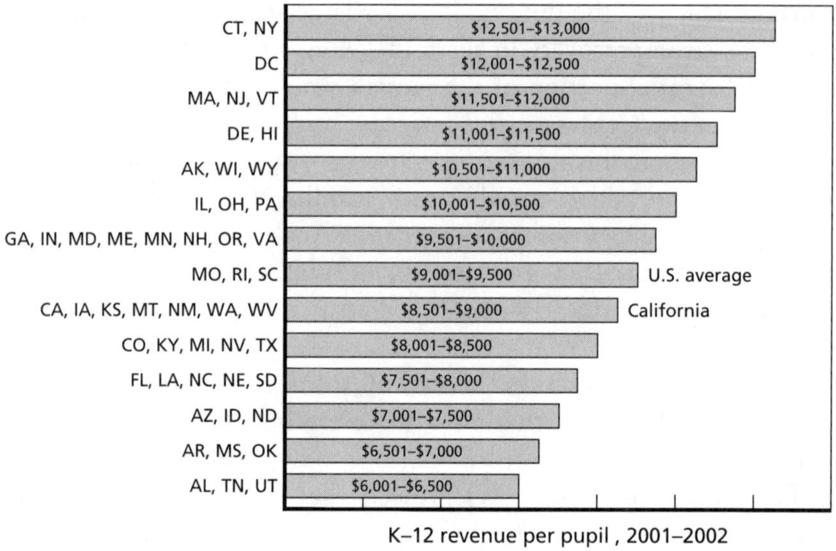

SOURCE: National Education Assoc., Rankings of the States, 2002.
RAND *MG186-3.5*

fornia's per-pupil revenues were above those of Texas and Florida and below those of New York and Illinois.[16]

---

[16] Comparisons with other states provide a valuable but limited perspective. States may put large investments into activities that are not counted in the NEA data or other data. For example, California has directed substantial funds to professional development for teachers and additional instructional time outside the regular school day. These monies are not included in the NEA data for California or any other state. At the same time, such investments may have a big payoff in the classroom (EdSource, 2001a). The National Center for Education Statistics (NCES) and NEA produce the two national indices of K–12 funding that are most widely used by researchers and policymakers. Because of differing methodologies, the two indices provide somewhat different measurements of California and national funding for K–12 education (e.g., NCES includes state administrative expenditures for K–12 education; NEA does not). Despite these differences, however, the two indices tend to track together (Legislative Analyst's Office, 2001a). In addition, some of the variation in per-pupil funding across states is accounted for by differences in the costs of educational services, the property wealth of the state, the amount the state is willing to spend for education, and the funding formula used by the state (U.S. General Accounting Office, 1995b). See EdSource 2001a for a more detailed discussion of why comparison data can be misleading.

Figure 3.6 presents more information on the size of the differences in per-pupil revenues among the five largest states, as well as information on how real per-pupil revenues in those states have changed over the past decade. In 2001–2002, per-pupil revenues were about $4,100 higher in New York than in California, even though real per-pupil revenues remained relatively constant in New York over the 1990s. From 1990–1991 to 2001–2002, both California and Texas saw real growth in per-pupil revenues of about 24 percent, and Illinois saw real growth of about 29 percent.

Categorical Aid as a Share of K–12 Revenues

An important trend in California school revenues is the rise in state categorical aid.[17] As described earlier, "categorical aid" is the catch-all term used to describe money earmarked for specific programs and purposes. In contrast to revenue limit, or general purpose, funding, most categorical aid is accompanied by conditions for its use. Some categorical aid is targeted for particular pupils, and some is targeted for specific programs. The state distributes categorical aid in a variety of ways, including across-the-board grants to all schools, reimbursements for specific services, incentives to encourage particular activities, and competitive grants (EdSource, 2001b). In 1969–1970, state categorical aid constituted 6 percent of all K–12 education revenue. In contrast, state discretionary aid plus property tax revenue—the sum that would become subject to revenue limits—constituted 87 percent of all revenues in 1969–1970 (Sonstelie, Brunner, and Ardon, 2000).[18]

Figure 3.7 shows revenue limit (general purpose) funding as a percentage of total K–12 Proposition 98 funding from 1988–1989 through 2000–2001.[19] During this period, discretionary spending

---

[17] Since Proposition 13 and SB 154, state categorical aid is all state aid not included in the district's revenue limit (general purpose) funding.

[18] The remainder was federal aid and other local aid.

[19] This includes funding in excess of Proposition 98's minimum requirement.

Figure 3.6
Public K–12 Revenue per Pupil, Five Most Populous States, 1990–1991 and 2001–2002

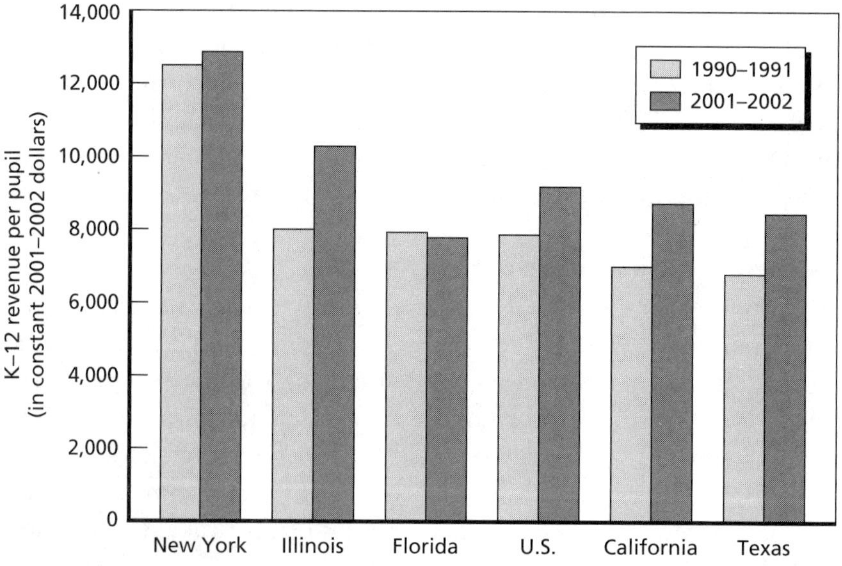

SOURCE: National Education Assoc., Rankings of the States, various years.
RAND *MG186-3.6*

declined from 78 percent of total Proposition 98 funding to 67 percent. This means that by 2000–2001, more than one-third of total Proposition 98 school funding was earmarked by the state for specific programs and purposes. In 2000–2001, the state funded about 70 categorical programs, most of which were relatively small. Five programs spent more than $500 million each in 2000–2001 and accounted for about 55 percent of all funds expended through categorical programs.[20] The largest state categorical program is special education, which accounted for about $2.5 billion in state funds in 2000–2001 (EdSource, 2001b).

---

[20] These five programs are Special Education, Class Size Reduction, Childcare and Development, Targeted Instruction Improvement Grants (TIIP, formerly Desegregation Grants), and Adult Education.

Figure 3.7
K–12 Proposition 98 Discretionary Spending Share, 1988–1989 to 2000–2001

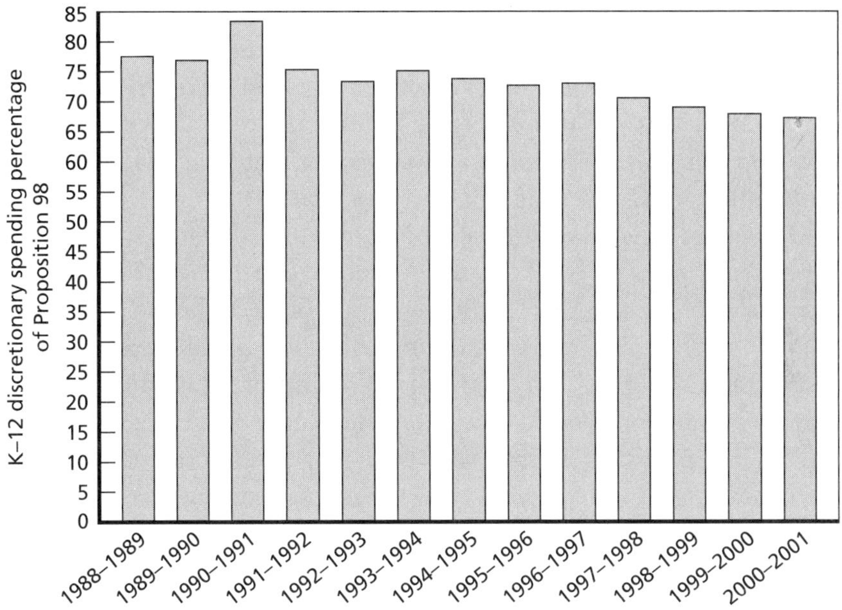

SOURCE: Legislative Analyst's Office, 2001a.
RAND *MG186-3.7*

The governor and the state legislature determine the division of Proposition 98 funds between categorical and general purpose aid, as well as how categorical aid is allocated. A significant feature of the 2000–2001 budget bill was its failure to provide any additional general purpose funds for local school districts and county offices above increases required by law. For 2003–2004, state leaders took the unusual step of reducing revenue limits by not giving districts the cost-of-living adjustment they were due and by cutting revenue limit amounts by 1.2 percent. In recent years, California used categorical funds to further its standards-based reform agenda. In 2003–2004, however, state leaders, faced with a large state deficit, reduced or even eliminated programs they had created and funded just a few years earlier, such as programs for instructional materials and professional development. In addition, to help districts absorb the general purpose cuts, state policymakers granted districts some limited-term financial flexibility, including the use of a large portion of their unspent 2002–2003 categorical fund reserves (EdSource, 2003).

Education analysts and researchers have raised concerns about the growing dependence on categorical aid. For example, the LAO expressed the view that the decline in local discretion over spending runs counter to the increased emphasis the state has placed on accountability in K–12 education in recent years. If the state is going to hold school districts accountable for improving student performance, the districts need to be given the resources and the local budgetary discretion to allocate their resources based on local need (Legislative Analyst's Office, 2001). In addition, Sonstelie, Brunner, and Ardon (2000) raise concerns about the equal distribution of funding and the growth in categorical aid. While revenue limits have become more equally distributed, they have also become a smaller fraction of total funds, leading to the question of whether total revenues have become more equally distributed.[21] The courts do not require categorical aid to be evenly distributed, which gives the state latitude in allocating resources across school districts. At the same time, lawmakers continue to explore ways to provide districts greater flexibility in the expenditure of categorical funds (EdSource, 2001b).[22]

---

[21] It is difficult to determine how the move to a state system of school finance and the growth in categorical aid have affected different kinds of districts and populations of students. Under state finance, general revenue is more equally distributed across school districts, with any remaining differences due to categorical programs. Sonstelie, Brunner, and Ardon (2000) conclude that large unified districts have benefited from both the equalization of revenue limits and the allocation of categorical aid. They also conclude that total revenues under the state funding system are distributed similarly to how they were distributed under local funding, and that state finance has not promoted more revenue for disadvantaged children.

[22] For example, the Governor's 2003–2004 budget proposed that 64 categorical programs be consolidated into a $5.1 billion block grant for the general purposes of professional development, instructional materials, technology, specialized and targeted instructional programs, school safety, and student services. The administration proposed that most of the programs' statutory requirements be eliminated and that school districts be given significant flexibility in how they used these funds (Legislative Analyst's Office, 2003).

California K–12 School Expenditures

We have looked at one part of California's K–12 school finance picture: school revenues, or how much money schools receive and from what sources. The other part of the picture is school expenditures, or how much schools spend and for what purposes.[23]

While it is generally accepted that California schools are spending less than the national average, estimates of how much less vary. Part of why these estimates vary is that they take different expenditures into account. Expenditures can be categorized based on whether they are funded from state, local, and/or federal revenues. And, clearly, per-pupil estimates will vary widely depending on the extent to which these sources are included or excluded. Expenditures can also be categorized by narrowly defined purposes—such as spending on teacher salaries, instructional materials, administration, or facilities. A broader distinction is made between spending on capital outlay and operating expenditures. The expenditure category most often referenced in the NEA and NCES indices is "current expenditures," which consists of operating expenditures, or those expenditures made in the day-to-day operation of schools (Legislative Analyst's Office, 2001a).[24]

---

[23] The measure of spending per pupil used in this section is spending per pupil in fall enrollment. Per-pupil spending is often cited as the ratio of current expenditures to the number of pupils in average daily attendance (ADA), but this measure may be misleading for California because prior to 1998–1999, at which point California joined the other states in how it counted daily attendance, it was the only state to count students with excused absences as being in attendance. Consequently, ADA may have been higher in California schools relative to ADAs in other states, thus understating California's spending per pupil in ADA. An alternative measure to ADA is to take a one-time, snapshot look at enrollment—the number of pupils enrolled in a school at one point in time (Sonstelie, Brunner, and Ardon, 2000). Expenditures per student in fall enrollment are available historically for California and other states and are used as the measure in this section.

[24] It should be noted that expenditures reflect the actual spending of local school districts and education agencies, which are reported after a given school year has been completed. The latest reliable school expenditure data lag two to three years behind the present.

Per-Pupil Expenditures in K–12 Public Schools

Figure 3.8 shows current expenditures per pupil over the past three decades in constant dollars.[25] In comparison to 1970, the per-pupil spending of U.S. public K–12 schools in 1999–2000 was about 100 percent higher than what would have been necessary simply to keep pace with inflation. About two-thirds of the increase can be largely

Figure 3.8
Current K–12 Public School Expenditures per Pupil, 1969–1970 to 1999–2000, California and the United States

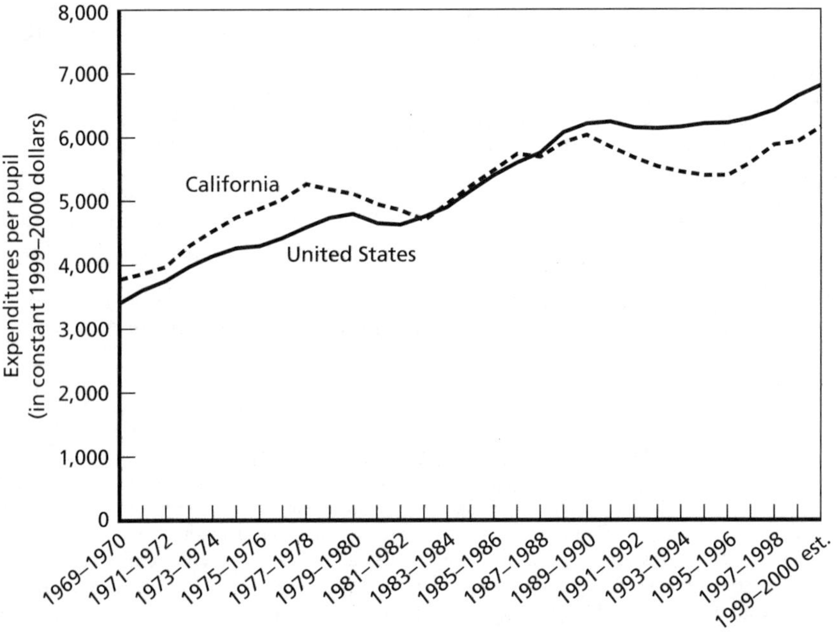

SOURCE: U.S. Department of Education, NCES, Digest of Education Statistics, various years.
RAND *MG186-3.8*

---

[25] These figures cover K–12 educational operations only, defined as "current expenditures of education." This means that for California, as well as other states, some significant expenditures may not be included in the numbers. For instance, summer school, noneducational after-school or Saturday programs, adult education, services to private schools or the community, and professional development institutes provided for teachers are excluded (EdSource, 2001a).

explained by higher numbers of instructional staff.[26] The remainder, about $1,000 per pupil, may reflect increases in personnel other than instructional staff, the cost of personnel benefits, and expenditures for supplies and materials, including technology (Augenblick, 2001). In California, the public school per-pupil spending in 1999–2000, compared to that in 1970, was about 62 percent higher than what would have been necessary to keep pace with inflation.

For the decade before Proposition 13 passed, per-pupil expenditures were about 10 percent higher in California than in the rest of the country (Sonstelie, Brunner, and Ardon, 2000). After 1978, however, per-pupil expenditures grew more slowly in California than in the rest of the country, reaching the level of other states by 1982–1983. From 1982 to 1990, California's level of per-pupil expenditures continued to be about equal to the level in other states. During the economic recession that occurred in the first half of the 1990s, California's average per-pupil expenditures fell below those of other states, reaching 85 percent of the level in other states in 1994–1995. They then rebounded somewhat, reaching 90 percent of the level in other states in 1999–2000. This upturn at the end of the century helped, but California's ranking in per-pupil spending was hampered for two primary reasons: Other states were also improving their education expenditures during that time, and California gained more students than the other states did. In fact, California's enrollment grew by 1.8 percent from 1998–1999 to 1999–2000 (more than 100,000 students), far exceeding the national rate of 0.6 percent (EdSource, 2001a).

Figure 3.9 shows the difference between California's per-pupil expenditures and the national average per-pupil expenditures in constant 1999–2000 dollars. Per-pupil school spending in California, in constant 1999–2000 dollars, went from about $400 above the national average in 1969–1970 to over $600 below the national average in 1999–2000. And despite recent funding increases for K–12 educa-

---

[26] Higher teacher salaries explain some of the increase, but most of the rise in aggregate teacher salaries was because of higher numbers of teachers, not higher teacher salaries.

Figure 3.9
California's K–12 Public School Per-Pupil Spending Relative to the National Average, 1969–1970 to 1999–2000

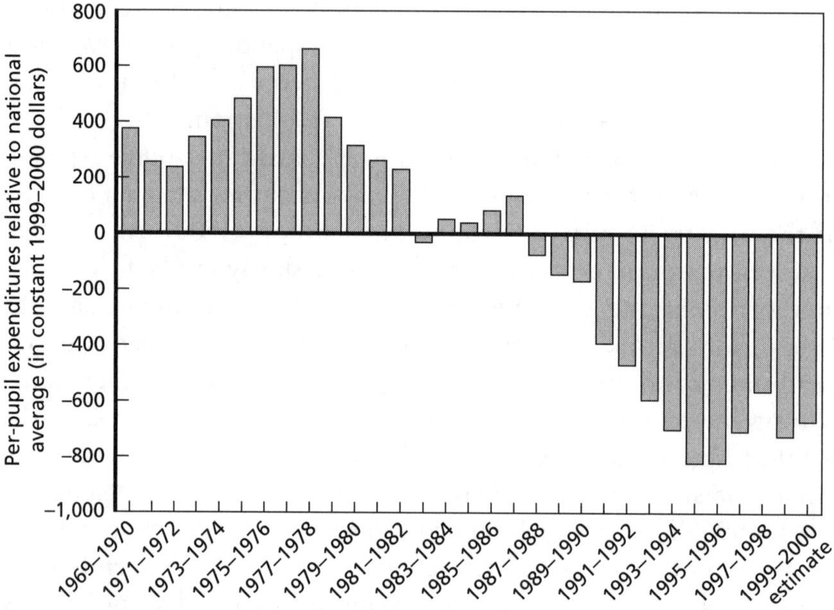

SOURCE: U.S. Department of Education, NCES, Digest of Education Statistics, various years.
RAND *MG186-3.9*

tion, California schools have continued their decade-long pattern of spending below the national average per student.

K–12 School Spending on Various Categories

When school district officials in California decide how to spend funds, they do so within constraints. Employee salaries and benefits make up more than 80 percent of most district budgets and are subject to collective bargaining, and about one-third of the remaining operating money is earmarked by the state for special purposes.[27] Figure 3.10 shows California's per-pupil spending in 1991–1992 and

[27]Some of those special purposes include paying for employee salaries and benefits.

Figure 3.10
California's K–12 Public School Per-Pupil Spending on Various Expenditure Categories, 1991–1992 and 1999–2000

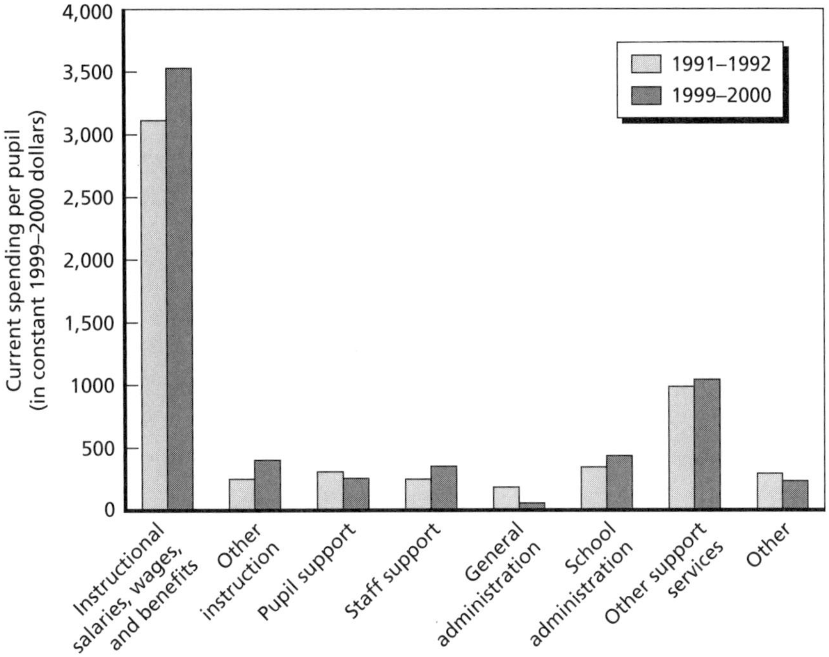

SOURCE: U.S. Census Bureau, Public Education Finances, various years.
RAND *MG186-3.10*

1999–2000 by spending categories. Instructional salaries, wages, and benefits accounted for about $3,500 per pupil and grew about 14 percent in real (adjusted for inflation) dollars during that period. The next largest category, "other support services," accounted for about $1,000 per pupil and stayed about the same size over time in real dollars.[28] The category "other instruction" includes expenditures for

[28] Other support services include business support services, central support services, and other forms of support services. Business support services include payments for fiscal services (budgeting, receiving and disbursing funds, payroll, internal auditing, and accounting), purchasing, warehousing, supply distribution, printing, publishing, and duplicating services. Central support services include planning, research, development, and evaluation services, as

supplies, materials, and contractual services;[29] staff support includes expenditures for curriculum development, instructional staff training, and media, library, and computer-assisted instruction services. Pupil support, which decreased over time, includes expenditures for attendance recordkeeping, social work, counseling, student appraisal, and placement services, as well as medical, dental, nursing, psychological, and speech services. In particular, general administration, which includes expenditures for board of education and executive administration (office of the superintendent) services, decreased considerably over time.

Figure 3.11 shows the change in current spending per pupil between 1991–1992 and 1999–2000 for each spending category in California and the United States. Compared to the United States as a whole, California experienced relatively large dollar growth in "other instruction" spending and school administration over the 1990s. A possible explanation for this relatively large growth could be that the school districts invested in materials and contractual services to support the standards-based reforms instituted by the state; another possibility could be that the districts needed to invest in supplies and materials deleted during the tight budget years in the early 1990s. California per-pupil expenditures on pupil support and general administration, compared to those of the United States, fell by relatively large dollar amounts over the 1990s. This suggests that California experienced a sizable reduction in student counseling and in social and health services over this period. In 1999–2000, California ranked 29th in the nation in current per-pupil spending on instructional salaries, 37th in current per-pupil spending on pupil services, 11th in current per-pupil spending on school administration, and 50th in current per-pupil spending on general administration.

---

well as information services, staff services (recruitment, staff accounting, noninstructional in-service training, staff health services), and data processing services.

[29] Instruction covers regular, special, and vocational programs offered in both the regular school year and summer school. It excludes instructional, student, and other support activities.

Figure 3.11
Change in K–12 Public School Per-Pupil Spending Between 1991–1992 and 1999–2000, California and the United States

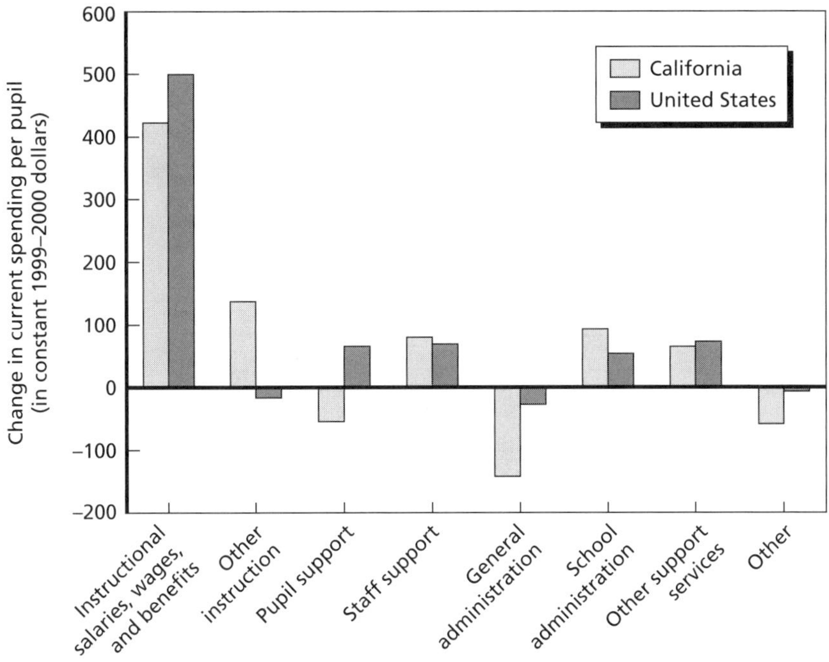

SOURCE: U.S. Census Bureau, Public Education Finances, various years.
RAND *MG186-3.11*

California's K–12 Funding Capacity and Effort

Per capita personal income is a traditional measure of a state's capacity to fund its schools, and measuring state public school expenditures against per capita personal income is a way to compare capacity with effort.[30] Figure 3.12 presents per capita personal income in the five

[30] The term *effort* is commonly used and is intended to be ability-neutral in that states with higher income can contribute more, but these differences in ability are controlled for by examining spending relative to a fixed amount of personal income.

Figure 3.12
Per Capita Personal Income, Five Most Populous States, 1999–2000

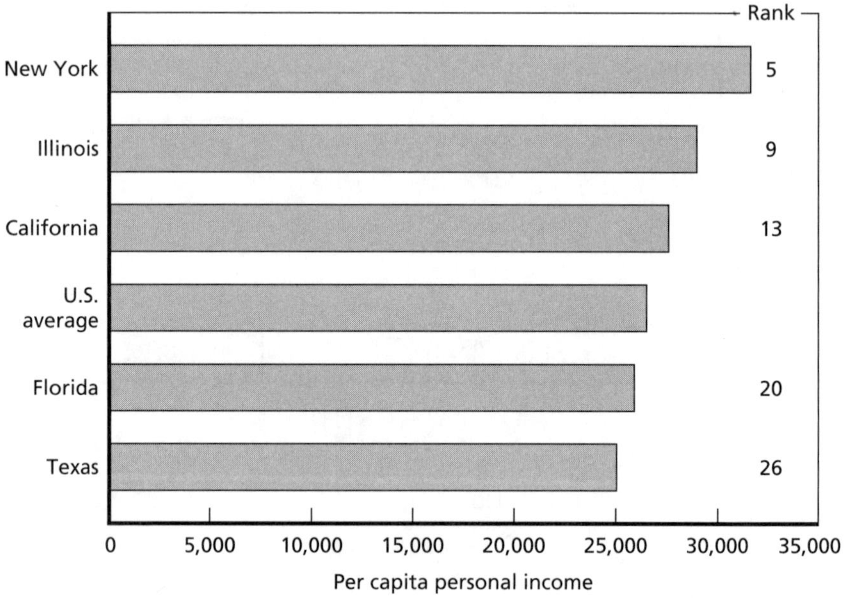

SOURCE: U.S. Bureau of Labor Statistics.
RAND *MG186-3.12*

most populous states. California's 1999–2000 per capita personal income, about $27,600, put it at 13th in the nation.

To measure effort, we looked at how much California actually spent on education for every $1,000 of per capita personal income. Figure 3.13 shows that in 1999–2000, California spent about $46 on K–12 public education per $1,000 of personal income. California ranked 36th in the nation on this measure, putting it behind Texas and New York and ahead of Illinois and Florida. In short, despite its high per capita personal income, California ranked low in K–12 spending.[31]

---

[31] California consistently ranked relatively high in per capita personal income throughout the 1990s. At the same time, California's rank in K–12 per-pupil spending relative to $1,000

Figure 3.13
Relation of K–12 Public School Per-Pupil Spending to $1,000 Personal Income, Five Most Populous States, 1999–2000

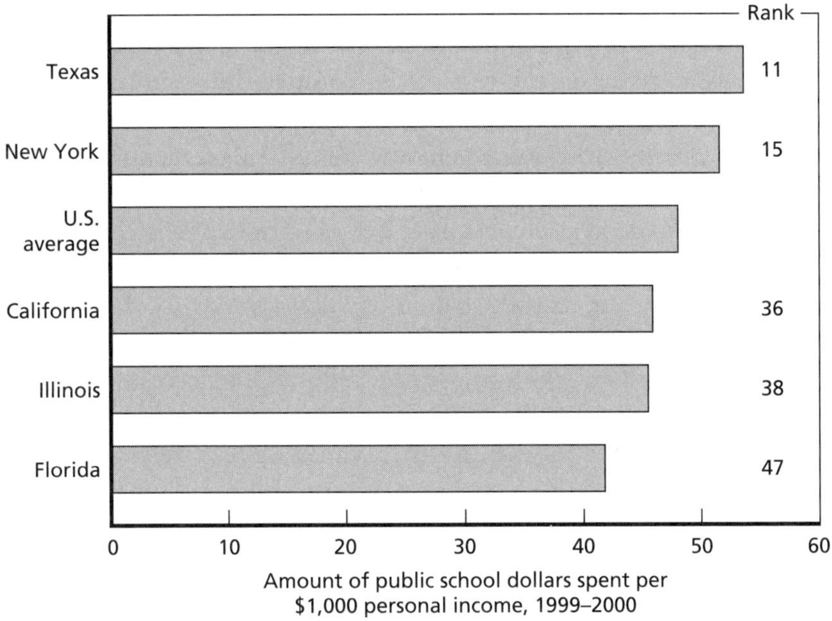

SOURCE: U.S. Census Bureau, Public Education Finances, 1990–2000.
RAND *MG186-3.13*

States of similar size may not have similar per capita personal income, however, so we also compared California's K–12 spending with that of states having similar per capita personal income. The four states whose per capita personal income was most similar to California's were Minnesota, Washington, Virginia, and Nevada. Of these, California ranked higher than three in K–12 spending, but only Minnesota ranked above the national average. It is not clear why these states, with relatively high per capita personal income, rank relatively low on K–12 spending per $1,000 in personal income.

---

in personal income was 48th in 1991–1992, 48th by 1995–96, and then 36th in 1999–2000 (National Education Association, Rankings and Estimates, various years).

Figure 3.14 shows public school spending as a percentage of personal income.[32] By the standards indicated by the rest of the country's spending, California could have afforded to spend more on its public schools in the 1990s than it actually did. In the early to mid-1970s, California spent about the same share of its personal income on public education as the rest of the country did—about 4.5 percent. In the late 1970s through the mid-1990s, however, California's share was considerably less, generally about 1.2 percentage points lower than that of the United States. Proposition 13 may have caused a comparatively rapid decline in K–12 expenditures as a percentage of personal income in California in the late 1970s and early 1980s.

In addition, the relative share of elementary and secondary education spending as a percentage of personal income began decreasing nationally in the late 1970s and early 1980s. This decrease occurred partly because of increased spending on other state functions, such as Medicaid and corrections, but also because of relatively weak economic growth and the budget effects of state and federal mandates in areas other than education (U.S. General Accounting Office, 1995b).

As Figure 3.15 shows, compared to the U.S. average, California has a relatively high level of per capita financial commitment to state services such as corrections and police and fire protection, and a relatively low level of per capita financial commitment to education. In the mid-1990s, California ranked relatively high in per capita spending on corrections and on police and fire protection—11th and 4th,

[32] The discrepancy between the estimate of California's school spending as a percentage of personal income presented in Figure 3.13 and the comparable ratio presented in Figure 3.14 reflects differences in the data sources we used. The data for Figure 3.13 were taken from the U.S. Census Bureau, which uses its own annual survey of government finances; the data for Figure 3.14 were taken from NCES, which uses the common core survey data. These two surveys define state public elementary and secondary school spending differently, the Census Bureau using state public school "finance amounts" and NCES using state public school "spending." The difference lies in the fact that actual spending for a year might be lower than what is initially financed. We cannot use the Census Bureau data for Figure 3.14 because they do not go back to 1970. However, because the Census data are commonly used for ranking states in terms of the ratio of public school per-pupil spending to personal income, we elected to use them for Figure 3.13.

Figure 3.14
K–12 Public School Per-Pupil Spending as a Percentage of Personal Income, California and the United States, 1970–2000

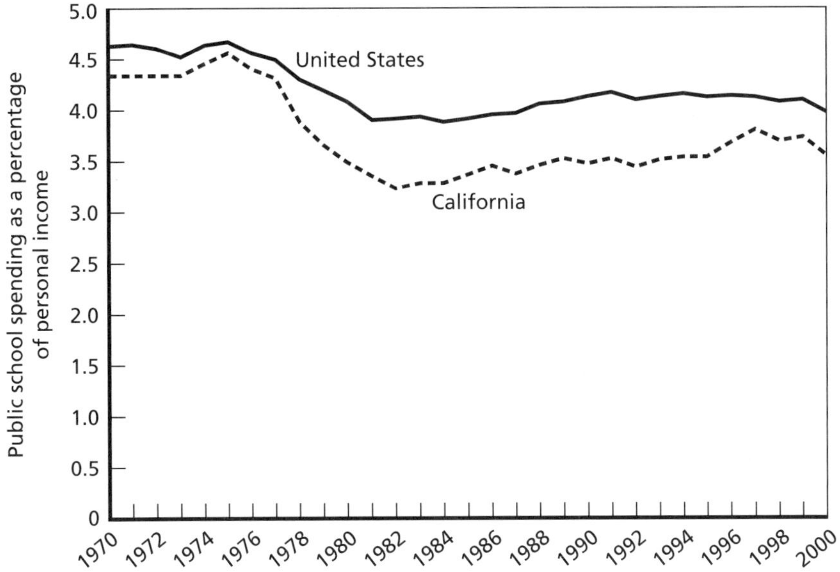

SOURCE: U.S. Bureau of Labor Statistics, and U.S. Department of Education, NCES, Digest of Education Statistics, various years.
RAND *MG186-3.14*

respectively (EdSource, 2001a)—but it ranked 30th in per capita spending on both higher and K–12 education.

There are a number of possible explanations for the difference between California's effort and the efforts of other states to fund K–12 education. One possible explanation is that Californians place a relatively low priority on funding education; another might be that California's demographics call for relatively high expenditures on social services, or that relatively high crime rates have propelled spending on police and corrections. Or California may have relatively more state mandates in areas other than education, or perhaps differing tax rates across states or differences in the percentages of people paying taxes are playing a role. There is really no way to know without doing additional research.

Figure 3.15
Per Capita Spending on Various State Functions, California and the United States, 1997–1998

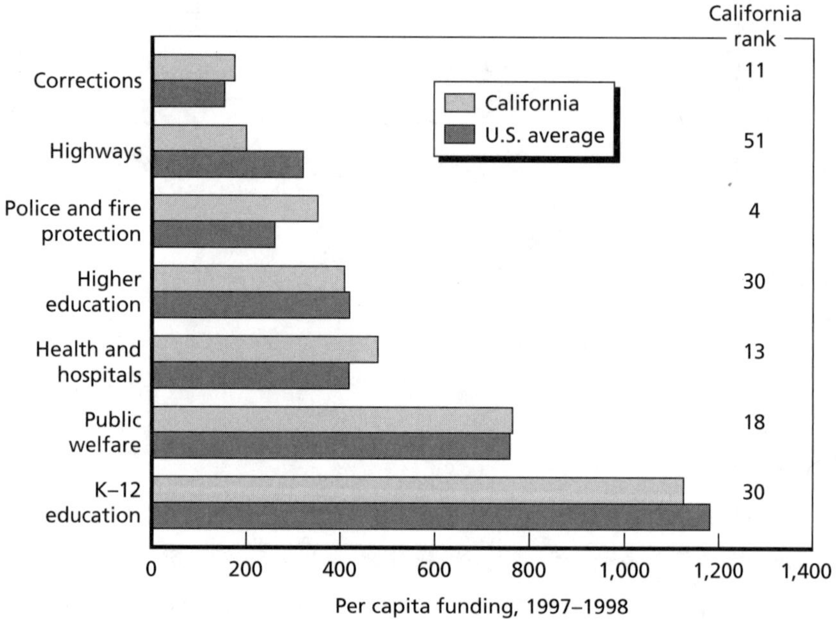

SOURCE: National Education Assoc., Rankings of the States, 2001.
RAND *MG186-3.15*

Conclusions

Concerns about the distribution of revenue prompted school finance reform in California in the 1960s and 1970s. More recently, there has been concern about the amount of resources provided to California's schools, the volatility of California's system of school finance, and the possible consequences of moving a larger share of state dollars away from general purpose aid to distribute them through categorical, or restricted, programs. Table 3.1 provides a quick summary of California's school financing compared to the school financing of all the

Table 3.1
Comparative Summary of California's K–12 Public School Finances

	California Compared to:		How California's Trend in the 1990s Compared to That of:	
Measures	**All States**	**Next Four Largest States**	**All States**	**Next Four Largest States**
Total per-pupil revenues (federal, state, and local)	Lower than average	Lower than average	Lower than average	Average
Fluctuations in total per-pupil revenues	Not applicable	Not applicable	Higher than average	Higher than average
State's capacity to fund K–12 public schools	Higher than average	Average	Not applicable	Not applicable
State's effort to fund K–12 public schools	Lower than average	Lower than average	Not applicable	Not applicable
Per-pupil expenditures on instructional salaries, wages, and benefits	Lower than average	Average	Lower than average growth	Average growth
Per-pupil expenditures on other instructional spending and school administration	Higher than average	Higher than average	Higher than average growth	Higher than average growth
Per-pupil expenditures on pupil support and general administration	Lower than average	Lower than average	Lower than average growth	Lower than average growth

states. Our review of school finances over time in California and in other states points to several conclusions:

- Passage of Proposition 13 by California voters in 1978 (combined with passage of Proposition 98 in 1988) produced a number of consequences for K–12 education. In particular, since Proposition 13, the K–12 funding has varied with fluctuations in the state economy. School districts now have limited local revenue options and, like the state as a whole, have to deal with extreme fluctuations in revenues, such as those that have occurred in recent years.
- California's decline in per-pupil K–12 funding relative to the U.S. average began in the late 1970s and early 1980s, following

passage of Proposition 13. Before that, California's per-pupil funding had been consistently above the national average. Since then, however, it has been consistently at or below the national average. K–12 real revenues and expenditures per pupil grew fairly rapidly in California and the United States over the mid- to late 1980s, with California per-pupil spending largely tracking that of the United States. California then fell well behind other states in the late 1980s. Beginning in the mid-1990s, California steadily added to education funding, as did other states, with real growth between 1994–1995 and 2001–2002 estimated at 27 percent. Now, though, after several years of more positive finances, local schools in California are again confronting the challenges that go with severe budget constraints.

- A growing share of California's education dollars is being distributed as categorical, or restricted, aid, as opposed to revenue limit, or general purpose, aid. This has raised concerns about a decline in local discretion, as well as concerns about equalization.
- California has a relatively high capacity to fund its schools (as measured by per capita personal income), but its level of effort in funding its schools is below the national average.

CHAPTER FOUR

California's K–12 Public School Teachers

In this chapter, we describe trends and patterns in teacher qualifications and salaries and in pupil-teacher ratios in California's K–12 public schools.

Teachers and Other Staff

Education—particularly K–12 education—is a labor-intensive industry. About 85 percent of all K–12 expenditures go to personnel salaries and benefits, and close to 40 percent of all expenditures go to teacher salaries and benefits. In 1999–2000, public elementary and secondary schools in the United States employed about 2.9 million teachers, who were paid an average salary of $41,700 (excluding benefits). In addition, the nation's K–12 public schools employed nearly 2.7 million other people: about 94,000 school district administrative staff, 900,000 instructional staff other than teachers (such as instructional aides, principals and assistant principals, librarians and guidance counselors), and about 1.7 million support staff (such as secretarial support, transportation staff, food service staff, health staff, and plant operation and maintenance staff). These figures suggest that teachers account for about 52 percent of public school employees, district staff for about 2 percent, other instructional staff for about 16 percent, and support staff for about 30 percent (U.S. Department of Education, NCES, Digest of Education Statistics, 2001).

Table 4.1 shows that public school staffing across the nation and in California has changed dramatically in the last 30 years. As the table indicates, the number of teachers has risen substantially both in absolute terms and in comparison to the number of students. In addition, this period saw a doubling in the number of staff other than teachers. Various factors may explain this increase in teachers and other staff relative to pupils—for example, growth in the number of pupils who have special education needs and therefore need more teacher attention, the expansion of programs and services for pupils (e.g., for those at risk of failure) and the resulting need for adult staff, and the tendency for school districts to maintain staff even through periods when enrollments decrease (Augenblick, 2001).

In general, California staffing of public schools has followed the national trend in terms of both growth in the absolute number of teachers and other staff and growth in teachers and other staff relative to pupils. But in contrast to the national trend, California's growth in staff per pupil has been relatively slow, and its public schools employ

Table 4.1
Teachers and Other Staff in K–12 Public Schools, United States and California, 1969–1970 and 1999–2000

	United States		California	
	1969–1970	1999–2000	1969–1970	1999–2000
Number of teachers (in thousands)	2,016	2,911	190	287
Number of teachers for every 1,000 students	44	62	41	47
Number of staff other than teachers (in thousands)	1,345	2,721	128	245
Number of staff other than teachers for every 1,000 students[a]	30	58	28	41

SOURCE: U.S. Department of Education, NCES, Digest of Education Statistics, various years.

[a]For the United States from 1969–1970 through 1999–2000, instructional staff rose from 6 to 19 per 1,000 students, school district administrative staff rose from 1.4 to 2.0 per 1,000 students, and support staff rose from 22.2 to 36.6 per 1,000 students (U.S. Department of Education, NCES, Digest of Education Statistics, various years).

relatively few staff per pupil—particularly with respect to teachers per pupil.

In 1999–2000, about 287,000 teachers, earning an average salary of $47,680 (excluding benefits), were employed in California schools. California has about 10 percent of the nation's public school teachers and, as Table 4.1 indicates, has about 47 teachers for every 1,000 pupils.

Most California school districts had leaner budgets following the switch to a state finance system for K–12 education in the late 1970s. They had several options—all with drawbacks—for adjusting to the lower revenues. They could limit their hiring, particularly of teachers, although this would increase class sizes. They could reduce teacher salaries, although this would hamper their ability to attract and retain teachers. They could economize on other expenditures, such as supplies and school facilities, which would impair teachers' ability to teach effectively. California school districts generally chose the first option, and the outcome was that California's pupil-teacher ratios grew relative to those in the rest of the nation (Sonstelie, Brunner, and Ardon, 2000).

To deal with the high ratios of pupils to teachers, California implemented its Class Size Reduction (CSR) program, beginning in 1996–1997, to reduce class sizes to 20 students per teacher in grades K–3. Class sizes were reduced across districts in California in the ensuing years, but one effect of this reduction was that the existing shortages of people interested in teaching, particularly in the most challenging schools, grew worse. California has been struggling for several years with how to address these shortages while simultaneously addressing concerns about both the quality of those who enter the classroom to teach and the challenges of meeting demanding new academic standards. California's policies related to teacher recruitment and to programs supporting teacher quality have changed dramatically since 1997–1998. Lawmakers have put increased focus and hundreds of millions of dollars into the preparation, recruitment, and support of new teachers, as well as into the establishment of a new state-directed approach to teacher training (EdSource, 2001b).

Profile of Teachers

By the 2002–2003 school year, California had a public K–12 teacher workforce of almost 310,000. As Figure 4.1 shows, the number of California teachers grew dramatically between 1990 and 2000, increasing by about 38 percent, compared with a 23 percent increase over that period for the national workforce of K–12 teachers.[1] This growth was at its highest between 1995–1996 and 1998–1999, when the workforce increased by more than 50,000 teachers, or about 7 percent annually (Shields et al., 2003). Two main factors spurred this growth: (1) a growth in student enrollment between 1991–1992 and 2000–2001 that increased the number of students enrolled in California's public schools by approximately 1 million, or 21 percent, to a total of more than 6 million students; and (2) the need for more K–3 teachers that accompanied implementation of the program of class size reduction in California beginning in 1996–1997.

The growth California experienced in the number of teachers slowed considerably in the early 2000s—moving closer to the annual growth rates of around 1 percent that had been seen in the early 1990s—primarily because class size reduction had reached full implementation and the state economy had slowed (Shields et al., 2003). Looking forward, the expectation is that the number of teachers in California will to grow, albeit at a continued slower pace (Esch and Shields, 2002). Student enrollment is estimated to rise over the medium term, which means that additional teachers will be required if current average class sizes are to be maintained. Attrition and retirement will further fuel the need for new teachers, even as enrollment flattens. Recent estimates suggest that teacher retirement rates will increase consistently—and perhaps dramatically—as baby boomers now reaching the height of their careers begin to retire. According to the annual report of the California State Teachers' Retirement System (STRS), almost 40 percent of all active STRS members were 50

[1] Growth in the teacher workforce in the four other most populous states (Texas, New York, Florida, and Illinois) has also been about 23 percent over the past decade.

Figure 4.1
Number of Teachers in California's K–12 Public Schools, Fall 1969 to Fall 2002

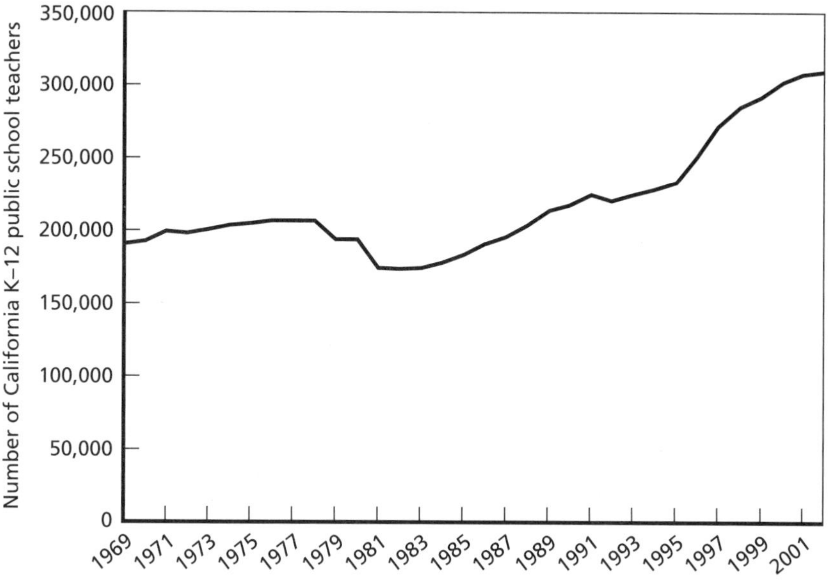

SOURCES: U.S. Department of Education, NCES, Digest of Education Statistics, various years; Shields et al., 2003.
RAND *MG186-4.1*

years of age or older in 1999–2000, so if they retire at their average retirement age of 60, the majority of these members will no longer be teaching by 2010. An estimate based on conservative assumptions and STRS membership data is that the annual retirement rate for teachers will peak in 2007–2008 at 4.9 percent. Thereafter, the retirement rate will begin to decline; but in 2009–2010, it will still be approximately 4.1 percent of the workforce, compared with today's estimated rate of 1.7 percent (Esch and Shields, 2002).

As a group, California's public elementary and secondary teachers are formally trained, state-certified professionals. In the 2002–2003 school year, 88 percent of the state's classroom teachers were fully credentialed (Shields et al., 2003).[2] Even though the requirements have changed somewhat over the past few years, being fully credentialed generally means that the teacher (1) holds at least a bachelor's degree, (2) has demonstrated his/her knowledge by passing the California Basic Educational Skills Test (CBEST) and satisfying subject matter requirements through coursework or evaluation, and (3) has completed schooling or training that includes classroom practice (such as student teaching) and class work in various state-required areas (such as reading instruction and the use of technology). The majority of California's teachers are also quite experienced, having spent an average of 13 years in the classroom (EdSource, 2002b).

Teachers Without Full Credentials

By 1999–2000, a substantial portion—about 15 percent—of the teacher workforce was newly employed, with not more than two years on the job (EdSource, 2002b). A majority of these new teachers were in classrooms without having completed the education-specific training noted above (Esch and Shields, 2002). These percentages are of serious concern to those who view certification as an indicator of teacher quality.[3]

This group of newly employed, not fully certified teachers encompassed interns, pre-interns, and individuals on emergency permits, or waivers. Participants in intern programs have a bachelor's degree, have passed subject matter requirements, and while working as the teacher of record, are enrolled in a planned course of study and receive support from mentor teachers and/or faculty at an institution of higher education. Pre-interns are full-time teachers who may or may not be enrolled in a preparation program, have not met subject matter requirements, and receive limited support through a pre-intern program while being the teacher of record. The pre-intern program was enacted in 1997 in response to a serious teacher short-

[2] Fully credentialed includes first-time, new-type, multiple- and-single subject, preliminary, and professional clear credentials.

[3] The debate over certification and student performance is represented in Goldhaber and Brewer, 2000, 2001; and Darling-Hammond, Berry, and Thoreson, 2001.

age. For an emergency single- or multiple-subject teaching permit, the minimum requirements are completion of a bachelor's degree, passage of the CBEST, and verification of subject matter competence at a level established by regulation for the emergency permit. Individuals serving on an emergency permit must enroll in a professional preparation program for the credential and complete coursework each year to renew the permit. People on emergency permits can renew them for only five consecutive years, after which they must obtain a full credential if they wish to continue teaching.

The proportion of first-year teachers without full credentials peaked in the 1999–2000 school year at over 50 percent. As of 2002–2003, that number had decreased to about 42 percent (Shields et al., 2003). Figure 4.2 shows the credential status of first-year teachers in California public schools for the six school years from 1997–1998 to 2002–2003.

As the 1990s progressed, teacher candidates entered positions in K–12 public school systems earlier, through emergency, intern, and other noncredentialed routes. The composition of the group of noncredentialed teachers changed over this period as more individuals entered intern and pre-intern programs and fewer individuals taught on emergency permits. While the pre-intern program was originally seen as a short-term response to a severe teacher shortage, it has expanded over time: The percentage of noncertified teachers in the program rose from 3 percent in 1998–1999 to about 24 percent in 2002–2003. The pre-intern program is likely to decrease in size over the next few years, however, because the federal No Child Left Behind (NCLB) provisions seek to ensure that all children are taught by a "highly qualified" teacher. Generally, this means that all teachers in core subject areas are required either to have a full credential or to be working to obtain one by 2005–2006 while participating in a structured intern program. Because NCLB does not consider pre-interns to be highly qualified, school districts will have little incentive to hire pre-interns as teachers. Intern programs, in contrast, will likely continue to grow. Participation in intern programs has increased steadily over the past several years; individuals participating in intern pro-

Figure 4.2
Percentage of First-Year Teachers in California, by Credential Status

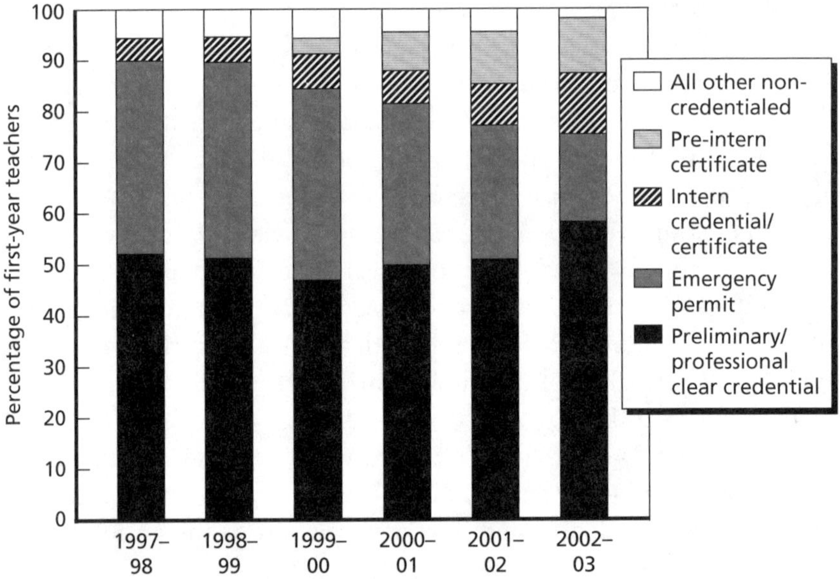

SOURCE: Shields et al., 2003 (the raw data are from the California Department of Education, Educational Demographics Unit, CBEDS Professional Assignment Information Form).

NOTE: "All other noncredentialed" includes first-year teachers on waivers and first-year teachers who have more than one certificate or credential (other than a preliminary/professional clear credential).

RAND *MG186-4.2*

grams went from 11 percent to 20 percent of all noncertified teachers between 1997–1998 and 2002–2003 (Shields et al., 2003).

Figure 4.3 shows the total number of K–12 public school teachers and the number of fully credentialed teachers in California over time. The gap between these two numbers grew from the mid-1990s until 2000–2001, when it reached a high of 42,427 teachers, or 14 percent of the teacher workforce. In the following two years, however, the gap declined somewhat, with the result that in 2002–2003,

Figure 4.3
Gap Between Total Number of K–12 Teachers and Number of Fully Credentialed Teachers in California Public Schools, 1991–1992 to 2002–2003

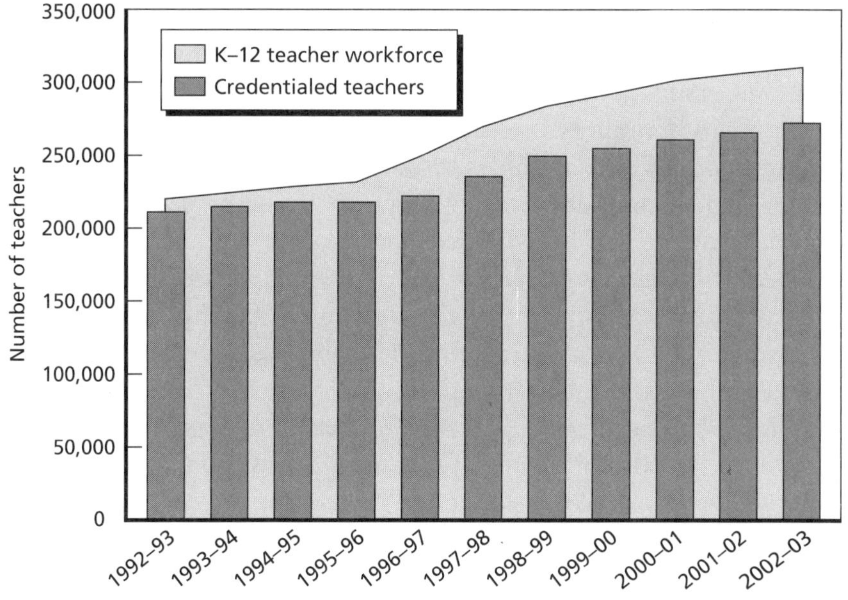

SOURCE: Esch and Shields, 2002; Shields et al., 2003 (the raw data are from the California Department of Education, Educational Demographics Unit; the California Commission on Teacher Credentialing; and the California State Teachers' Retirement System).
RAND *MG186-4.3*

37,111 teachers, or 12 percent of the workforce, had not completed a credential (Shields et al., 2003).[4]

Although the number of California's teachers who have not completed a credential remains relatively high, these teachers may have benefited from state efforts aimed at improving teacher prepara-

[4] An examination of a few of the state's large school districts suggests that the 2003–2004 school year may have seen the number of teachers without full certification decline considerably more (Shields et al., 2003).

tion and recruitment, supporting new teachers, and training teachers. Over the past few years, the California legislature has put considerable resources into programs to entice people to become teachers—ranging from creating regional recruitment centers to paying the student loans of teachers who work in particular schools. For example, the state spent a little more than $14 million on teacher recruitment programs in 1998–1999, but had increased that amount to nearly $160 million two years later. In addition, lawmakers directed hundreds of millions of dollars to supporting new teachers and establishing a new state-directed approach to training them. California now has a large and well-funded induction program for beginning teachers. Legislation passed earlier, in 1992 (SB 1422), supported the statewide development of the Beginning Teacher Support and Assessment (BTSA) program; and other legislation, passed in 1998 (SB 2042), raised the standards for new teacher preparation and established an induction program for teachers' first two years of teaching. The allocation for BTSA in 1992 was $4.9 million. By 2003–2004, it was $86 million, and there were 145 BTSA programs serving more than 21,000 beginning teachers, with participation by nearly every district in the state (Shields et al., 2003).[5]

The state's policy toward teacher quality has also changed significantly since 1997–1998. In that year, California's approach to teacher quality issues was based on long-standing programs: The state allowed school districts to use up to eight instructional days to provide locally selected staff development programs, and school districts received $77 million for a mentor teacher program to support new teachers. Over the past few years, however, this approach has changed, with the state now asserting greater control over both the eight days' worth of funds that local districts once used as they wished and the investment of hundreds of millions of dollars in teacher training. Between 1999 and 2001, much of the state's assistance came

[5] The BTSA program primarily supports new teachers with full credentials. New teachers with emergency permits and pre-intern certificates are not eligible for BTSA, and intern eligibility is a complicated issue.

through either the state's Subject Matter Projects[6] or the Professional Development Institutes,[7] both administered by the University of California's Office of the President.

Currently, however, funding for many of the programs begun only a few years ago is being reduced or entirely cut as a result of the state's weak economy and soaring budget deficit. For example, all funding for the Professional Development Institutes and a substantial portion of the funding for the Subject Matter Projects were recently cut from the budget.[8] Moreover, the state has severely reduced its spending on teacher recruitment because of the current budget shortfall. And the California university system responsible for preparing most of the state's new teachers is facing budget reductions of its own.

Distribution of Teachers Without Full Credentials

Although the percentage of new teachers lacking full credentials decreased over the past two years, certain subject areas faced more severe shortages of fully credentialed teachers than did others and, as a result, continued to have disproportionate percentages of teachers without full credentials. Table 4.2 provides the details. In elementary schools, which have the largest percentage of all K–12 teachers—63

---

[6] The state's network of California Subject Matter Projects (CSMPs) was established in 1988 and reauthorized in 1998 with a new structure. CSMPs aim to improve teachers' content knowledge in their subject area and to identify teacher leaders. They incorporate California content standards, a team approach to training teachers, and a focus on teachers in the state's lowest performing schools. Projects in nine subject areas—writing, mathematics, etc.—provide teachers with an intensive summer institute and follow-up activities during the school year (Shields et al., 2003).

[7] Several California Professional Development Institutes (CPDIs) were established in 2000. They offer teacher training in reading, mathematics, and English language development in the form of summer institutes and follow-up work. CPDIs prioritize teachers from schools scoring in the 40th percentile or lower in the state's Academic Performance Index (API) (Shields et al., 2003).

[8] While state dollars have been cut from these two programs, professional development dollars sent directly to school districts have increased, with strings attached. The legislature created the Reading and Mathematics Professional Development Program (AB 466), which allows school districts to purchase training from organizations that have met state guidelines and been approved by the California Department of Education.

Table 4.2
K–12 Public School Teachers Without Full Credentials, by Assignment Area, 1997–1998 and 2002–2003

Assignment	Percentage of Teachers Without Full Credentials,[a] 2002–2003	Percentage Point Increase (Decrease) in Teachers Without Full Credentials from 1997–1998 to 2002–2003	Teachers with This Assignment as Percentage of All K–12 Teachers
Elementary	10	(1)	63
All secondary	10	4	31
Mathematics	15	10	7
Physical science	13	8	4
Life science	12	7	5
English	8	5	13
Social science	6	3	12
Special education	18	5	12

SOURCE: Esch and Shields, 2002; Shields et al., 2003.
NOTE: The raw data are from the California Department of Education, Educational Demographics Unit Professional Assignment Information Form. The percentage of teachers without full credentials is calculated as the percentage of full-time teachers by assignment who report not having a full credential. Teachers may report more than one assignment.
[a]Teachers without full credentials are those in pre-intern and intern programs and those on emergency permits or waivers.

percent—10 percent were not fully credentialed in 2002–2003. In the secondary schools, the subject areas of mathematics and physical science suffered the largest shortages of credentialed teachers. And the worst situation was in special education, where 18 percent of teachers lacked full credentials.

Changes in the percentage of teachers without full credentials between 1997–1998 and 2002–2003 varied by assignment area. Elementary teachers without full credentials decreased one percentage point during the 1997–1998 to 2002–2003 period. By contrast, secondary teachers of mathematics and physical science without full credentials went up 10 and 8 percentage points, respectively, over this period. In addition, fully credentialed special education teachers remained in short supply, and in a time when the numbers of special education students continued to increase. In 1994–1995, for example, there were 550,000 special education students in California; in 2002–2003, there were more than 675,000.

Besides being concentrated in certain subject areas, teachers lacking full credentials are concentrated in certain types of schools serving certain populations of students. Prior to the mid-1990s, the percentages of inexperienced and uncertified teachers per school showed very little difference with respect to the student population's race/ethnicity and income level. And in 1995–1996, the year before class size reduction began, schools with high percentages of nonwhite and low-income students were only slightly more likely than other schools to have inexperienced teachers lacking full certification and post-graduate schooling. By 1999, however, there were large gaps between teacher qualifications in schools attended by nonwhite and low-income students versus other schools. These differences reflect the various levels of difficulty schools had in attracting and retaining teachers following implementation of class size reduction (Jepsen and Rivkin, 2002).

Although the picture has improved somewhat in the past two years, noncredentialed teachers are still found in disproportionate numbers in urban schools, low performing schools, and schools serving high numbers of low-income and minority students or English learners.[9] In 2002–2003, for example, urban districts had an average of 12 percent of noncredentialed teachers on staff (14 percent in 1998–1999), whereas suburban schools had 10 percent (11 percent in 1998–1999) and rural schools had 7 percent (7 percent in 1998–99). In addition, analysis of school-level scores on the state's API showed that, on average, the lowest performing schools had 18 percent of teachers without full credentials in 2002–2003, which is about 3.5 times the proportion of such teachers at the highest performing schools (Shields et al., 2003). Again, these differences have recently

---

[9] It should also be noted that new teachers with emergency permits and pre-intern certificates are not eligible for the state's extensive system of beginning teacher support through BTSA, and the eligibility of interns for BTSA is a somewhat complicated issue. Consequently, these new teachers in the state's schools with the highest poverty, highest minority students, and the lowest test scores often lack a structured support system during their early years in the teaching profession. For example, 26 percent of teachers in schools where 20 percent or more teachers lacked full credentials reported participating in BTSA, compared with 66 percent of teachers in schools where few teachers lacked full credentials.

been reduced somewhat: In 2000–2001, the lowest performing schools had five times the proportion of teachers without full credentials that the highest performing schools had.

The percentage of teachers lacking full credentials is also directly related to the percentage of students receiving free or reduced-price lunch (a proxy for the poverty level of the student population) and to the percentage of students who are minorities at a school. As shown in Figure 4.4, in 2002–2003, schools with the highest percentages of

Figure 4.4
Distribution of California's K–12 Public School Teachers Without Full Credentials, by Student Poverty Level, 1997–1998 to 2002–2003

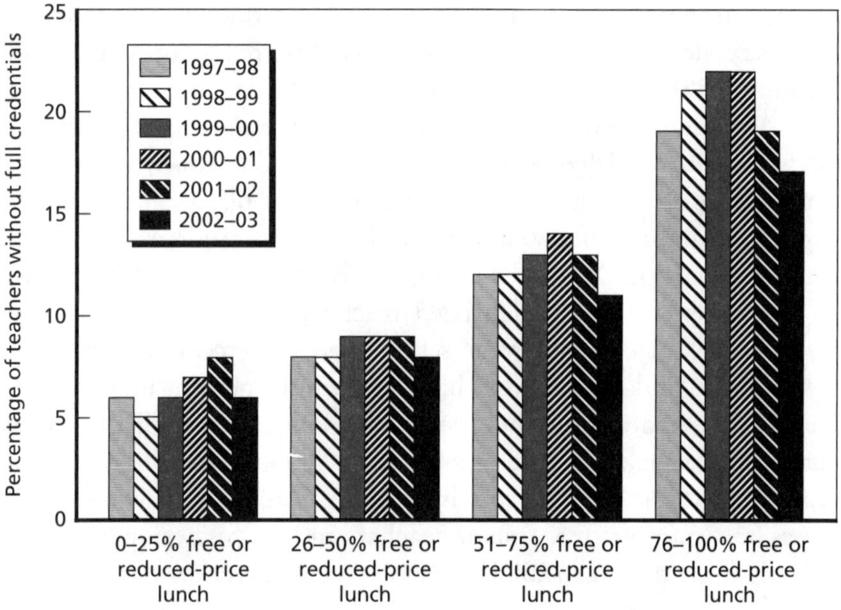

SOURCE: Shields at al., 2003 (the raw data are from the CDE, Educational Demographics Unit, Teacher Credentials and Experience by School; CDE, Educational Demographics Unit, List of California Public Schools and Districts; and CDE, Educational Demographics Unit, Free and Reduced Price Meals/CalWORKS (AFDC)).

RAND *MG186-4.4*

students receiving free or reduced-price lunch continued to have almost three times the percentage of teachers without full credentials that schools with the lowest percentages of such students had. At the same time, the percentage of teachers without full credentials at the highest poverty schools had come down: Schools in which more than 75 percent of students received a free or reduced-price lunch had, on average, 17 percent of teachers without full credentials, down from 19 percent in 1997–1998 and 2001–2002.[10]

A similar trend is found in data for schools with high percentages of minority students. Schools serving high percentages of minority students have seen a decrease in the percentages of teachers without full credentials, but those percentages still remain close to five times higher in high-minority schools than in low-minority schools. As shown in Figure 4.5, in 2002–2003, high-minority schools had an average of 20 percent of teachers without full credentials on staff compared with 4 percent in low-minority schools.

In addition to looking at teacher qualification requirements in California and how those requirements have changed over time, we also looked at how the requirements vary across states. Table 4.3 examines the percentage of school districts in California and in the United States in 1999–2000 that required various teacher qualifications when considering teacher applicants. The most marked difference is that 82 percent of districts in the United States required full standard state certification in field to be taught, whereas only 46 percent of districts in California did. In addition, 30 percent of California's districts required a major or minor in field to be taught, compared with 63 percent of districts nationally. By contrast, 95 percent of districts in California required a passing score on a state test of basic skills, compared with 64 percent nationally, largely reflecting the absence of a state test of basic skills in some states.

---

[10] Over 2,000 schools in California (or about 25 percent of all schools in California) have more than 75 percent of students receiving free or reduced-price lunch.

Figure 4.5
Distribution of California's K–12 Public School Teachers Without Full Credentials, by Percentage of Minority Students, 1997–1998 to 2002–2003

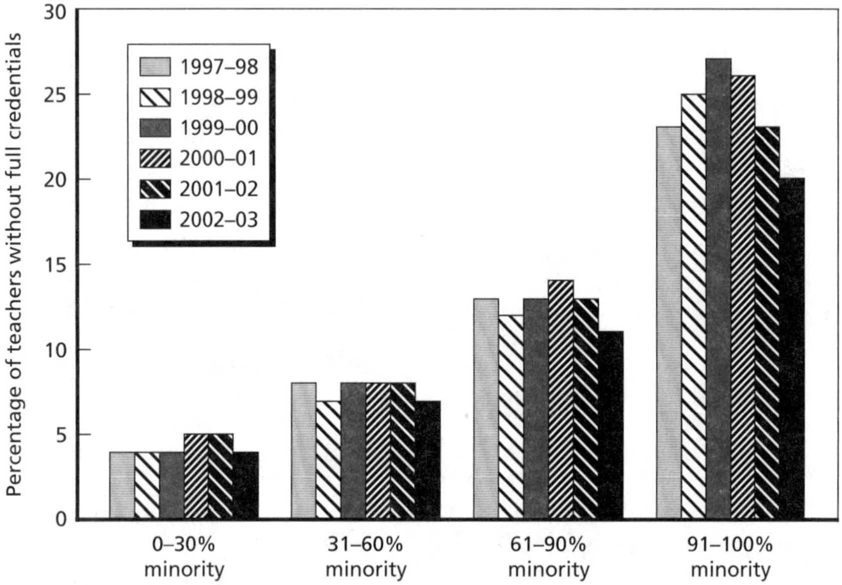

SOURCE: Shields et al., 2003 (the raw data are from CDE, Educational Demographics Unit, Teacher Credentials and Experience by School; CDE, Educational Demographics Unit, Enrollment by Ethnic Group by school; and CDE, Educational Demographics Unit, List of California Public Schools and Districts).

RAND *MG186-4.5*

Teacher Salaries

Because teacher salaries and benefits make up about 40 percent of a typical district budget, they are a critical part of public school costs.[11]

[11] Teacher salaries and benefits as a percentage of total K–12 current expenditures have decreased over time in California and nationally. Teacher salaries and benefits represented about 40 percent of K–12 expenditures in California and the United States in 2000, down from about 50 percent in 1969 (U.S. Department of Education, NCES, Digest of Education Statistics, various years).

Table 4.3
Percentage of Public School Districts Requiring Various Teacher Qualifications When Considering Teacher Applicants, California and the United States, 1999–2000

Teacher Qualifications	Percentage of Districts in 50 States and Washington, DC	Percentage of Districts in California
Full standard state certification in field to be taught	82	46
Graduation from state-approved teacher preparation program	70	60
Major or minor in field to be taught	63	30
Passing score on state test of basic skills	64	95
Passing score on state test of subject knowledge	54	44
Passing score on local district test of basic skills or subject knowledge	3	11
Passing score on either Praxis Core Battery or Praxis II: Subject Assessment	25	21

SOURCE: U.S. Department of Education, Schools and Staffing Survey (SASS), 1999–2000.

In addition, it is clear that over the long term, relative teacher compensation plays an important role in influencing people's decisions to enter and leave the teaching profession (Goldhaber, 2000). In sheer dollar terms, the average salaries of California's teachers have consistently placed them in the top 10 in the nation, suggesting that California teachers are well paid in comparison to most of their counterparts across the country. But since California's cost of living is considerably higher than that of most other states, the purchasing power of these higher salaries is less in California than it would be in most other states. Once average teacher salaries are adjusted for regional cost differences, California's average teacher salaries end up below the national average. We now turn to average teacher salaries in California and the nation with no adjustment for regional cost of living, after which we present average teacher salaries for California compared to other states once cost-of-living differences are taken into account.

Figure 4.6 shows that average teacher salaries in California rose over the 30-year period from 1969–1970 to 2000–2001 from about $10,000 to about $49,000 in current dollars. Once adjusted for inflation,[12] however, average 2000–2001 teacher salaries in California are about what they were in 1969–1970. Real average salaries fell in the early 1980s, reflecting a state economic downturn, and then began to

Figure 4.6
Average Annual Salaries of K–12 Public School Teachers, California, 1969–1970 to 2000–2001

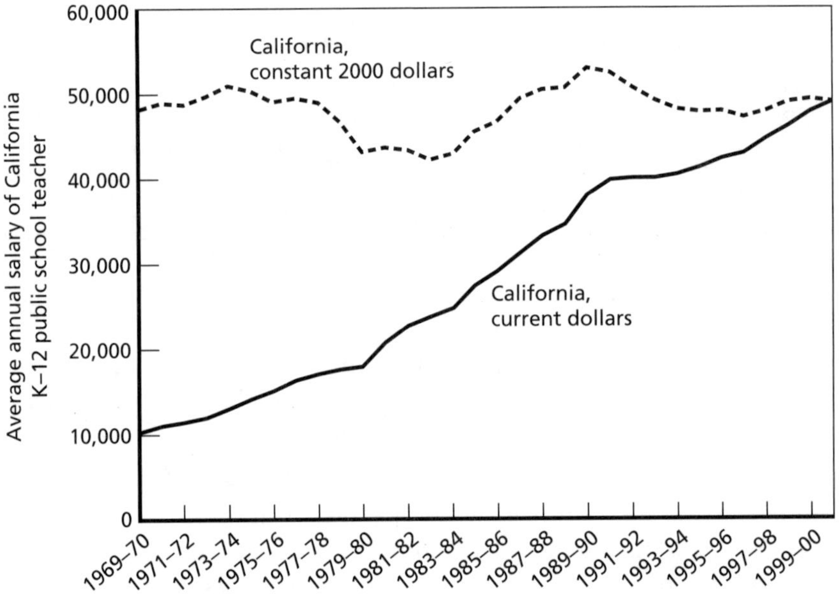

SOURCES: U.S. Department of Education, NCES, Digest of Education Statistics, various years.

RAND *MG186-4.6*

---

[12] Adjustments for inflation are done using the CPI. Some analysts argue that because productivity growth in service industries, such as education, is typically slower than in other sectors of the economy, the CPI may not be the most appropriate statistic to use in adjusting teacher salaries for inflation. Different price deflators may have a relatively significant impact on the calculation of real teacher salaries. Still, the differences are not pronounced enough to change the overall pattern. See Goldhaber, 2000, for a detailed discussion.

rise again in the mid-1980s. They then fell again, though only somewhat, in the early 1990s, reflecting another state economic downturn, and then rose slightly in the mid- to late 1990s. It is important to note in looking at teacher salaries that they also reflect changes in the demographics of the teacher labor force over time, such as teacher education and experience levels. The 1990s fall in average annual teacher salaries stems partly from a decline in teacher education and experience levels over that period. For example, about 45 percent of teachers in California had a master's degree or higher in 1987, compared with 41 percent in 1990 and 38 percent in 1999. In addition, approximately 67 percent had 10 or more years of full-time teaching experience in 1987, compared with 60 percent in 1990 and 51 percent in 1999 (U.S. Department of Education, NCES, Digest of Education Statistics, various years).

Average teacher salaries (not adjusted for cost-of-living differences) in California were sixth highest in the nation in 2000–2001 (U.S. Department of Education, NCES, Digest of Education Statistics, 2002). Compared to average teacher salaries in the four other most populous states and the United States, California's salaries have consistently been below those in New York (which ranked third in the nation in 2000–2001) and above those in Texas, Florida, Illinois, and the United States as a whole, although the gaps in these cases have grown and shrunk over time. One fact that stands out is that even as spending per pupil in California fell well below the U.S. average over time, the average salary of California's teachers remained above the U.S. average (Sonstelie, Brunner, and Ardon, 2000).[13]

Most teachers are subject to a uniform salary schedule that provides automatic salary increases for years of experience and education beyond the bachelor's degree. This means that certain factors can affect the computation of average salary. For instance, the aging of

---

[13] A study by the Legislative Analyst's Office (1991) reached a similar conclusion. It found that increases in K–12 funding in the 1980s had gone mostly to teacher salaries. Sonstelie, Brunner, and Ardon (2000) found that California districts were responding to market forces and paid teachers what was necessary to remain competitive.

teachers can greatly increase the average salary, and a lowering of the education distribution of teachers can greatly decrease it. Because of this, comparisons of starting salaries over time or of some other consistent place on salary schedules are generally considered to be more precise information than averages are.

As an example, consider the following. In 1997–1998, statewide average salaries in California varied from $29,873 for new teachers with a bachelor's degree to almost $56,000 for highly experienced teachers with a bachelor's degree and 90 additional units of coursework (Sonstelie, Brunner, and Ardon, 2000). The school district with the highest salary for new teachers paid almost twice as much for its new teachers as the lowest-paying district did, and the difference between what the highest- and the lowest-paying districts paid their experienced teachers was even larger. With that said, salary variation at each level of education and experience was relatively modest across districts.[14] Regional differences were an important factor in teacher salary differences for teachers at a given experience level. For example, compared to the new-teacher salaries in Southern California, those in Northern California and the Central Valley were relatively low (and private sector salaries were also correspondingly low). The local demand for teachers may affect teacher salaries as well. Teacher shortages were most severe in Southern California, so that area's relatively high starting salaries probably reflected the need to attract a greater number of teachers. Another factor in teacher salary differences is district size, with salaries generally tending to be higher in larger districts (Sonstelie, Brunner, and Ardon, 2000).[15]

---

[14] About 90 percent of districts paid new teachers at each level of educational attainment salaries that fell within 15 percent of the average. A similar portion of districts paid more-experienced teachers salaries that fell within 20 percent of the listed averages (Sonstelie, Brunner, and Ardon, 2000).

[15] In accounting for salary variation, however, Sonstelie, Brunner, and Ardon (2000) found that district size was only half as important as regional differences. Under the current finance system, the state allocates funds to districts on a per-pupil basis. The state does not consider regional cost differences, including those that affect teacher salaries. Like salaries, nonsalary benefits varied according to region and district size. Teachers in regions with low salaries tended to receive larger district contributions for nonsalary benefits. This variation seems to be driven more by the lower costs of a given benefit in urban areas than by differences in

Figure 4.7 shows beginning teacher salaries in the 1990s in California and nationally, in constant 2000 dollars (not adjusted for regional cost differences). Real beginning teacher salaries across the United States stayed relatively constant throughout the 1990s at about $28,000. In California, after falling from about $32,000

Figure 4.7
Beginning K–12 Public School Teacher Salaries, California and the United States, 1990–1991 to 1999–2000

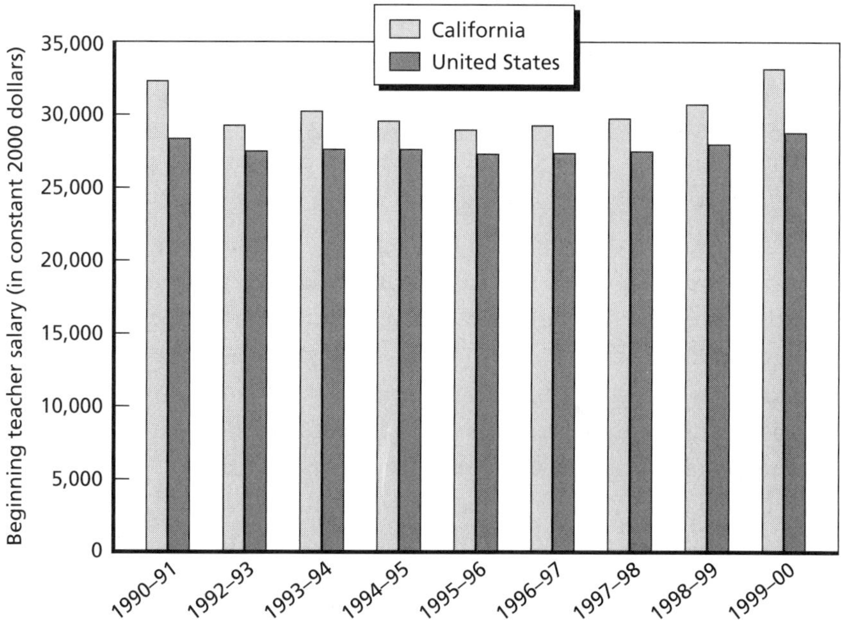

SOURCE: U.S. Department of Education, NCES, Digest of Education Statistics, various years.
RAND *MG186-4.7*

types of benefits offered. In general, large districts faced lower benefit costs than smaller districts. Differences in nonsalary benefits tended to narrow (but not eliminate) differences in total compensation across regions. Other states (including Texas, Colorado, Florida, Ohio, and Wyoming) now adjust school district funding to account for such differences in educational costs, including those related to teacher compensation (Sonstelie, Brunner, and Ardon, 2000).

in 1990–1991 to about $29,500 in 1991–1992, real beginning teacher salaries remained relatively constant throughout most of the 1990s. In 1999–2000, beginning teacher salaries rose to about $33,300. This increase may reflect the need to attract beginning teachers, particularly in Southern California, where shortages were the most severe. In addition, throughout the 1990s, beginning teacher salaries in California were above those nationally, ranging from a low of about $1,600 more in 1994–1995 to a high of about $4,300 more in 1999–2000.

Figure 4.8 shows average teacher salaries in California and the United States (not adjusted for regional cost-of-living differences) for various levels of experience and earned degrees in 1999–2000 for those public school districts with a salary schedule.[16] In 1999–2000, California's average teacher salaries were $29,601 for those with a bachelor's degree and no experience, and $56,028 for those at the highest step on the salary schedule. Across levels of experience and earned degrees, California paid teachers more than teachers were paid nationally. The absolute differences in dollars grew with more years of experience and higher degrees earned, although the percentage differences in dollars were similar across years of experience and degrees earned. In both California and the nation as a whole, average salaries increased due to higher degrees and additional credits, but there was a large jump in average salaries for years of experience.

This picture of California teachers being well paid in comparison to teachers across the country does not hold up, however, when regional cost-of-living adjustments are made, because the relatively higher cost of living in California affects the purchasing power of salaries. Table 4.4 provides comparisons to show the effect of adjust-

---

[16] Note that salary schedules do not always reflect total wages. Teachers can earn additional income by, for example, coaching, teaching in summer school programs, and helping with extracurricular programs.

Figure 4.8
Average K–12 Public School Teacher Salaries for Various Levels of Earned Degrees and Experience, California and the United States, 1999–2000

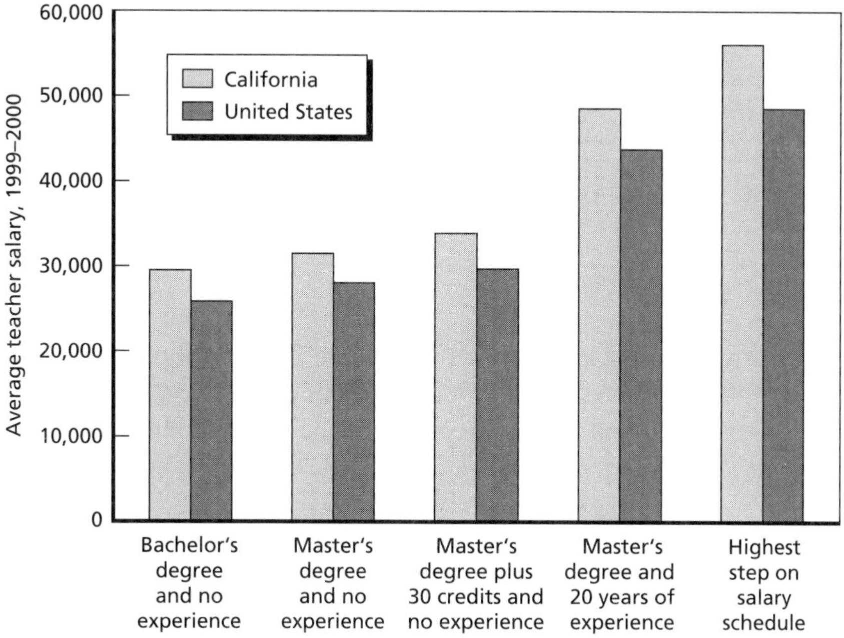

SOURCE: U.S. Department of Education, NCES, Schools and Staffing Survey (SASS), 1999–2000.
RAND *MG186-4.8*

ing dollars to reflect purchasing power.[17] Once regional cost differences are accounted for, California falls from 7th to 32nd in the nation in average teacher salaries for 1999–2000, or from an unadjusted average teacher salary of $47,680 to an adjusted average teacher salary of $38,845.

---

[17] The cost-of-living index we used is based on that of Nelson (1991). (Detailed information on the calculation of the interstate cost-of-living index is available at http://www.aft.org/research/reports/col/colpape3.htm.) No government agency regularly calculates either an interstate or interarea cost-of-living adjustment.

Table 4.4
Average K–12 Public School Teacher Salaries, Adjusted and Unadjusted, Five Most Populous States and United States, 1999–2000

	Unadjusted Average Salary, 1999–2000	Rank	Adjusted Average Salary, 1999–2000	Rank
U.S. average	$41,820		$41,820	
California	$47,680	7	$38,845	32
Texas	$37,567	27	$41,758	17
New York	$51,020	8	$46,731	6
Florida	$36,722	28	$38,912	30
Illinois	$46,480	11	$47,396	4

SOURCE: Nelson et al., 2000.

Edweek provides another source of adjusted national salary data in its 2000 edition of Quality Counts. Using U.S. Census data from 1992–1999, the authors calculated average national annual salaries for public and private school teachers with only a bachelor's degree at $30,074, with a master's degree at $40,703, and for all teachers with at least a bachelor's degree at $35,480. The adjusted salaries for California teachers were $30,332, $37,372, and $32,930, respectively. In general, the conclusions based on adjusted salary data are that California teacher salaries are generally lower than the national average (EdSource, 2002b).

Pupil-Teacher Ratios

Class size represents a measure of interaction between students and their teachers—presumably, on average, a student will get more attention from a teacher if there are fewer students in that teacher's classroom. In addition, the ratio of pupils to teacher can serve as a general instructional resource indicator, even though it does not directly indicate average class size. Pupil-teacher ratios are calculated by dividing the total enrollment by the number of full-time equivalent teachers. Because resource teachers, such as art or physical education teachers, do not have their own classes but are counted in pupil-teacher ratios, average class sizes are almost always larger than pupil-teacher ratios.

In 1999–2000, California had the second highest ratio of pupils per teacher in the nation.[18] That ratio was 20.9 pupils to one teacher; the U.S. average was 16.1. The widespread reduction in K–3 class sizes that began in California in 1997 was not enough to bring the state down to the level of the other states, many of which were also decreasing their class sizes. Figure 4.9 displays pupil-teacher ratios in California and the United States over the past 30 years. As can be seen, these ratios largely tracked each other until 1979, which was when California's school districts, faced with leaner budgets partly caused by the adoption of Proposition 13, had several options, including limiting the hiring of teachers, reducing teacher salaries, and reducing other expenditures. There was no large decline in teacher salaries, nor was there a large decline in other expenditures, which left class size to absorb the decline in spending (Sonstelie, Brunner, and Ardon, 2000). In 1996–1997, California's pupil-teacher ratios began to fall in response to the class size reduction program.

Like Figure 4.9, Figure 4.10 shows pupil-teacher ratios over the past 30 years, this time for California relative to the national average. In 1969, pupil-teacher ratios in California were about 7 percent higher than the national average. They then climbed to a high of almost 40 percent above the national average by 1994–1995, after which they fell to about 28 percent above the national average by 1998–1999 and then rose in 1999–2000.[19]

We also looked at the breakdown of class size in California in terms of school grade levels. Classes are considerably larger in middle

---

[18] It should be noted that in 1999–2000, California also had relatively low numbers of other staff to pupils. Of all the states in the nation, California ranked 50th in total school staff to students, 48th in number of district officials/administrators to students, 50th in number of school principals and assistant principals to students, and 51st in number of guidance counselors and librarians to students (EdSource, 2002a).

[19] Federal funds for reducing class sizes became available for the first time in the 1999–2000 school year.

Figure 4.9
Pupil-Teacher Ratios in K–12 Public Schools, California and the United States, Fall 1969 to Fall 1999

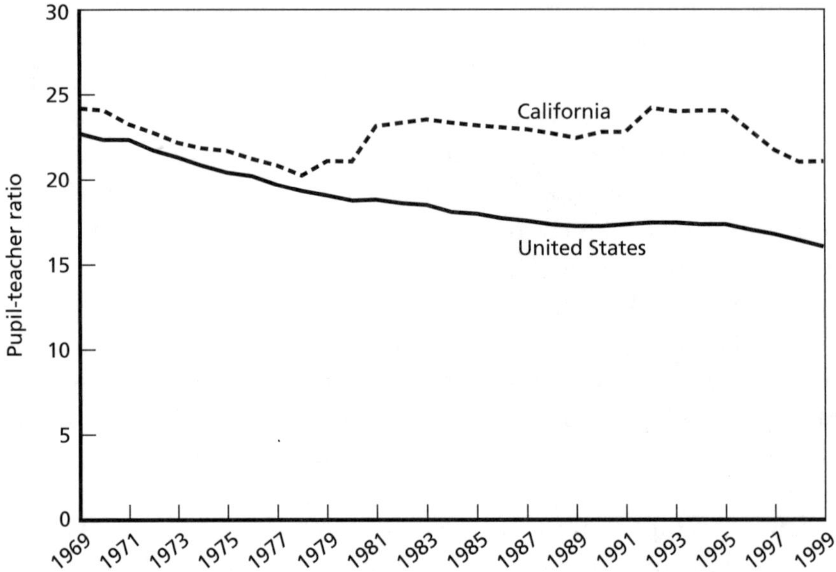

SOURCE: U.S. Department of Education, NCES, Digest of Education Statistics, various years.
RAND *MG186-4.9*

and high schools than in primary schools.[20] One important reason for this is that the class size reduction initiative focused on grades K–3.[21] Figure 4.11 compares median pupil-teacher ratios in primary, middle, and high schools in California and the United States. As can be seen, California pupil-teacher ratios in 2000-2001 were about 20:1 in the

---

[20] The Common Core Data Public Elementary School Universe Survey divides instructional levels into primary, middle, and high, and provides an "other" category for any configuration not falling within those three levels, including ungraded schools. NCES also uses these distinctions for reporting median pupil-teacher ratios.

[21] The program did not focus on all the primary grades. Funding was provided for implementation first in grade 1, then in grade 2, and then in grade 3 and kindergarten. A less extensive program, established in 1998, offers $135 for each student in grade 9 in courses having an average of no more than 20 students.

Figure 4.10
Pupil-Teacher Ratios in K–12 Public Schools, California Relative to National Average, 1969–1970 to 1999–2000

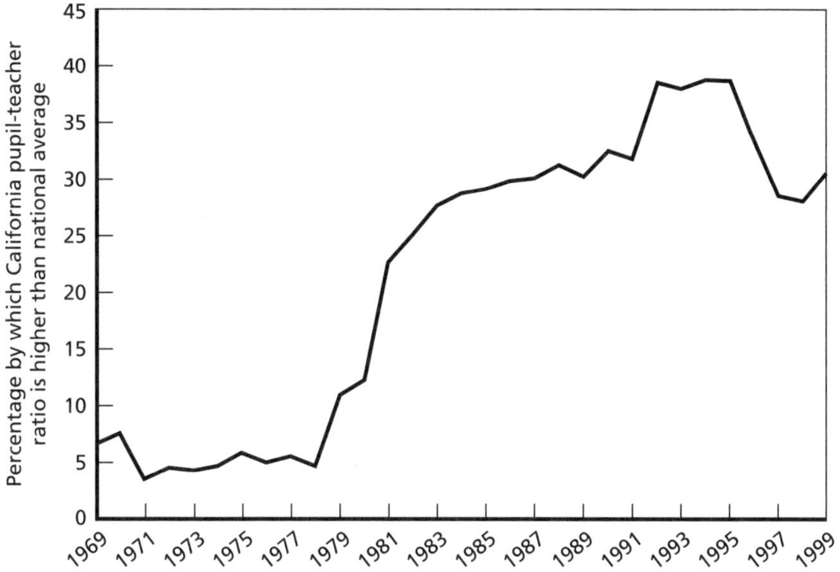

SOURCE: U.S. Department of Education, NCES, Digest of Education Statistics, various years.
RAND *MG186-4.10*

primary grades, about 23:1 in the middle grades, and about 21.5:1 in the high school grades. The national pupil-teacher ratios for that school year, however, were consistently lower for all school grade levels, and there was a drop between the primary and high school grades from about 16:1 to just below 15:1.

Figure 4.12 compares the pupil-teacher ratios of California and the four other most populous states for 1969–1970, 1979–1980, 1989–1990, and 1999–2000. As can be seen, each of these states reduced its pupil-teacher ratio between 1969–1970 and 1999–2000, with Texas reducing it the most, from 24:1 to 15:1. California, Florida, and Illinois continued to have pupil-teacher ratios above the national average of 16.1 in 1999–2000. In addition, California's pupil-teacher ratio remained above the ratios of the four other most popu-

Figure 4.11
Median Pupil-Teacher Ratios in Public Primary, Middle, and High Schools, California and the United States, 2000–2001

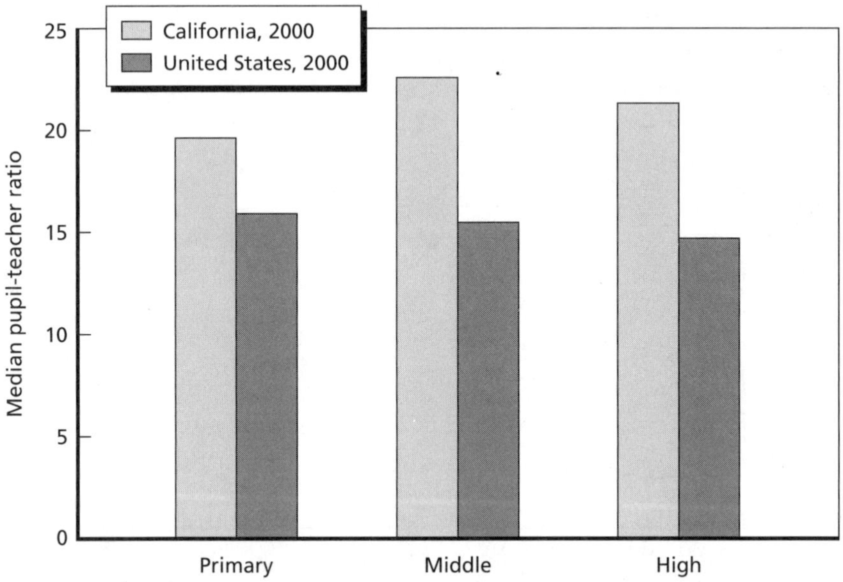

SOURCE: U.S. Department of Education, NCES, Common Core of Data, 2001.
RAND *MG186-4.11*

lous states in all years, with the other states generally reducing class sizes more rapidly over time. In the final year shown, 1999–2000, California, Florida, Illinois, Texas, and New York ranked, respectively, 50th, 45th, 33rd, 21st, and 15th in lowest pupil-teacher ratios across the United States.

Conclusions

The comparisons we made in this chapter for California over time and in comparison to other states and to the nation as a whole are complex, but they nevertheless point to several conclusions about teachers in California's K–12 public schools:

Figure 4.12
Pupil-Teacher Ratios in K–12 Public Schools, Five Most Populous States, 1969–1970, 1979–1980, 1989–1990, and 1999–2000

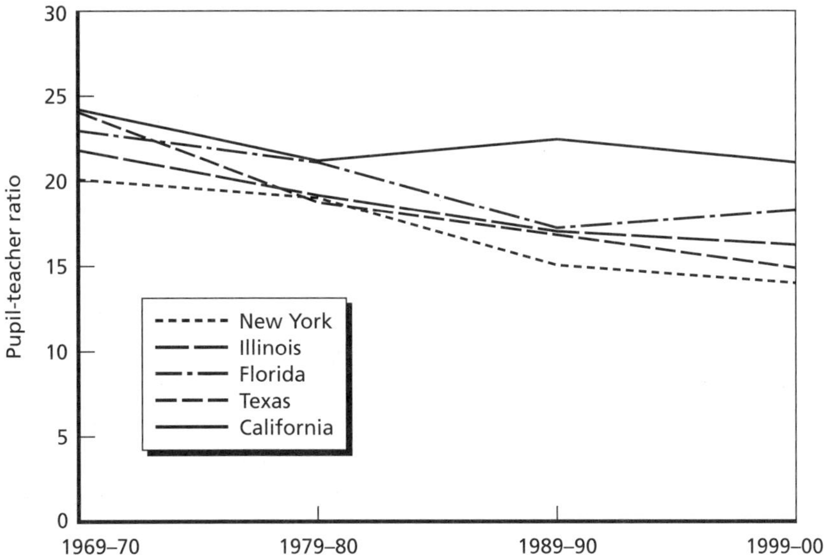

SOURCE: U.S. Department of Education, NCES, Digest of Education Statistics, various years.

RAND *MG186-4.12*

- California on the whole appears to employ highly educated and experienced K–12 public school teachers whose salaries can potentially double over their professional careers.
- The 1990s saw dramatic growth in the number of new K–12 teachers in California's public schools. The state's demand for new teachers is expected to continue to grow, although at a considerably slower pace than that experienced in the 1990s.
- A substantial portion of California's public K–12 teacher workforce—about 15 percent—is newly employed. In 2000, a majority of these first-year teachers were not formally trained, state certified teachers. In the1990s, the number of individuals entering teaching with pre-intern, intern, and emergency permits grew, causing the gap between the total number of teachers and

the number of teachers with preliminary or professional clear credentials to enlarge.

- Between 2000–2001 and 2002–2003, the number of first-year teachers in California's K–12 public schools who lacked full credentials fell from over 50 percent to about 42 percent.
- Prior to the mid-1990s, there were few differences in the percentages of inexperienced and uncertified teachers by school characteristics. Since then, however, teachers lacking preliminary or professional clear credentials have been concentrated in urban schools, the lowest performing schools, and schools with high percentages of low-income and minority students.
- Teacher qualification requirements are generally lower in California than in other states. For example, 82 percent of public school districts in the United States require that anyone hired as a teacher have full standard state certification in the field to be taught; in California, only 46 percent of districts do.
- Since 1997–1998, California lawmakers have increasingly directed their attention and hundreds of millions of dollars to the preparation, recruitment, and support of new teachers and to the establishment of a new state-directed approach to teacher training. However, the current weak state economy and budget deficit have resulted in reductions in several of the programs.
- The real average annual salaries for K–12 public school teachers in California in 2000–2001 were about the same as they were in 1969–1970 and have remained relatively flat over time.
- In terms of average annual salaries for public K–12 teachers, California has consistently placed in the nation's top ten highest-paying states over time. When the dollar amounts are adjusted to reflect regional cost-of-living differences, however, teacher salaries in California are actually lower than the national average.
- California continues to have the second highest ratio of K–12 public school students per teacher of any state: about 20.9 students to one teacher, compared to the U.S. average of 16.1:1. California pupil-teacher ratios largely tracked the national average until 1979–1980, which was when California's public

schools were faced with leaner budgets, due in part to the adoption of Proposition 13.

Table 4.5 provides a summary of this chapter's discussion about California's K–12 public school teachers.

Table 4.5
Summary of Outcomes for California's K–12 Public School Teachers

	How California Compares (in latest year data available) to:		How 1990s Trend in California Compares to That in:	
Measures	**All States**	**Four Other Most Populous States**	**All States**	**Four Other Most Populous States**
Growth in number of teachers	Higher than average	Average	Higher than average	Higher than average
School districts requiring full standard state certification in field to be taught	Lower than average	Not available	Not available	Not available
Average teacher salary, unadjusted	Higher than average	Higher than average	Higher than average	Higher than average
Average teacher salary, adjusted	Lower than average	Lower than average	Not available	Not available
Pupil-teacher ratio	Higher than average	Higher than average	Higher than average	Higher than average

CHAPTER FIVE

California's K–12 Public School Facilities

Concerns about public elementary and secondary school facilities in California mirror those at the national level. A national study conducted about 10 years ago (U.S. General Accounting Office, 1995a) suggested that schools had reached the breaking point in terms of facilities, and that conditions in California schools were among the worst. Over the past decade, California and the rest of the nation have made encouraging progress in addressing this problem, but sizable facility needs remain. For example, California's Legislative Analyst's Office estimates that 33 percent of all students attend an overcrowded school or one in need of significant modernization (Legislative Analyst's Office, 2001a). And the California Department of Education estimates statewide construction needs of about $23 billion, or $4.6 billion per year, from 2002 to 2007—of which about $17 billion is for construction needs and about $6 billion is for modernization needs.[1]

California's needs for new facilities and school facility improvements arise from a variety of sources. One is the growth in the state's student population, which today exceeds the student population of the peak years of the "baby boom" by over one million. (California's

[1] Projections of the need for school facility funding are based on assumptions about various intangibles, including, for example, future growth in student population, the condition of existing buildings, and anticipated changes in school programs that affect facilities. As a result, vast differences in projections are both possible and plausible. Most observers agree, however, that California's public school facility needs are monumental and call for a large funding effort (EdSource, 1998).

student population is described in detail in Chapter Two's discussion of demographics.) In addition, much of the growth in the student population since 1980 has not been in the areas where the baby boom generation grew up, which means some school districts have old school sites that are being leased out, while others have seen rapid growth in their student population and have no school buildings with which to accommodate that growth.

Another source of the need for facility improvements is the number of older school buildings requiring repair. The majority of California's public schools were built during the post–World War II boom, between 1950 and 1965,[2] and many have been poorly maintained.[3] These aging buildings are costly to keep up, no longer meet educators' ideas of a good learning environment, and usually lack the commonplace amenities found in newer structures, such as modern wiring and lighting. Moreover, the condition of school facilities makes it difficult for many schools to improve public education through such measures as class size reduction[4] and greater use of technology (EdSource, 1998).

Finally, in order to understand school facility funding and needs, it is necessary to examine how revenue sources for school construction and modernization have changed over time. (School financing is discussed in more detail in Chapter Three.) Prior to the passage of Proposition 13, California financed school construction

---

[2] California had a total of 7,872 public schools and 60,000 public school buildings in 1995–1996. The California Department of Education reports that 55 percent of those buildings are over 30 years old.

[3] Districts have likely responded to declines in general school funding over the past 20 years by deferring preventive maintenance (see Chapter Three). According to U.S. General Accounting Office, 1995a, district officials attributed the declining physical condition of America's schools primarily to insufficient funds, which resulted in decisions to defer maintenance and repair from year to year. In addition, they reported having difficulty raising the money for needed repairs and renovations because an anti-tax-raising sentiment among voters resulted in both the failure of bond issues and passage of property tax limitations.

[4] In the first two years of the California class size reduction program—1996–1997 and 1997–1998—California's public elementary schools used a variety of strategies to add about 28,000 new classroom spaces, including a heavy reliance on portable classrooms. These schools were able to reduce class sizes for an estimated 85 percent of the state's K–3 students (EdSource, 1998).

and renovation primarily with funds raised through local general obligation bond elections.[5] As of its passage in June 1978, however, Proposition 13 took away from school districts and other local governments the power to set their own property tax rates, thus eliminating the ability of local agencies, including school districts, to issue general obligation bonds. As a result, the primary responsibility for financing new school construction and modernization shifted from local school districts to the state. The state responded to the ongoing needs of California's school districts by implementing a number of new programs, most significantly asking voters to approve state bonds to finance new school facilities. However, by 1984, it had become increasingly clear that revenue raised through state bond issues was insufficient to meet California's school infrastructure needs.[6] As a result, beginning in 1984, voters and the state legislature passed a number of new programs designed to reinstate the authority of local school districts to raise revenues for new school construction and modernization.

Since 1984, spending on school facilities has risen over time due to events that include

- Passage of a number of state bond issues.
- Reestablishment of the authority of local districts to issue general obligation bonds with the support of two-thirds of the voters within a district in 1984 (Proposition 46).
- Ability of school districts to impose developer fees beginning in 1986 (AB2926).
- Passage of Proposition 39 in 2000, which reduced the voter approval requirement for passage of local general obligation bonds from two-thirds to 55 percent.

---

[5] Local bond revenue was supplemented by the State School Building Aid Program, which provided loans to school districts that were both bonded to their debt capacity and facing high growth in their enrollments.

[6] Brunner and Rueben (2001b) demonstrate that school facility expenditures were falling even before Proposition 13 passed, but they suggest that the dramatic decline in school facility spending between 1978 and 1984 is directly attributable to Proposition 13.

Condition of Schools

Up until a 1995 national study completed by the U.S. General Accounting Office (1995a), there were no systematic, national data on the status of school facilities. While most states maintain some information about school facilities, only about one-half of them maintain information on the condition of school facilities. In addition, of those states that do collect information on the condition of facilities, some collect it on an ongoing basis while others have done one-time studies (U.S. General Accounting Office, 1995c).

The large-scale national survey that the GAO completed in 1995 documented the condition of school facilities in each state.[7] The survey results suggested unsuitable conditions in many of America's schools in the mid-1990s and showed that California schools were in the worst condition—in terms of the percentage of schools reporting inadequate buildings and features—in the country. For example, California school officials reported 43 percent of schools as having at least one inadequate building,[8] whereas the comparable proportion nationally was one-third. In addition, California school officials reported over 70 percent of schools as having at least one inadequate building feature,[9] compared with about 57 percent being reported nationally.

In addition, both the GAO survey and a follow-up survey in 1999 by the National Center for Education Statistics (NCES) asked school officials about the adequacy of specific building features and environmental factors. In the 1994–1995 GAO survey, California

---

[7] The survey was sent to a nationally representative stratified random sample of about 10,000 schools in 5,000 school districts. The physical condition of schools is described in a series of GAO reports based on the 1994–1995 survey.

[8] An inadequate building is one entire building in need of extensive repair or replacement. Respondents were asked to rank the overall condition of buildings and of selected building features on an adequacy scale: excellent, good, adequate, fair, poor, or need to replace. The GAO report includes school officials' ratings of fair, poor, and need to replace in the category of "inadequate."

[9] An inadequate building feature is a major building feature needing extensive repair, overhaul, or replacement.

school officials reported relatively large percentages of schools, compared with the national average and the percentages of the four other most populous states, as having specific inadequate building features (such as roofs, plumbing, and interior finishes) and specific inadequate environmental factors (such as lighting, heating, and physical security). For example, the results of the survey suggested that 41 percent of school roofs in California were in "inadequate" condition (compared with 27 percent nationally) and over 30 percent of schools in California had inadequate lighting (compared with 16 percent nationally).[10]

The more recent data from NCES suggest that substantial progress has been made in addressing school facility needs, both nationally and across different regions of the country (U.S. Department of Education, National Center for Education Statistics, 2000).[11] Given the smaller sample size of the 1999 survey, the results are reported for regions of the country, not individual states. Figure 5.1 compares the percentage of schools reporting specific inadequate building features in 1994–1995 and 1999–2000, both in the western portion of the United States[12] and in the nation as a whole.

---

[10] Kozol (1991) and others, such as Corcoran, Walker, and White (1988), and Lewis et al. (1989), highlight the point that the condition of the nation's schools varies widely. Some schools are in poor condition, some are in exceptional condition, and most fall somewhere in the middle—they are in "adequate" or "better" overall condition, as found in the GAO 1995 national study. School conditions often vary by location. The GAO 1996 study (U.S. General Accounting Office, 1996), for example, found that, in 1994–1995, the largest proportion of schools reporting unsatisfactory physical and environmental conditions were in central cities serving more than 50 percent minority students or 70 percent or more low-income students. However, the study also found that poor conditions exist in many rural areas. Brunner and Rueben (2001a) also raise concerns about possible inequities in the distribution of capital revenue per pupil across districts in California.

[11] These results are supported by the growth in construction expenditures in the mid- to late 1990s (see Figure 5.3, below).

[12] Western states include Montana, Idaho, Wyoming, Colorado, New Mexico, Arizona, Utah, Nevada, Washington, Oregon, California, Alaska, and Hawaii. California's public elementary and secondary public school enrollment in fall 1999 represented 54 percent of the total public elementary and secondary school enrollment in all western states.

Figure 5.1
Percentage of K–12 Public Schools Reporting "Inadequate" Building Features, the West and the United States, 1994–1995 and 1999–2000

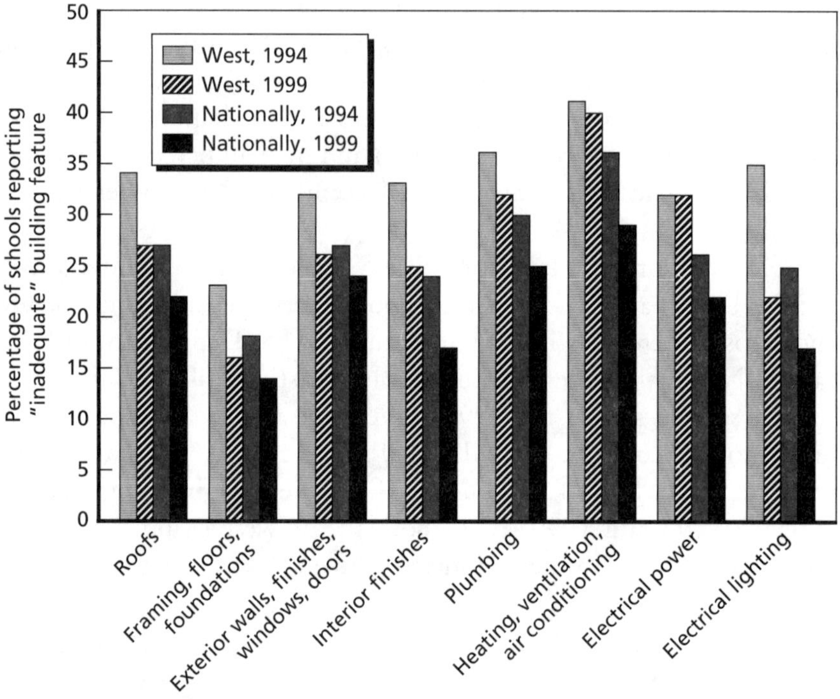

SOURCE: U.S. General Accounting Office, 1995a; and U.S. Department of Education, NCES, 2000.
RAND *MG186-5.1*

In general, school building conditions improved between 1994 and 1999, both in the West and nationally. For example, about 34 percent of schools in the West reported an inadequate roof in 1994, compared with 27 percent in 1999. In addition, it appears that sizable improvements were made in the condition of electrical lighting in the mid- to late 1990s. While improvements were made over this period, Figure 5.1 suggests that California, included in the West, still lagged the rest of the nation in the condition of building features. Across every building feature, the West continued in 1999 to report considerably larger percentages of schools with inadequate features than did the United States. In addition, in the GAO's 1994 survey, California schools reported greater occurrences of inadequate building features than did the western states as a whole. Therefore, it is likely that the number of California schools with inadequate building features in 1999 is somewhat higher than the number of such schools for the nation as a whole.

Similarly, Figure 5.2 suggests significant improvements were made in several environmental features of public schools between 1994 and 1999. For example, about 31 percent of schools in the West reported "inadequate" physical security in 1994, compared

Figure 5.2
Percentage of K–12 Public Schools Reporting "Inadequate" Environmental Factors, the West and the United States, 1994–1995 and 1999–2000

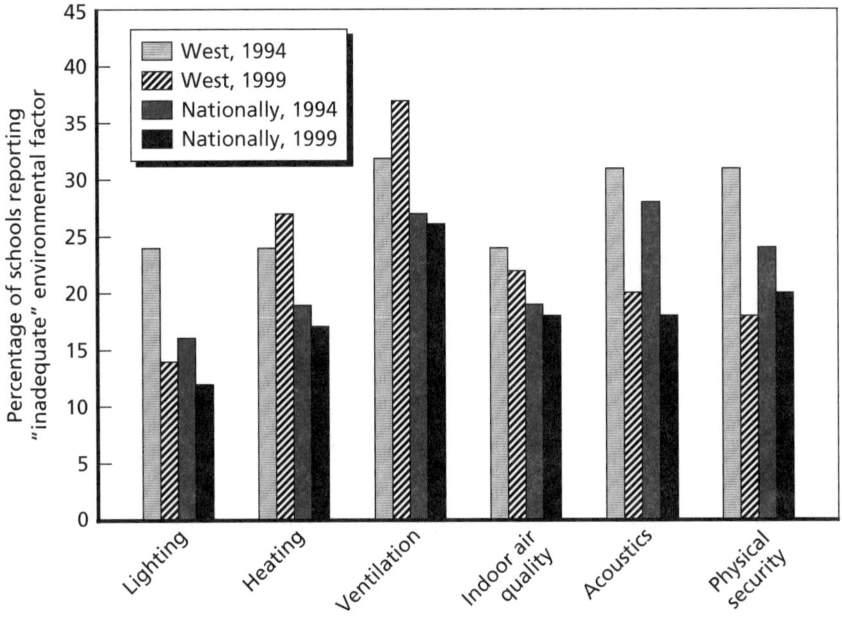

SOURCE: U.S. General Accounting Office, 1995a; and U.S. Department of Education, NCES, 2000.

RAND *MG186-5.2*

with18 percent in 1999. The surveys also suggest improvements were made in lighting, indoor air quality, and acoustics, both in the West and nationally. At the same time, the percentage of schools in the West reporting inadequate heating and ventilation was larger in 1999 than it was in 1994. And across every environmental factor except physical security, the West continued to report considerably larger percentages of schools as having inadequate factors than did the United States.

Growth in Construction Expenditures

School construction expenditures have grown significantly in recent years. Annual construction expenditures for K–12 schools across the nation grew by about 76 percent from 1991–1992 through 1999–2000, to about $33 billion after adjusting for inflation. This increase was more substantial than the rise in enrollment, which was about 12 percent over the same period. As shown in Figure 5.3, the growth in construction expenditures was concentrated in the mid- to late 1990s. This trend reflects a variety of factors, including higher enrollments, a strong economy, and an increasing need to replace old buildings.

Figure 5.4 shows California's growth in annual construction expenditures and in enrollment over this same period. Annual construction expenditures for elementary and secondary schools grew at a faster rate in California than they did nationally, increasing by about 157 percent from 1991–1992 through 1999–2000 to reach about $4 billion after adjustment for inflation. The growth between 1992–1993 and 1993–1994 reflects a $2.8 billion state bond measure passed in 1992. Similar to the growth seen nationally, the large growth in construction expenditures in California occurred in the mid- to late 1990s.[13] Enrollment growth was also relatively rapid in

[13] The state also approved large bond measures in 1996, 1998, and 2002.

Figure 5.3
Percent Growth in K–12 Public School Construction Expenditures and Enrollment, United States, 1991–1992 to 1999–2000

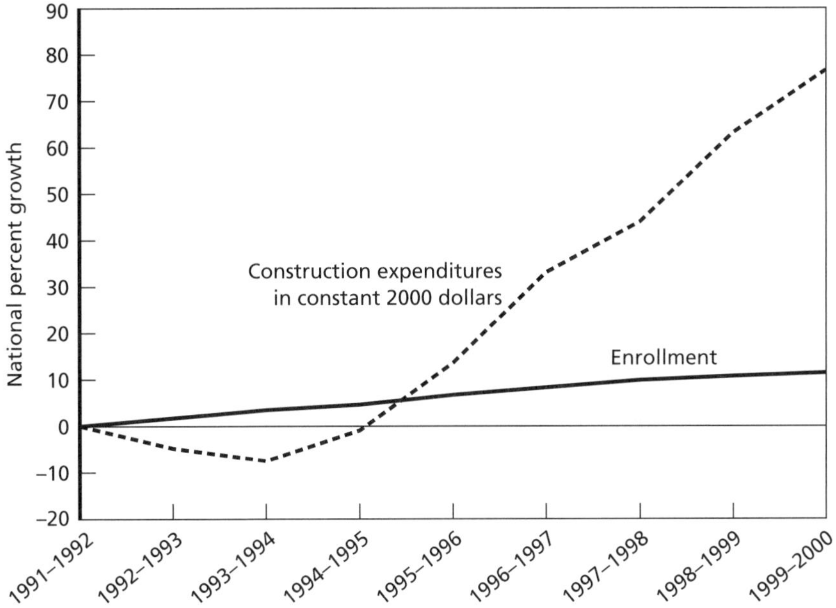

SOURCE: U.S. Census Bureau, Public Education Finances, various years.
RAND *MG186-5.3*

California compared to the nation as a whole, increasing by about 20 percent over this period.

Average annual construction expenditures per pupil vary widely by state. In general, states with the largest expenditures per pupil tend to also have the highest enrollment growth rates, and those with the lowest expenditures per pupil tend to have relatively low enrollment growth rates (U.S. General Accounting Office, 2002). As Figure 5.5 shows, California's real per-pupil construction expenditures in 1991–1992 were $304, about $140 below the national average. Per-pupil construction expenditures grew both nationally and in California throughout the mid- to late 1990s. From a peak deficit of about $235 below the national average in 1995–1996, California's per-

Figure 5.4
Percent Growth in K–12 Public School Construction Expenditures and Enrollment, California, 1991–1992 to 1999–2000

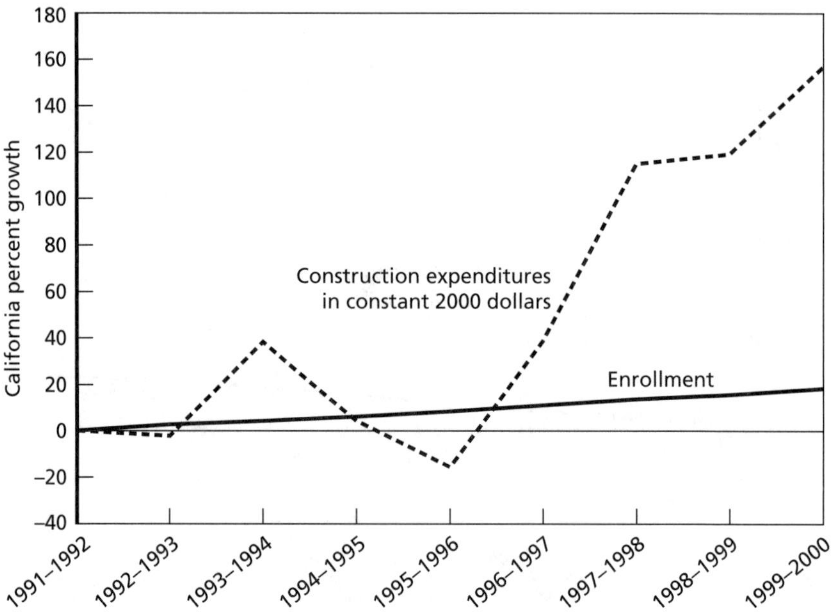

SOURCE: U.S. Census Bureau, Public Education Finances, various years.
RAND *MG186-5.4*

pupil construction expenditures had moved to about $40 below the national average by 1999–2000.

Another way to compare per-pupil construction expenditures in California and the United States is to cumulate the differences in per-pupil expenditures over time. Figure 5.6 shows the cumulative differences in per-pupil construction expenditures between California and the United States when the annual differences between 1991–1992 and 1999–2000 are added up.

As shown in Figure 5.5, California's per-pupil construction expenditures for any individual year fell behind those of the United States—ranging from about $5 per pupil below in 1997 to about

Figure 5.5
K–12 Public School Construction Expenditures per Pupil, California and the United States, 1991–1992 to 1999–2000

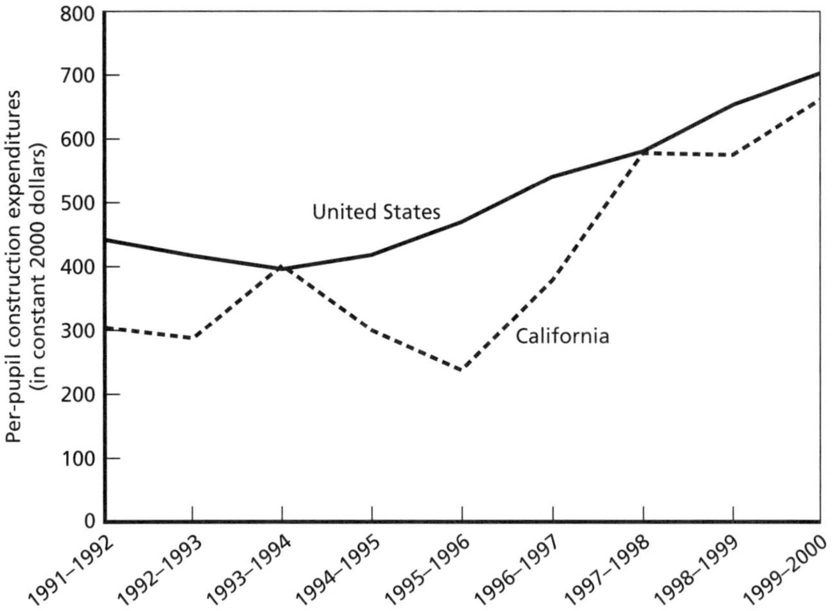

SOURCE: U.S. Census Bureau, Public Education Finances, various years.
RAND *MG186-5.5*

$235 per pupil below in 1995. Adding those differences up over time shows California's spending to be about $890 less per pupil cumulatively over the 1991–1999 period.

California's per-pupil construction expenditures were also below those of each of the four other most populous states in 1991–1992, as Table 5.1 shows. For example, in 1991–1992, they were $505 below those of Florida. Over the 1990s, California and the four other most populous states increased their per-pupil construction expenditures, with California closing some of the spending gap that had existed between it and all but one of the four other states.

Figure 5.6
Cumulative Differences in K–12 Public School Construction Expenditures per Pupil, California and the United States, 1991–1992 to 1999–2000

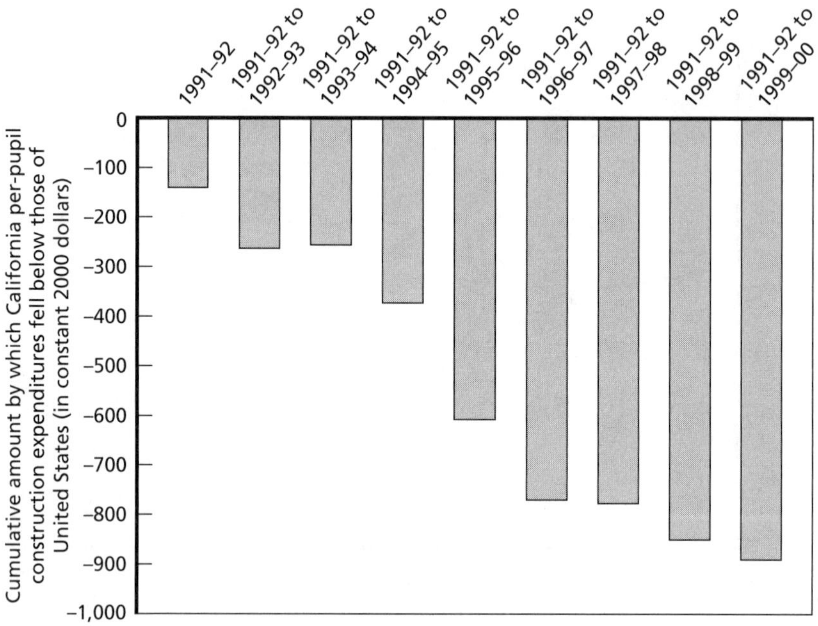

SOURCE: U.S. Census Bureau, Public Education Finances, various years.
RAND *MG186-5.6*

Table 5.1
Amount by Which California Trails the Four Other Most Populous States in K–12 Public School Construction Expenditures per Pupil, 1991–1992 and 1999–2000

	Amount by Which California Trails in Construction Expenditures per Pupil (in dollars)	
	1991–1992	**1999–2000**
Texas	288	279
New York	353	287
Florida	505	252
Illinois	34	316

SOURCE: U.S. Census Bureau, Public Education Finances, various years.

Financing of School Facilities

K–12 public schools nationwide receive funding for construction and renovation of facilities from two main sources—state and local general obligation bonds. The construction of school buildings was traditionally a local responsibility, but nearly all states now have some role in school facility construction, renovation, and major maintenance. Until the 1940s, only 12 states provided any financial assistance for school construction. And during the baby boom of the 1950s, state participation increased when local communities needed classrooms and states had surplus revenues. Even with such increases, however, localities were mainly responsible for school facility construction.

In the 1970s, school finance litigation began highlighting disparities in school districts' ability to raise money for public education. (Chapter Three discusses school finance reform in more detail.) Resulting court decisions caused many states to increase their funding levels and to play a larger role in lessening financial disparities between high- and low-wealth districts. Although these decisions have pertained mainly to the state's role in providing for instruction rather than buildings, the past 25 years have seen a general increase in state involvement with facilities-related matters as well (U.S. General Accounting Office, 1995c).[14]

In California, the cost of building and modernizing schools is met through a partnership between school districts and the state. Through the issuing of general obligation bonds, California provides money for school districts to buy land and to construct, renovate, and modernize K–12 school buildings. General obligation bonds are backed by the state, meaning that the state is obligated to pay the principal and interest costs of these bonds. General Fund revenues,

---

[14] GAO (U.S. General Accounting Office, 1995c) reported that by 1991, state funding for school facilities totaled more than $3 billion, or about 20 percent of all funds used for public school construction. In addition to funding levels varying among states in any one year, construction funding can vary dramatically within states from year to year, making it difficult to capture the complete picture of state support in one snapshot. In addition, no current and complete database shows the sources of funding for school construction. As a result, nationwide data on how amounts and portions of funds are divided between localities and states are not available.

primarily from state income and sales taxes, are used to pay these costs. The cost of school construction projects financed through state general obligation bonds is shared between the state and the local school district.[15]

In addition, school districts are authorized to issue local general obligation bonds to fund school construction projects with the approval of 55 percent of the voters in the district. These local bonds are paid off by taxes on property located within the district. Although school facilities have been funded primarily from state and local general obligation bonds, school districts also receive significant funding from developer fees. State law authorizes local governments to impose these fees on new residential, commercial, and industrial developments. Statewide, school districts report having received an average of over $300 million a year in developer fees over the last ten years. In addition, beginning in 1983, school districts were able to form special local districts in order to sell bonds for school construction projects (known as Mello-Roos bonds).[16] Statewide, school districts have received on average about $150 million per year in special local bond proceeds over the past decade.

Figure 5.7 shows the share of school facility funds raised from various sources from 1987–1988 to 1998–1999. About 72 percent of

---

[15] For example, the Leroy Greene School Facilities Act of 1998 was funded with state bond revenue from passage of Proposition 1A in November 1998. Under this act, the state provided per-pupil funding for new school construction and modernization on a matching basis. New school construction grants were funded on a 50/50 state and local matching basis; modernization grants were funded on an 80/20 state and local matching basis. Proposition 47, passed in November 2002, requires districts to use local resources to pay for 50 percent of new construction costs and 40 percent of modernization costs.

[16] The Mello-Roos Community Facilities District Act, passed in 1982, allows any county, city, special district, school district, or joint powers of authority to establish a "Community Facilities District" as a way to finance public services and facilities. The services and facilities that Mello-Roos districts can provide include streets, police protection, elementary schools, parks, and libraries. Establishment of a Mello-Roos district must be approved by a two-thirds margin; property owners in these districts are then responsible for payment of the "special tax." These districts are often formed by a developer that wants to build a housing or business development and needs public funding to put in roads, school facilities, or other types of facilities, or by an existing community that needs to have new services provided or new facilities built.

Figure 5.7
Sources of Funds Raised for California's K–12 Public School Facilities, 1987–1988 to 1998–1999

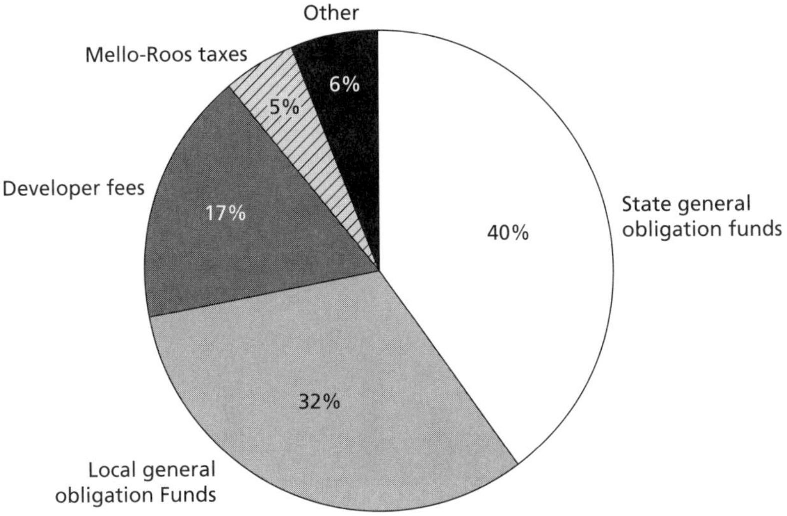

SOURCE: Legislative Analyst's Office, 2001.
RAND *MG186-5.7*

school facility funds were raised from state and local general obligation bonds.

Over the past two decades, voters have approved a total of about \$28.1 billion in state bonds for K–12 public school construction, as shown in Figure 5.8.[17] In November 1998, voters approved Proposition 1A, a \$9.2 billion state bond initiative with \$6.7 billion earmarked for the construction and repair of K–12 schools over four years. In November 2002, voters approved Proposition 47, which allows the state to issue \$13.05 billion of general obligation bonds for construction and renovation, \$11.4 billion of which is earmarked for K–12 school facilities. Of this \$11.4 billion, approximately \$6.35 billion is for buying land and constructing new school buildings, \$3.3

[17] Since 1982, only one statewide school bond issue (in 1994) has failed to win approval.

Figure 5.8
California Voter Decisions on Statewide School Bonds, 1982 to 2002

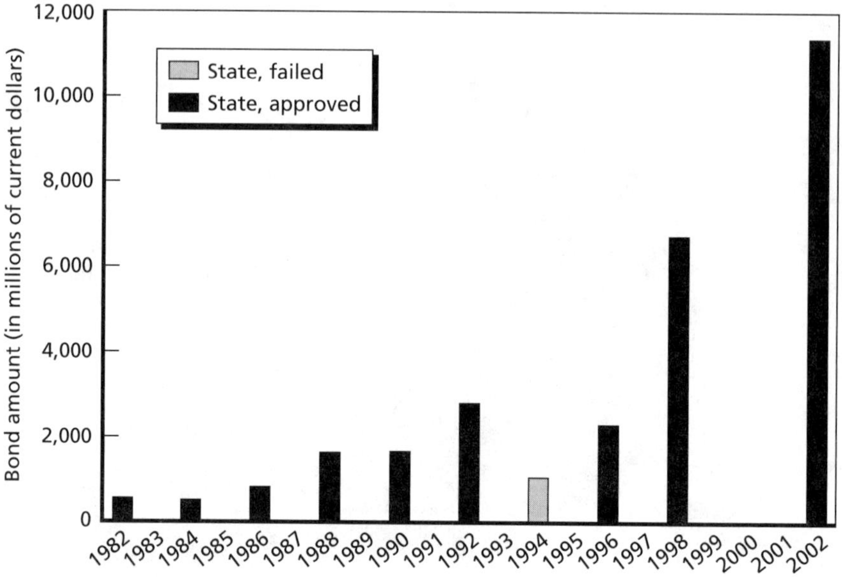

SOURCE: www.cashnet.org.
RAND *MG186-5.8*

billion is for the reconstruction or modernization of existing school facilities, and $1.7 billion is for critically overcrowded schools (schools that have a large number of pupils relative to their site size). However, the measure permits changes in this allocation with the approval of the legislature and governor.

As Figure 5.9 shows, from 1982 to 2002, California school districts received voter approval to issue more than $28 billion of local general obligation bonds. In 1997, the Los Angeles Unified School District passed a $2.4 billion bond issue, and in 2002 alone, voters approved close to $10 billion in local general obligation bonds. During this same period, voters failed to approve more than $15 billion of general obligation bonds.

Figure 5.9
California Voter Decisions on Local School Bonds, 1982 to 2002

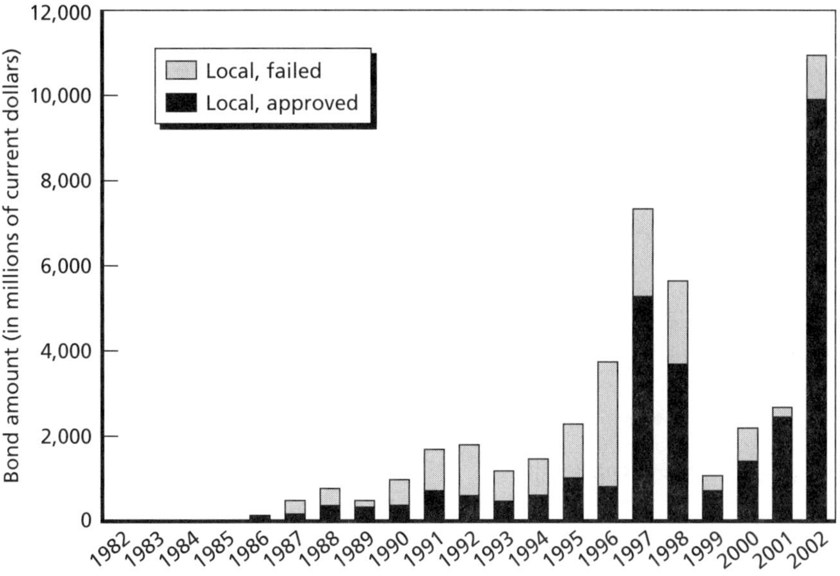

SOURCE: www.cashnet.org.
RAND *MG186-5.9*

One pattern that stands out in Figure 5.9 is the growing approval rate of local school bond initiatives. Bond measure approval rates were generally around 50 percent until the mid-1990s, rose to about 65 percent in the late 1990s, and were seen to hit 80 percent in the early 2000s. These high rates in the 2000s likely stem from the November 2000 passage of Proposition 39, which altered the ground rules for passage of general obligation bonds. Prior to Proposition 39, these bonds had to have a two-thirds voter approval to pass. Now, however, local governing boards can present a general obligation bond to voters that requires either a two-thirds approval or a 55 percent approval. If they choose the latter, they must meet a number of conditions—such as limiting the tax burden on property owners, conducting two independent audits, and listing the specific projects for which the funds will be used—but they nevertheless do have the option now.

Figure 5.10 compares the first 18 months of bond elections after Proposition 39 went into effect with the 18 months immediately preceding the change (Legislative Analyst's Office, 2002). From January 2001 to June 2002, school districts raised $6.17 billion for facilities through local bonds, in contrast to the $3.36 billion they had raised in the previous 18 months. Further, 84 percent of local bond measures passed, compared to about 60 percent in the earlier period. In about 70 percent of the elections held under the new law, districts

Figure 5.10
Passage of Local Bond Measures in California Before and After Proposition 39 Took Effect

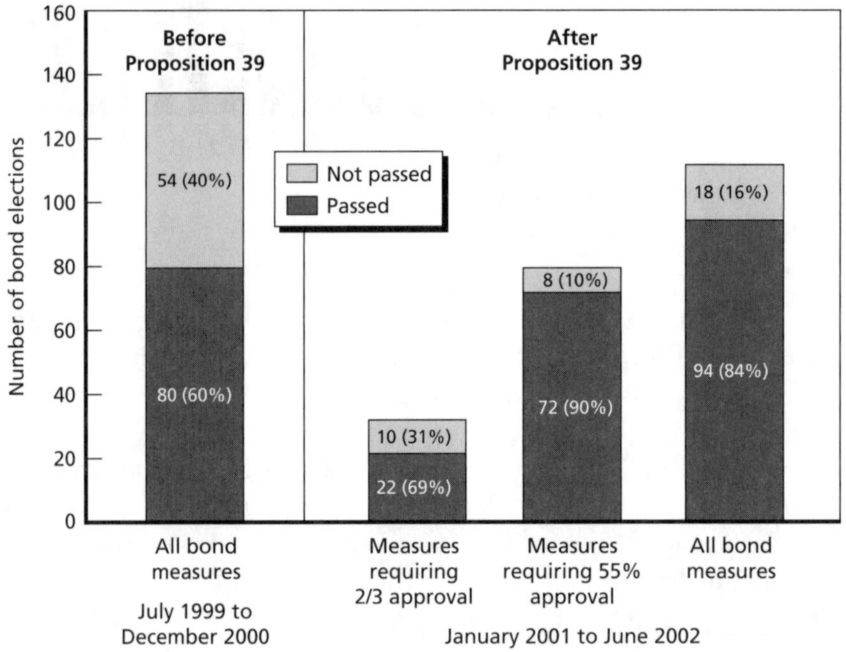

SOURCE: EdSource, 2002c.
RAND *MG186-5.10*

opted for the lower threshold. Those successful elections represent $4.88 billion, or almost 80 percent of bond proceeds.

There is little information available on current disparities in the local funds that are raised for facilities across California's different types of districts. The reliance on local bonds to finance new school construction and modernization has caused concern about the equity of school facility finance in many states and has led to a new wave of school finance litigation (Brunner and Rueben, 2001b).[18] Two studies completed in California using data from the late 1990s examine how disparities in capital expenditures across California's districts are related to districts' growth in enrollment, districts' property wealth per pupil, and income (Brunner and Rueben, 2001a,b). The studies suggest that enrollment growth, income, and assessed value per pupil all play an important part in explaining variation in school facility spending by local school districts. For example, districts with higher assessed value per pupil have significantly higher capital revenue per pupil. However, these findings do not incorporate the significant changes in school facility finance in California since the late 1990s, including passage of two multibillion-dollar statewide school bonds and Proposition 39.

Conclusions

Over the past decade, California has made substantial progress in addressing K–12 public school facility needs. This progress is primarily due to voter approval of several large state general obligation bond issues, as well as a variety of legislative changes that have enabled districts to approve local general obligation bond issues. In 2002 alone, voters approved over $11 billion in state general obligation bonds and close to $10 billion in local general obligation bonds. Evidence from the late 1990s on the condition of school building features and environmental factors and on per-pupil spending for construction sug-

[18] For example, both Arizona and Colorado have had their systems of financing school facilities questioned in court actions.

gests that California was making progress but still lagged the nation and the other large industrial states in dealing with the state's facility needs. And the differences between California and the rest of the nation in responding to facility needs were likely concentrated in central cities serving high minority and poor populations and in rural areas. California's recent passage of Proposition 39 and approval of several large state and local bond issues suggest that progress in addressing the state's facility needs has continued in recent years. Unfortunately, data and studies are not currently available to document the most recent progress in California's schools in any detail. As school facility funding shows a pattern of greater reliance on local funding, questions will likely be raised about how political and economic differences across communities affect the ability and willingness of school districts to locally finance school facilities and how state facility funding addresses these differences.

Table 5.2 provides a summary of this chapter's discussion about California's K–12 public school facilities.

Table 5.2
Summary of Outcomes for California's K–12 Public School Facilities

	How California Compares (in latest year data available) to:		How 1990s Trend in California Compares to That in:	
Measures	**All States**	**Four Other Most Populous States**	**All States**	**Four Other Most Populous States**
Adequacy of building features	Lower than average	Not available	Lower than average	Not available
Adequacy of environmental features	Lower than average	Not available	Lower than average	Not available
Percent growth in school construction expenditures	Higher than average	Higher than average	Higher than average	Higher than average
Per-pupil school construction expenditures	Lower than average	Lower than average	Lower than average	Lower than average

CHAPTER SIX

California's K–12 Public School Student Academic Achievement

In this chapter, we discuss student academic achievement in California's K-12 public schools. We compare the performance of California's K–12 public school students with that of their counterparts in the nation as a whole and in the four other most populous states—Texas, New York, Florida, and Illinois. We also describe trends over time in student achievement in California and compare them to the corresponding trends in both the nation and the four other most populous states.

We begin with an overview of the various state assessment programs and tests administered to public school K–12 students in California, noting the shortcomings of the data that make them unreliable for trend and comparative analyses. We present the results for the most recent set of state assessments. We then present results from the National Assessment of Educational Progress (NAEP). We review overall scores, scores for groups of students disaggregated by race/ethnicity, and trends over time. We point out the importance of controlling for demographic characteristics in these analyses and show how results differ when such characteristics are controlled for. We then end the chapter with our conclusions, focusing heavily on the NAEP results because of the unreliability of the state assessment data. A more detailed discussion of the results from the earlier assessments is provided in Appendix A.

Data Sources

We analyzed data from two different sources. The first is California's state assessment programs, which consist of the three standardized tests administered in California at various points in time: the Survey of Basic Skills, administered under the California Assessment Program (CAP), the SAT/9, and the CAT/6. The second is the NAEP.

California's Statewide Testing Programs

California has a long history of using statewide assessment programs to monitor the academic outcomes of its public school students. The longest running statewide testing program, the California Assessment Program (CAP),[1] began in 1973 and ended in 1992. In 1993 and 1994, California tested students under the very short-lived California Learning Assessment System (CLAS).[2] There was no statewide testing in 1995. In 1996 and 1997, the Pupil Testing Incentive Program (PTIP) was in place, but it was a voluntary testing program.[3] The current testing system, the Standardized Testing and Reporting (STAR) program, began in 1998 and continues to collect standardized test score data.

SB 376 authorized STAR in 1997, requiring all students in grades 2–11 to participate in statewide testing. In 2001, SB 233 reauthorized STAR for three more years. As of 2003, STAR has four components: (1) the California Standards Tests (CST), criterion-referenced or standards-based tests,[4] which measure the proficiency of

[1] For an overview of the available CAP data, see Appendix A. These data were taken from California Department of Education reports. Our analysis of the available data found no reliable evidence of California students' performance relative to students' performance in the nation or over time.

[2] Data from CLAS are not available. We were not able to locate data or publications related to CLAS.

[3] Data from PTIP are also not available. For a chronology of California's statewide assessment programs, see www.cde.ca.gov/ta/tg/sr/documents/pkt03media.pdf and www.cde.ca.gov/ta/tg/sa/documents/cas0304.pdf.

[4] A criterion-referenced test measures student performance relative to fixed levels of performance. A standards-based test measures student performance relative to fixed levels of

California students relative to California's academic content standards; (2) the California Achievement Test, 6th edition survey (CAT/6), a nationally norm-referenced test[5] of student achievement published by CTB/McGraw-Hill; (3) the California Alternative Performance Assessment (CAPA), which is designed for students with learning disabilities; and (4) the Spanish Assessment of Basic Education, 2nd edition (SABE/2), published by CTB/McGraw-Hill, which is a test in Spanish for limited English proficient (LEP) students enrolled in California schools for less than one year.

Beginning in 1998 and running through 2002, California administered the Stanford Achievement Test, 9th edition, Form T (SAT/9), a nationally norm-referenced test of student achievement published by Harcourt Educational Measurement.[6] The test was administered statewide in reading, writing, spelling, and mathematics in grades 2–8; in reading, writing, mathematics, and science in grades 9–11; and in history–social science in grades 8, 10, and 11 (California Department of Education, 2004). The CAT/6 replaced the SAT/9 in 2003.

Several shortcomings of California's state assessment data make them questionable for trend analysis and for examining performance relative to other states.

---

subject mastery described in content standards. For a discussion of the types of tests used to measure student achievement, see Hamilton and Koretz, 2002.

[5] Norm-referenced tests report scores in terms of a larger distribution of scores, and the scores reflect not what a student knows but where a student places in the larger distribution. National norm-referenced scores are reported as national percentile ranks (NPRs), placing students according to their performance relative to the national performance (norm group). See Hamilton and Koretz, 2002.

[6] We focused our research on the SAT/9 and CAT/6 because the results from these tests can, theoretically, be used to compare the performance of California's students to that of students in the nation. We discuss the limitations of using these tests in the second section of this chapter. The CSTs are specific to California and therefore cannot be used for comparisons to the nation or the other most populous states. The CAPA is California specific, tests a small, specialized population of students, and is not included in our analysis. Finally, since California school districts have the option of using the SABE/2 to test all LEP students regardless of their length of enrollment in California schools, there is uncertainty in the sample of students tested with the SABE/2. For this reason and because the most recent national norm is 1988, we chose not to report the SABE/2 data.

First, California's earliest statewide testing program (CAP) administered California-specific tests. Accordingly, they cannot support comparisons of the performance of California students with that of students in other states. Further, the CAP data are not available, which prevents any analysis of the performance of California students over time.

Second, when states administer tests that have been developed by third-party publishers (e.g., the SAT published by Harcourt Educational Measurement) that are normed to a national comparison group, the resulting test scores can be compared to each other and to scores nationwide. However, when tests are developed by different publishers, the results are not directly comparable. Thus, although California administered the SAT/9 statewide from 1998 to 2002, the performance of California students on that test cannot be used to make comparisons with the performance of students in the four other most populous states—Texas, New York, Florida, and Illinois—because none of them administered the SAT/9 statewide from 1998 to 2002.

Similarly, the SAT/9 data from 1998 to 2002 cannot be used to compare California's student achievement to that of students nationally, because these results also rely on outdated national norms. The SAT/9 results reported for 1998–2002 are based on a 1995 national norm.

Given the limitations described above, we chose to rely on the 1998–2002 SAT/9 scaled scores[7] and the 2003 CAT/6 results that

---

[7] SAT/9 results are available in raw scores, national percentile ranks, and scaled scores. Raw scores report the number of questions a student answered correctly on a given test in a given subject. Test items, or questions, vary in degree of difficultly and in content tested. Simply reporting the number or percentage of questions answered correctly does not reflect these differences and therefore does not allow comparisons to be made between students or groups of students. Scaled scores are scores that control for the varying degrees of difficulty of the questions and the content being tested by each question. Scaled scores place student achievement along a common scale with a designated mean so that student performance can be compared to the average score obtained on a given test. Along the range of scaled scores, each one-point difference is equivalent. SAT/9 scaled scores are equated across grades so that comparisons can also be made across grades. More importantly, scaled scores allow comparisons of test scores and test score gains over time.

are the most current state data available. To provide a snapshot of California's recent trends in student achievement and the relative national performance, we use scaled scores from the SAT/9 to show the trend in student achievement over time, and we use national percentile ranks (NPR) from the 2003 CAT/6 results to gauge California's student performance relative to that of the nation using the most up-to-date national norms.

When making comparisons of California's student performance in 2003 to the 2000 national norms, we were mindful of the fact that any inferences made about relative standing may be inaccurate.

Appendix A presents findings from our analysis of the limited CAP data available and reports the available national percentile rank SAT/9 data for interested readers.

National Assessment of Educational Progress (NAEP)

Currently, the only assessment that allows for reliable comparative analyses among states is the NAEP. The NAEP state tests have been administered since 1990, which means states can be compared from 1990 to 2003.[8] The NAEP main assessment has also been administered nationally since 1990, which allows up-to-date national comparisons for each NAEP state test administered between 1990 and 2003.

The NAEP is a nationally administered norm-referenced and criterion-referenced test of student achievement. NAEP tests are given to representative samples of students across the nation and within states, making these data the only data available that allow valid comparisons of California student achievement relative to other large states. NAEP state assessments have been given to representative samples of students at grades 4 and 8, in mathematics and reading.

[8] The NAEP state assessments test representative samples of students in participating states. NAEP state tests are designed in the same way as the NAEP Main Assessment, which tests a nationally representative sample of students. Participation in NAEP state tests was voluntary until 2003. Between 1990 and 2002, approximately 44 states participated in at least two NAEP tests.

Table 6.1 lists the 17 tests that have been given at these two grade levels in mathematics and reading from 1990 to 2003.

Complex sampling techniques are used in the NAEP test design and data collection to reduce the amount of time it takes each student to complete a test in a given subject, to maintain a broad range of tested knowledge, and to reduce the bias from question placement within booklets. NAEP tests are both multiple choice and constructed response, testing students' basic and critical thinking skills. A multistage design is used to sample students: The design first chooses the geographical area, then the schools within that area, and finally

Table 6.1
California's Participation in the NAEP, 1990–2003

				California		
Year	Subject	Grade	No. of States Tested	Participation	Student Sample	School Sample
1990	Math	8	38	Yes	2,424	98
1992	Math	8	42	Yes	2,516	108
1992	Math	4	42	Yes	2,412	104
1992	Reading	4	42	Yes	2,365	109
1994	Reading	4	39	Yes	2,252	91
1996	Math	4	44	Yes	2,063	99
1996	Math	8	41	Yes	2,290	101
1998	Reading	4	39	Yes	1,722	84
1998	Reading	8	35	Yes	1,944	90
2000	Math	4	38	Yes	1,656	81
2000	Math	8	39	Yes	1,628	76
2002	Reading	4	43	Yes	4,016	143
2002	Reading	8	41	Yes	3,124	125
2003	Math	4	50	Yes	8,544	N/A
2003	Math	8	50	Yes	5,512	N/A
2003	Reading	4	50	Yes	8,297	N/A
2003	Reading	8	50	Yes	5,510	N/A

SOURCE: http://www.nces.ed.gov/nationsreportcard/naepdata/.
NOTE: The full set of documentation for the 2003 NAEP is not available. Missing data are noted as "N/A."

the students within those schools. Public school samples[9] are stratified to achieve increased minority representation so that truly representative samples of students are chosen from small populations, the goal being to ensure the reliability of the score estimates for subgroups. Since participation was voluntary between 1990 and 2002, the sample of states changes from test to test; but every state except South Dakota participated in at least one NAEP test during that period.[10] Each time the state assessments were administered, the main assessment was also administered to a nationally representative sample of students. Each subject and grade has a national sample in the same year to which it can be compared.

Mandatory participation in 2003 (as a result of NCLB) increased the sample sizes in all states.[11] Table 6.1 shows California's student sample size for each administration. Between 1990 and 2000, NAEP tested approximately 2,000 of California's students; in 2003, California's sample size increased to over 8,000 fourth graders and over 5,000 eighth graders in each subject. The average sample size for the nationally administered NAEP tests in mathematics and reading, grades 4 and 8, increased from approximately 6,000 students per test between 1990 and 2000 to an average of 134,000 students per test in grade 4 and 166,000 in grade 8 in 2002 and 2003.

Before trying to compare California with the four other most populous states, it is important to consider changes that have occurred in NAEP administration and states' participation in NAEP testing. These changes need to be kept in mind when looking at the scores and results presented.

---

[9] Beginning in 1994, NAEP began collecting data on private schools, reporting scores for all schools and for public schools only.

[10] For a complete summary of NAEP sample design and potential biases, see Grissmer and Flanagan, 1998.

[11] Between 1990 and 1998, the state NAEP samples and the national sample were independent of one another. In 2002, the NAEP national sample was drawn from the state samples plus samples of students from nonparticipating states (Grigg, Daane, Jin, and Campbell, 2003, p. 134).

First, the pattern of state exclusion rates from NAEP test-taking changed differentially and significantly among states. The changes appear to have been the effect of an increase in the numbers of students accommodated on state tests. Until 1998, students accommodated on state tests were excluded from taking the NAEP. In addition, students designated as LEP students and students having an individualized education plan or disability (IEP/DS) can be excluded from NAEP participation. Unfortunately, changes in exclusion rates (discussed later in this chapter) make it difficult to compare California's performance with that of other states whose exclusion rates were also changing. These changes primarily affected the samples of fourth grade students.

In 1996, California excluded 16 percent of its students from taking the grade 4 mathematics NAEP, but in 2000, it excluded only 9 percent. In New York and Texas,[12] the pattern was in the opposite direction: New York excluded 8 percent in 1996 and 12 percent in 2000, and Texas excluded 5 percent in 1996 and 15 percent in 2000. Between 1998 and 2002, California's exclusion rate was the only one that changed for the grade 4 reading NAEP—it went from 14 percent of students to 5 percent.

If the scores of excluded students are assumed to be lower than those of included students, California's 2000 and 2002 scores in both mathematics and reading would have to be lower, making the state's gains from the earlier NAEP administrations appear smaller. We would expect the reverse to be true for the score gains in grade 4 mathematics (but not reading) for students in New York and Texas. The scores and results presented below should be viewed with these changes in mind.

NAEP began a program to accommodate the test-taking of students with special requirements in 1998, and reported both accommodated and nonaccommodated scores in 1998 and 2000.[13] These

---

[12] Florida did not participate in the 2000 NAEP, so no data on exclusions are available for Florida for 2000. The same is true for Illinois in 1996.

[13] Because the nation's proportions of minority students designated as LEP were increasing and the Individuals with Disabilities Education Act (IDEA) had been passed in 1997, more

accommodations include extended time for test-taking, one-on-one testing, small group testing, bilingual testing, and tests read aloud (Grigg, Daane, Jin, and Campbell, 2003; and Braswell et al., 2001). In 2002 and 2003, NAEP reported only the scores that included the accommodated test-takers and does not plan to report nonaccommodated scores in the future. On average, the difference between accommodated and nonaccommodated NAEP scores was no more than one or two points.

In our analysis of NAEP state trends, we used the difference between the reported accommodated and nonaccommodated NAEP scores in 1998 to adjust the 2002 and 2003 reading scores, and the difference between the 2000 accommodated and nonaccommodated scores to adjust the 2003 mathematics scores. By making this minor adjustment, we had a consistent set of data (nonaccommodated NAEP scores) for analyzing trends.

Results from State Assessments, 1998–2003

Although data from the STAR program have shortcomings, this section presents the most recent STAR data in order to provide a current snapshot of student academic achievement in California.

SAT/9 Results, 1998–2002

As mentioned earlier, California administered the SAT/9 statewide in mathematics, reading, writing, spelling, science, and history–social science. Figures 6.1 and 6.2 show the resulting SAT/9 mathematics

---

and more students needed to be accommodated on both state tests and the NAEP. One of NAEP's core principles is to provide truly representative test scores for the nation and the states, so as states began accommodating students, NAEP needed to do the same if its scores were to remain representative. Beginning in 1996, NAEP began conducting tests of the validity of becoming more inclusive and providing accommodations to students in order to maintain another of its core principles: provide accurate trend data on student achievement for the nation and the states. See Mazzeo, Carlson, Voelkl, and Lutkus, 2000.

Figure 6.1
California SAT/9 Scaled Scores, Mathematics, by Grade, 1998–2002

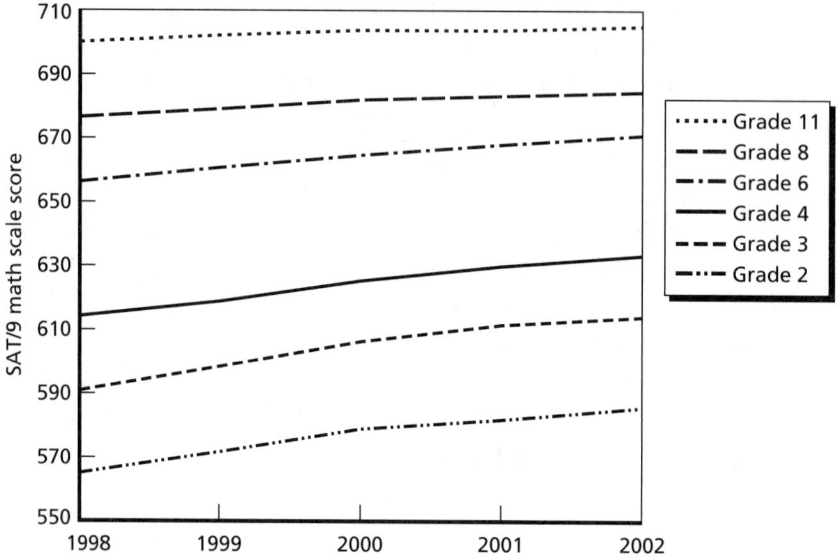

RAND *MG186-6.1*

and reading scaled scores for California students in grades 2, 3, 4, 6, 8, and 11.[14]

Mathematics scores in California, as measured by the SAT/9, showed some increases from 1998 to 2002. The gains were greater in the early grades (2, 3, and 4) than in the later grades: 21, 24, and 19 points, respectively. The gains diminish over grades, however, with eleventh graders making only a five-point gain over the period.[15]

Figure 6.2 shows a similar pattern for California's reading scores: larger gains in the early grades and smaller gains in the later grades. However, in this case, the gains at every grade were smaller

---

[14] The scaled scores for grades 5, 7, 9, and 10 show the same pattern across years and thus were omitted so that the results could be seen clearly in these two figures.

[15] Point differences refer to differences between reported SAT/9 scaled scores; the standard deviation for SAT/9 scores is approximately 40 (Stecher, McCaffrey, and Bugliari, 2002).

Figure 6.2
California SAT/9 Scaled Scores, Reading, by Grade, 1998–2002

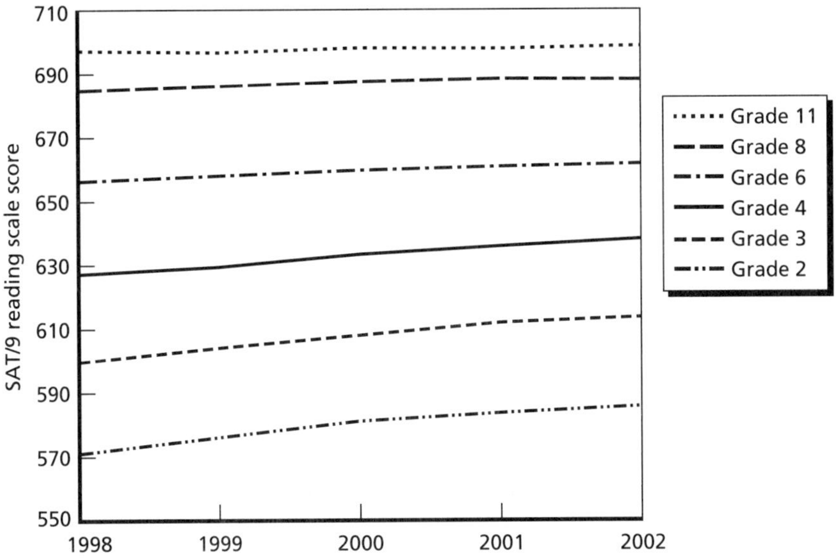

RAND *MG186-6.2*

than their counterparts in mathematics. From 1998 to 2002, second graders gained 15 points, third graders gained 13 points, and the gains continued to diminish in the higher grades, with eleventh graders making only a one-point gain.

CAT/6 Results, 2003

In 2003, California replaced the SAT/9 with the CAT/6. Table 6.2 shows the test results, presented as the percentages of California's students scoring at or above the 50th national percentile. These results indicate a mixed pattern of performance for students in California relative to students in the nation.

In nine out of the ten grades, California's students performed better in mathematics than they did in reading. For example, 57 per-

Table 6.2
Average Percentage of California Students Scoring At or Above the 50th National Percentile, 2003

Test	Percentage of California Students Scoring At or Above 50th National Percentile Rank				
	Grade 2	Grade 3	Grade 4	Grade 5	Grade 6
Math	57	52	48	49	51
Reading	46	34	35	40	45
	Grade 7	Grade 8	Grade 9	Grade 10	Grade 11
Math	46	48	46	51	46
Reading	45	41	50	49	47

SOURCE: http://www.cde.ca.gov

cent of second graders scored at or above the 50th percentile in mathematics, whereas only 46 percent did so in reading.

What makes the picture somewhat discouraging is the norm year being used for these comparisons. The CAT/6 results for 2003 were compared to a national sample of students in 2000 (the norm year). As a result, what is being compared here is the performance of California's students in 2003 to that of students in the nation in 2000. While national norms are considered "current" for several years, one must keep in mind that if students in the nation and in California are both making gains in student achievement over time, the fact that less than half of California's students are performing at or above the 50th national percentile may actually overstate California's position relative to the nation. The same is true for all grades, in both mathematics and reading. The degree to which these results overstate California's position depends on the relative rate of improvement in California compared to the nation.

Performance of Students Disaggregated by Race/Ethnicity

To illustrate the differences in scores by race/ethnicity, Figures 6.3 and 6.4 show the percentages of California students of four racial/

Figure 6.3
Percentage of California Students Scoring At or Above the 50th National Percentile Rank on CAT/6, Mathematics, by Race/Ethnicity, 2003

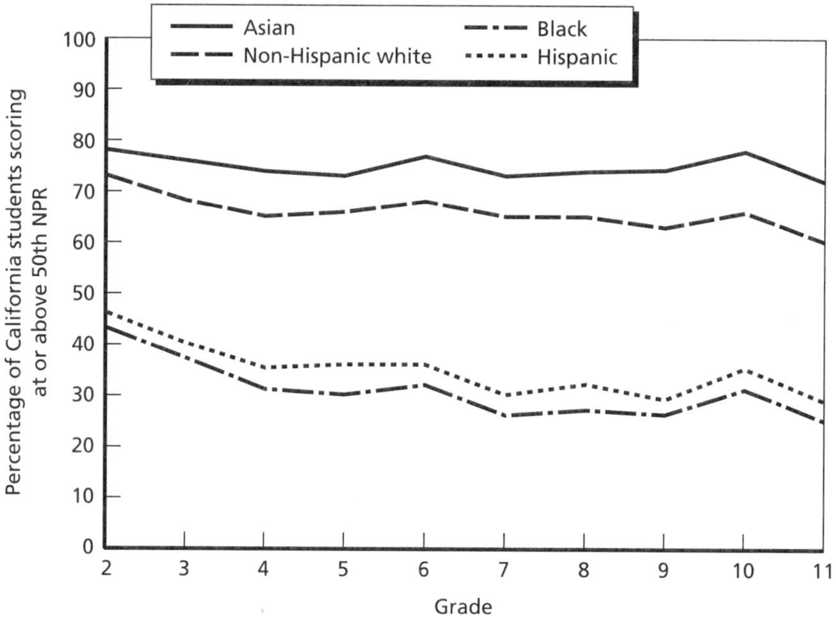

RAND *MG186-6.3*

ethnic groups at or above the 50th national percentile in mathematics and reading. The pattern of performance by race/ethnicity is striking.

In mathematics, the percentage of non-Hispanic white students and Asian students scoring at or above the 50th national percentile differed from the percentage of black and Hispanic students scoring at or above the 50th national percentile by approximately 30 to 40 percentage points. Roughly 70 percent of non-Hispanic white students and Asian students scored at or above the 50th national percentile on the CAT/6, whereas fewer than 40 percent of black and Hispanic students scored at or above that level. The gap between racial and ethnic groups is consistent across grades.

Figure 6.4
Percentage of California Students Scoring At or Above the 50th National Percentile Rank on CAT/6, Reading, by Race/Ethnicity, 2003

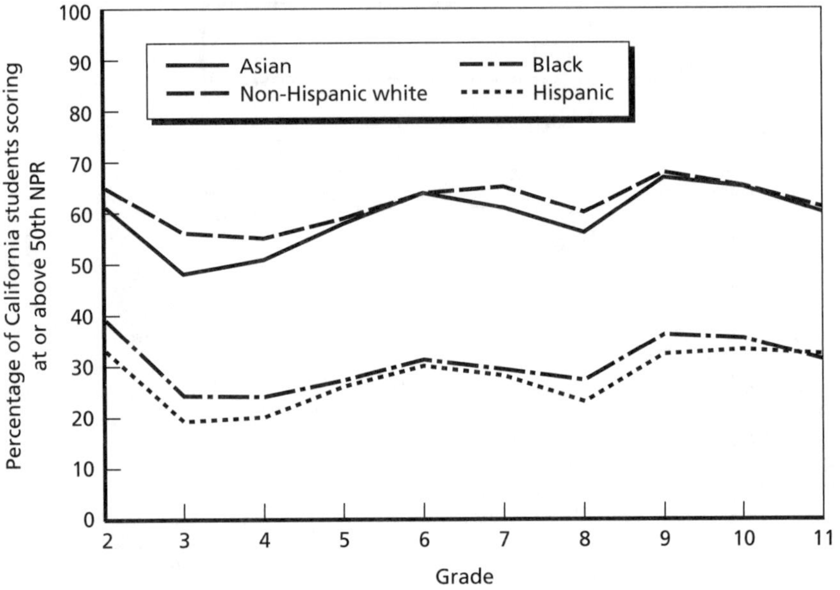

RAND *MG186-6.4*

Results from NAEP

As noted earlier, California participated in every state NAEP administration. We analyzed the following different measures using NAEP scores: reported NAEP scores by year, subject, and grade; average state scores across all 17 NAEP tests at grades 4 and 8; scores for students from similar families; and the gains made on the NAEP over time.

Overall NAEP Scores

Tables 6.3 and 6.4 present NAEP mathematics and reading scores for fourth and eighth grade public school students in California, the nation as a whole, and the four other most populous states. With few exceptions, California's scores are lower than those of the nation and

Table 6.3
Student Performance on NAEP, Difference Between the United States and California and Difference Between Each of the Four Other Most Populous States and California, Mathematics

	Mathematics								
	Grade 4				Grade 8				
	1992	1996	2000	2003	1990	1992	1996	2000	2003
U.S.	219**	222**	226**	236**	262**	267**	269**	274**	278**
California	208	209	214	228	256	261	263	262	269
Texas	218**	229**	233**	239**	258	265	270**	275**	279**
New York	218**	223**	227**	238**	261*	266	270**	276**	284**
Florida	214**	216**		234**	255	260	264		271**
Illinois			225**	235**	261*			277**	279**

SOURCE: http://www.nces.ed.gov/nationsreportcard/naepdata/.
NOTE: Statistical differences between either the nation or each of the four other states and California are shown. One asterisk (*) indicates a significant difference at the 5 percent level; two asterisks (**) indicate a significant difference at the 1 percent level. A blank indicates that a state did not participate in that NAEP test (e.g., Illinois did not participate in the 1992, 1996, and 2000 eighth grade math tests).

the other four states, and the general pattern is the same for both grades and both subjects.[16] Significant differences between California's test scores and those of the nation or any of the other states are noted in the tables.[17]

[16] These are the results reported by NCES and published in the official NAEP reports. Statistical significance is estimated using multiple comparison techniques based on sampling standard errors. These results are available at http://www.nces.ed.gov/nationsreportcard/naepdata/.

[17] NAEP began accommodating students with disabilities and reporting two sets of scores—accommodated and nonaccommodated—in 1998. For 2003, only accommodated scores are available. Tests of significance were conducted using both the accommodated and the nonaccommodated scores for 1996, 1998, 2000, and 2002; the significant differences reported are for the most-conservative comparisons. For example, if the 1996 nonaccommodated mathematics score for California fourth graders significantly differed from the 1996 accommodated equivalent but did not significantly differ from the 2003 accommodated equivalent, we would report no significant difference. In only one case did the statistical test based on nonaccommodated scores differ from the statistical test based on accommodated scores in the earlier year.

Table 6.4
Student Performance on NAEP, Difference Between the United States and California and Difference Between Each of the Four Other Most Populous States and California, Reading

	Reading							
	Grade 4					Grade 8		
	1992	1994	1998	2002	2003	1998	2002	2003
U.S.	215**	212**	213**	219**	218**	261**	263**	261**
California	202	197	202	206	206	253	251	252
Texas	213**	212**	217**	220**	218**	262**	263**	260**
New York	215**	212**	216**	223**	223**	266**	265**	266**
Florida	208**	205**	207	215**	219**	253	263**	259**
Illinois					216**			266**

SOURCE: http://www.nces.ed.gov/nationsreportcard/naepdata/.
NOTE: Statistical differences between either the nation or each of the four other states and California are shown. One asterisk (*) indicates a significant difference at the 5 percent level; two asterisks (**) indicate a significant difference at the 1 percent level. A blank indicates that a state did not participate in that NAEP test (e.g., Illinois did not participate in the 1992, 1994, 1998, and 2002 fourth grade reading tests).

As Table 6.3 shows, California's fourth graders trailed their counterparts in the other four most populous states in mathematics. Moreover, their scores were significantly lower in comparison not only to those of students in the four states, but also to those of students in the nation as a whole—and in every year. California's grade 4 mathematics scores did improve markedly between 2000 and 2003, but even that gain—14 points, one of the largest in the nation—was not enough to lift California's scores to the levels of those in Texas, New York, Florida, Illinois, and the nation as a whole.

As for California's eighth graders, their mathematics scores were significantly lower than the national scores. The performance of these students was comparable to that of students in Texas and Florida over the early 1990s. But, as can be seen in Table 6.3, Texas's performance improved significantly relative to California's by 1996; and by 2003, Florida's performance had, too.

California students also performed poorly on NAEP reading tests in both fourth and eighth grade (Table 6.4). California's reading scores were equal to Florida's in both grades in 1998; but by the next administration of the reading test, California had once again been outscored by Florida.

Performance of Students Disaggregated by Race/Ethnicity

An analysis of NAEP scores by race/ethnicity revealed consistently low performance for California students of all racial/ethnic groups (see Tables 6.5 and 6.6). California's non-Hispanic white students scored lower than their counterparts in the nation did on 15 out of 17 (nine mathematics and eight reading) NAEP tests. Moreover, they scored significantly lower on 11 of the tests.

Table 6.5
Student Performance on NAEP, Difference Between the United States and California and Difference Between Each of the Four Other Most Populous States and California, Disaggregated by Race/Ethnicity, Mathematics

	Mathematics								
	Grade 4				Grade 8				
Race/Ethnicity	1992	1996	2000	2003	1990	1992	1996	2000	2003
Non-Hispanic white									
U.S.	227**	230**	234**	243	269	276	280	284**	287**
California	221	223	229	243	270	275	277	278	283
Black									
U.S.	192**	199**	204**	216	236	236	241	245	252**
California	182	188	191	213	231	233	244	241	246
Hispanic									
U.S.	201**	204	209**	221**	245	247**	250	252	258**
California	190	196	200	216	236	239	245	245	250
Asian									
U.S.	231**	225		246	275	290		287	289
California	218	213	221	246	267	277	278	283	287

SOURCE: http://www.nces.ed.gov/nationsreportcard/naepdata/.
NOTE: Statistical differences between either the nation or each of the four other states and California are shown. One asterisk (*) indicates a significant difference at the 5 percent level; two asterisks (**) indicate a significant difference at the 1 percent level. A blank indicates that the sample size did not meet NCES standards and no score was reported by race/ethnicity.

Table 6.6
Student Performance on NAEP, Difference Between the United States and California and Difference Between Each of the Four Other Most Populous States and California, Disaggregated by Race/Ethnicity, Reading

	Reading							
	Grade 4					Grade 8		
Race/Ethnicity	1992	1994	1998	2002	2003	1998	2002	2003
Non-Hispanic white								
U.S.	223**	222**	224**	227**	227**	269	271**	270
California	217	212	217	223	224	268	265	265
Black								
U.S.	191**	184	192	198	197	241	244	244
California	181	182	188	196	193	243	242	239
Hispanic								
U.S	194**	186**	194**	199**	199**	243	245**	244**
California	180	171	178	192	191	238	238	237
Asian								
U.S.	215	217	218	223	225	265	265	268
California	207	207	210	220	224	257	257	266

SOURCE: http://www.nces.ed.gov/nationsreportcard/naepdata/.
NOTE: Statistical differences between either the nation or each of the four other states and California are shown. One asterisk (*) indicates a significant difference at the 5 percent level; two asterisks (**) indicate a significant difference at the 1 percent level. A blank indicates that the sample size did not meet NCES standards and no score was reported by race/ethnicity.

California's Asian students generally performed below the national average for all Asian students on all the NAEP tests. Although the scoring differences in this case were usually not significant,[18] the pattern of scores across all 17 NAEP tests suggests that Asian students in California were, on average, lower scoring than Asian students in the nation were.

In 11 of the 17 NAEP tests, California's black students scored below black students in the nation. And although the point differences between California's scores and those of the nation were smaller for black students than for Asian students, California's black students'

[18] The findings of significance are most likely due to the relatively small sample size for Asian students.

scores exhibited the same consistent pattern of lower scores on average.

Finally, the scores for California's Hispanic students were consistently below the scores for Hispanic students in the nation in both subjects and at both grade levels. In some cases, the score differences were quite large—i.e., 10–11 points.

Average State NAEP Scores and Family Characteristics

A consistent pattern of performance emerged when we looked at each of California's NAEP tests. The NAEP scores for California students were consistently lower than those for the nation and for the four other most populous states. Given the consistency of these results, we can now turn to discussing California's average NAEP scores across all 17 tests.

The average scores presented below do not hide variations in California's performance in mathematics or reading at either the fourth or the eighth grade level. As we just noted, California's students scored consistently lower than did the nation's students and students in the four other most populous states regardless of subject or grade level. California's ranking relative to all states and to the four other most populous states using the average score reflects this low performance. Average NAEP scores disaggregated by grade and subject are presented in Appendix A; they also consistently place California at the lower end of the distribution of states. Averaging scores across years and subjects offers a straightforward and shorthand way of summarizing the NAEP results.

Overall, California NAEP scores were well below the national average. Figure 6.5 shows the states ranked by the average performance of their students on NAEP tests between 1990 and 2003. NAEP scores were converted into standard deviation units so that we could compare scores across grades and subjects—fourth and eighth grade mathematics and fourth and eighth grade reading. The state scores are normalized on the national mean and standard deviation so that the each state's performance can be compared to the other's and to the nation's.

Figure 6.5
Average State NAEP Scores, Reading and Mathematics, Grades 4 and 8, 1990–2003

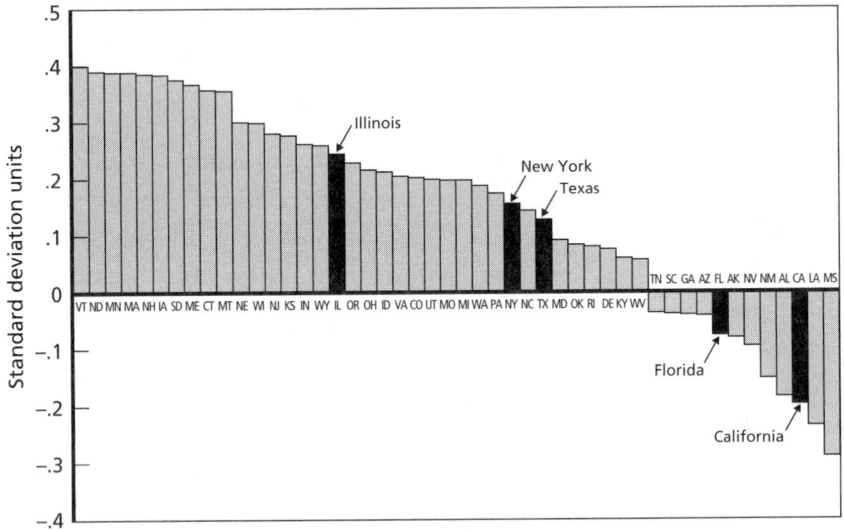

RAND *MG186-6.5*

California ranks at the bottom end of the distribution of states, just above Louisiana and Mississippi. At the top end of the distribution is a set of high-performing northern states—small, rural New England states and large, rural, sparsely populated Midwestern states. In the middle is a set of northern urban states whose students perform closer to the national average.

The pattern of performance generated using NAEP scores can be explained to some extent by the family characteristics within each state. Grissmer, Kirby, Berends, and Williamson (1994) identified family characteristics that were linked to test scores. They developed a model of education production using individual level data from the 1988 National Education Longitudinal Study (NELS) and the 1990 Census to estimate the effects of mother's education, father's education, family income, family size, age of mother at child's birth, family type, race/ethnicity, and mother's labor force status on children's test scores.[19] Grissmer and Flanagan (1998) refined this methodology, controlling for both family effects and the fixed effects of schools on student test scores.[20]

Table 6.7 shows California's 1990 and 2000 state averages for the family characteristics as well as how California ranks on these characteristics with respect to other states on key family characteristics. California is a relatively wealthy state, with a large proportion of parents who are college graduates and an average rate of births to teenage mothers and single mothers, which placed it at 25th out of 50 states in 2000. However, it has a very high minority population, and a large share of its population has less than a high school education. On these two characteristics, it ranks, respectively, first and eighth in the nation.

---

[19] The study found that parental education and minority status carry the greatest weight in predicting family influence on student test scores. That is, other things being equal, students with more-educated parents have, on average, higher test scores, and minority students have, on average, lower test scores. Median family income, having a single or teenage mother, and family size are less predictive of student test scores. Median income is positively related to test scores; single mother, teenage mother, and family size are negatively related to test scores—e.g., if all else is the same, students living in a female-headed household will have lower test scores on average. Mother's workforce status had no statistically significant effect on test scores.

[20] For more information on the technique used to create the composite socioeconomic status (SES) score, see Grissmer, Kirby, Berends, and Williamson, 1994; and Grissmer and Flanagan, 1998. This SES measure is obtained from a fixed effect regression with the following estimation equation: $y_{ij} = a + bx_{ij}' + u_j + e_{ij}$. The data are from the 1988 National Education Longitudinal Study (NELS:88). The y_{ij} are math and reading scores for the ith student (students age 8–10) in the jth school, and the x_{ij} are a set of parent reported family characteristics for the ith student in the jth school. To isolate the influence of family characteristics on test scores, fixed factors were incorporated into the model by the u_j's. This amounts to estimating a different intercept for each school in the NELS:88 data. The estimated regression coefficients, the b's, were then used to weight the same measures of family characteristics using a sample drawn from 1990 Census data for 8–10 year olds by state. The statewide average census values and the b's were used to predict a state-level test score, which was then defined as an estimated average family characteristic score, or an estimated composite SES score. The composite SES score was adjusted by weighting each state's value by the racial/ethnic percentages of its NAEP student population on each NAEP test from 1990 to 2003. This modification was an attempt to weight the SES variable with more-current demographic data, based on the assumption that this would adjust for LEP, Individualized Education Plans (IEP/DS), and private school students—students excluded from or not represented in the NAEP.

Table 6.7
Demographic and Economic Statistics for California, 1990 and 2000, and California's National Ranking, 2000

	California State Average		
Family Characteristic	2000	1990	California State Ranking, 2000
Median income (constant 2000 dollars)	53,025	52,076	14
Minority (percent)	66.0[a]	55.0[a]	1
Single mother (percent)	32.7	31.6	25
Teen births	2.7[c]	4.7[b]	19
Parent education, no high school diploma (percent)	18.8	23.8	8
Parent education, college degree (percent)	27.5	23.4	14

SOURCE: U.S. Census Bureau, 1990, 2000.
[a]http://www.nces.ed.gov/nationsreportcard/naepdata/.
[b]U.S. Department of Health and Human Services, Centers for Disease Control and Prevention, n.d.; teen birth rate data are for 1991.
[c]Allen Guttmacher Institute, n.d.

Using the methodology described above (see, especially, footnote 20), we predicted a test score for each state based on its family characteristics and the effects of schools. The weights given to each family characteristic when we simultaneously control for all of them better predict the link between test scores and family effects than does a simple listing and ranking of state demographics, as in Table 6.7. These composite socioeconomic status (SES) scores, depicted in Figure 6.6, are predicted test scores—i.e., the scores we would expect or predict for the states given their family characteristics (controlling for the effects of schools on student performance). While the general pattern of average NAEP scores mirrors that of average state family characteristics, Figure 6.6 indicates that California's weighted composite SES score was below the national average. It also shows California ranking 38th out of the 48 states used in the analysis.[21]

[21] Figure 6.6 reports the composite SES scores for states that participated in at least one NAEP test given between 1990 and 2000 when NAEP was voluntary. For that reason, all 50 states are not included in the figure. The District of Columbia is not reported because the

Figure 6.6
Estimated Average State SES Test Scores, 1990–2003

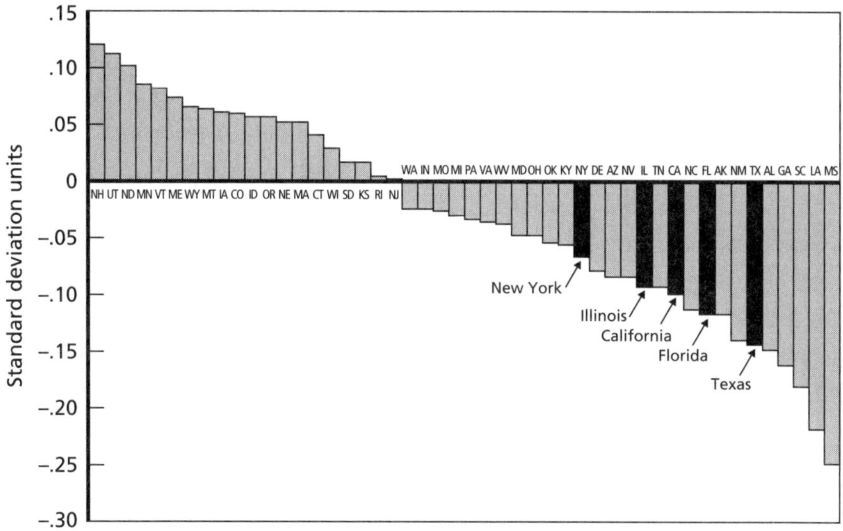

RAND *MG186-6.6*

Given the family characteristics in each of the five most populous states, we would predict test scores below the national average for all of them. Further, we would expect New York to be the highest-performing state, followed by Illinois, California, Florida, and Texas. Comparing Figure 6.5 with Figure 6.6, one can see the similarity in the distribution of NAEP scores and the SES scores. The rural, high-income, low-minority northern states at the top of the distribution in Figure 6.6 have some of the highest test scores in the nation; and the rural, low-income, high-minority southern states are the lowest scoring in the nation. California ranks in the lower end of the distribution, below the national average. Its position among the states suggests that its family characteristics are somewhat but not well below the national average. Based on this ranking, California's ranking as

---

family characteristics of relevant school-age children living in the District differ from the family characteristics of the students attending public school in the District. Similar demographic issues caused Hawaii and Alaska to be dropped from the analyses in Grissmer and Flanagan, 1998, and to be excluded here as well.

third from the bottom on actual NAEP scores (see Figure 6.5) is somewhat puzzling.

Scores for Students from Similar Families

We have argued elsewhere that it is more appropriate to compare scores across states for students with similar backgrounds and characteristics (Grissmer and Flanagan, 1998). The scores reported in Figure 6.7 are estimated average scores for similar students across 17 NAEP test administrations in mathematics and reading at the fourth and eighth grade levels. These scores were calculated by normalizing NAEP scores using the average national NAEP score and standard deviation. Once we had these scores that could be compared across grades and subjects, we then controlled for family characteristics.

Figure 6.7
Estimated Average NAEP Scores for Students from Similar Families Across States

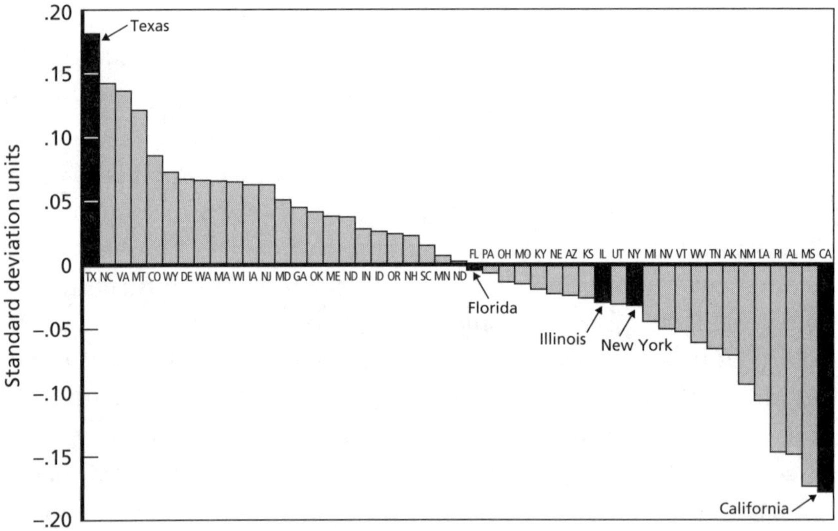

RAND *MG186-6.7*

Figure 6.7 reports the distribution of estimated scores for students from similar families across states. Because the effects of family have been largely controlled for, these scores are more closely linked to school quality.

Our results in Figure 6.7 show the following:

- California's scores for students from similar families are the lowest in the nation (–0.18 standard deviations below the mean). As shown in Figure 6.6, California students' family characteristics would predict that, all else being equal, the state would rank 38th in the nation. This suggests that these low scores are not simply a result of family characteristics in the state but that they reflect on schools as well.
- A comparison of Florida's average performance on NAEP scores and its scores for students from similar families suggests that Florida is performing at the level that its family characteristics would predict. Florida's rank among states changes very little when the average NAEP score and the estimated SES score are compared. Stated another way, in comparison to other states' schools, Florida's are adding average value to student perfomance.
- A comparison of California and Texas suggests that Texas's high scores are more likely school effects than family effects. Texas has the highest estimated average NAEP score for students from similar families (0.18 standard deviations above the mean) of all 48 states in the comparison, in spite of the fact that Texas families rank lower than families nationally on characteristics that are correlated with student test scores. Factors beyond family characteristics, such as schools, appear to add more than an average value to student performance in this case.

Another way of interpreting the data presented in Figure 6.7 is to ask, how would a student currently enrolled in a California school perform on the NAEP if he or she had been enrolled from the start in a Texas school? The data reported above suggest that California students' scores would increase by 0.36 standard deviations—from –0.18 to 0.18 standard deviations, or by approximately 12 NAEP points (12 points on NAEP scores) on average.[22]

Flanagan and Grissmer, in ongoing RAND work, have found that California's low performance is evident for students of all races/ethnicities. Black, Hispanic, and non-Hispanic white students in California are among the lowest-scoring students in the nation when compared to students in other states who have similar family characteristics.[23]

We have suggested that scores for students from similar families are better measures of school quality than reported scores are. Family effects on student test scores are substantial, and in some states, such as Texas and Florida, scores for students of similar families rank higher than either actual reported scores or scores predicted by average state family characteristics. Analyzing reported scores and scores for students from similar families makes it possible to identify states whose schools appear to be adding positive value to student test scores, as well as states, such as California, whose schools do not appear to be adding positive value.

Recent NAEP Score Gains

With each NAEP administration, the Department of Education, NCES, publishes official reports containing a table of all prior years' assessment data and an indication of statistical significance in the changes from one test to the next test in a given subject area.[24] Comparing the most recent year to the previous year provides one set of

[22] NAEP points refer to points on reported NAEP scaled scores. The scale for NAEP scores is 0 to 500. We calculated the number of NAEP points by taking the difference between Texas's and California's scores for students from similar families and multiplying it by the national standard deviation, which is equal to approximately 34.

[23] These data are also available at http://www.nces.ed.gov/nationsreportcard/naepdata/.

[24] These data are also available at http://www.nces.ed.gov/nationsreportcard/naepdata/.

information but may hide significant variations in test scores from one period to another. Simply comparing gains in reported scores suffers from the same problem as comparing the levels of reported scores, since neither approach controls for family characteristics, which are essential to any discussion of student achievement—whether it be in terms of gains or levels.

We first examine unadjusted gains in reported scores and then estimate the annualized trend across all 17 NAEP scores alone and controlling for the influence of family characteristics. When looking at trends in test scores, it is important to account for the demographic trends in California, especially the large increases in the percentage of minority students in the public school system.

The official reports show California making significant gains in eighth grade NAEP mathematics scores from 1990 to 1992, no significant gains from 1992 to 1996 and 1996 to 2000, and significant gains from 2000 to 2003. The same pattern is present at the fourth grade level for California mathematics gains. However, since there was no fourth grade mathematics NAEP in 1990, it appears that California made no significant gains until 2003.

Figure 6.8 plots both California's score gains in standard deviations and the score gains made at the national level between each NAEP administration in mathematics and reading for fourth and eighth grades. The remarkable gains made by the nation as a whole in mathematics at the fourth grade level are easy to see; and, in fact, the United States experienced significant gains in mathematics at this grade level from 2000 to 2003. Although not shown here, the four other most populous states all made large gains as well. Between 2000 and 2003, California fourth graders gained 14 NAEP points while the nation gained 10 NAEP points.

The reading scores show very small gains at the fourth grade level. Eighth grade reading performance from 1998—the first time the eighth grade reading NAEP was administered—to 2003 remained basically unchanged.

Figure 6.8
NAEP Gains for California and the United States, Mathematics and Reading, Grades 4 and 8, 1990–2003

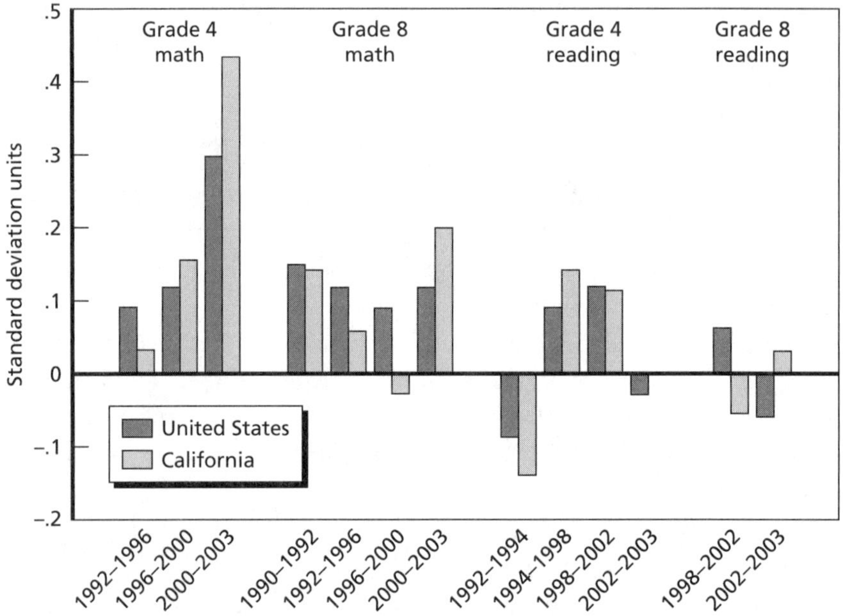

RAND *MG186-6.8*

Average Gains Adjusted for Family Characteristics

We calculated an average standardized gain among the states taking the NAEP between 1990 and 2003.[25] On average, with and without family controls, eighth graders gained approximately one NAEP point per year in mathematics (0.034 standard deviations), and fourth graders gained over one NAEP point per year (0.04 standard deviations). Fourth graders gained 0.01 standard deviations (0.34 points per year) in reading; for eighth graders, the trend in reading was negative. Eighth graders lost 0.014 standard deviations, or 0.44

[25] The overall trend is used as an approximation to the national trend. The overall trends reported here were obtained by estimating the trends for those states that participated in the NAEP.

points per year; with family controls, the eighth grade reading trend disappeared.

Table 6.8 presents the estimated annualized gains made by the five most populous states in mathematics and reading, as well as the gains for mathematics only and reading only. Mathematics and reading gains were estimated separately because of the large increases in mathematics scores, the smaller gains in reading scores, and the differential gains in both subjects across the set of states. Illinois is not included in the table because it did not participate in enough tests for us to estimate a trend.

It should be noted that, in this section, we have not made any adjustments for changing exclusion rates that are likely to affect both actual and gain scores. Flanagan and Grissmer, in ongoing RAND work, have found that approximately 25 percent of the gains made on the mathematics NAEP between 1992 and 2000 in grades 4 and 8 may be due to changing exclusion rates. Estimated gains across states

Table 6.8
Estimated Annual Gains in NAEP for the Five Most Populous States, Mathematics and Reading, 1990–2003, and Mathematics Only, 1990–2003

	Estimated Annual Gain			Estimated Annual Gain with Family Controls		
State	Math and Reading	Math	Reading	Math and Reading	Math	Reading
California	0.025**	0.034**	0.008	0.033**	0.040**	0.006
Texas	0.036**	0.047**(+)	0.015(**)	0.046**(+)	0.054**(+)	0.016(**)
New York	0.038**	0.050**(+)	0.019(**)	0.045**	0.053**(+)	0.019(**)
Florida	0.036**	0.041**	0.026(**)(++)	0.039**	0.040**	0.028(**)(++)
Illinois	N/A	N/A	N/A	N/A	N/A	N/A

NOTE: An asterisk (*) indicates a significant difference at the 5 percent level; two asterisks (**) indicate a significant difference at the 1 percent level. A plus sign (+) indicates a significant difference at the 5 percent level between California's score and the score for a given state; two plus signs (++) indicate a significant difference at the 1 percent level between California's score and the score for a given state. N/A means no data.

by race/ethnicity (since excluded students are primarily minority students) decline by approximately 0.01 standard deviations for white, black, and Hispanic students. If the trend in exclusion rates continues and reported scores are corrected for the variation in exclusion rates across states, we would expect to see an upward adjustment in California's relative ranking among the states when comparing the trend in NAEP scores. As noted earlier, California's NAEP exclusion rate has decreased while the rates for most other states have either increased or remained constant. The California gains reported in Table 6.8 are, therefore, conservative estimates.

From Table 6.8, we note the following:

- California, Texas, New York, and Florida all made significant gains on the NAEP. These state gains are equivalent to the gains being made by the nation as a whole.
- California's estimated combined mathematics and reading gains were comparable to those made by Texas, New York, and Florida. However, the mathematics gains of Texas and New York were significantly higher than those of California, and the reading gains of Florida were significantly higher than those of California.
- When the influence of family is taken into consideration, California's annual gain in mathematics and reading combined increased from 0.025 to 0.033 standard deviations and went from 0.034 to 0.04 standard deviations in mathematics.[26] Texas and New York both had larger gains in mathematics and reading when the effects of family were controlled for; Florida's gains increased as well but by a much smaller amount.

---

[26] The family adjustment is larger when mathematics and reading are combined. Reading scores are more affected by increases in the Hispanic population, and between 1990 and 2003, California's already large Hispanic population continued to increase. All else being equal, reading scores were lower for LEP students, the majority of whom are of Hispanic origin. Essentially, when we control for the influence of family, we are controlling for the changing demographics over time in each state. The result is an estimate of gain in the absence of these demographic changes.

California NAEP and SAT/9 Compared

Although, as we cautioned earlier, it is best not to compare results from norm-referenced tests developed by different test publishers, we decided to compare the gains in the scaled scores from the SAT/9 and CAT/6 with those from the NAEP. We wanted to see whether a comparison of state data to the NAEP data would produce any evidence to suggest that the scores from the state-administered tests follow the same patterns of improvement (or decline) that the NAEP test scores follow. We present these data in Figure 6.9.

California did not administer the SAT/9 in 1996 or 2003, so we compared the annualized gain in SAT/9 grade 4 mathematics measured between 1998 and 2002 to the annualized gain in NAEP grade

Figure 6.9
California Students' Annualized Gains on NAEP and SAT/9 for Comparable Test Years

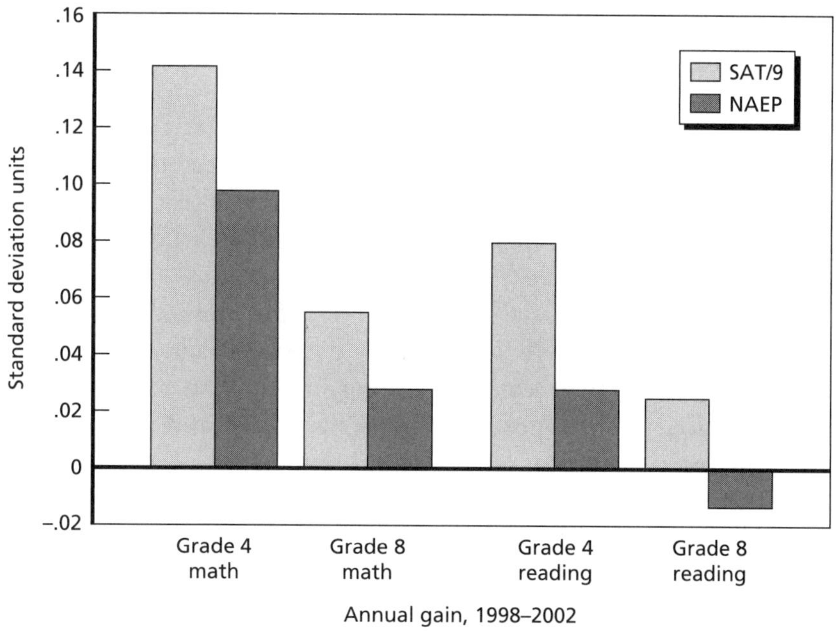

RAND *MG186-6.9*

4 mathematics measured between 1996 and 2003. Both tests have reading data for 1998 and 2002, so we calculated the annualized reading gain over the same period.

Figure 6.9 shows that California has made large gains in grade 4 mathematics—almost 0.14 standard deviations per year between 1998 and 2002 on the SAT/9, and 0.1 standard deviations annually between 1996 and 2003 on the NAEP. This amounts to a difference of approximately 1.3 NAEP points per year. The gains made on the SAT/9 are larger than the gains made on the NAEP at both the fourth and the eighth grade level in both mathematics and reading. Evidence from past research suggests that gains will be larger on "high-stakes" tests than on tests that are being used for monitoring achievement but that have no set education policy implications.[27] The results presented here are consistent with what that evidence suggests.

Conclusions

The state of California has administered several tests from 1973 to the present. However, limitations in the data collected and testing policies rule out the possibility of analyzing long-term trends in student achievement or the performance of California students relative to that of students across the country.

The NAEP provides a more accurate and representative look at student achievement. NAEP state tests have been administered approximately every two years, beginning in 1990, to representative samples of fourth and eighth graders in the nation and in the states. California participated in all NAEP administrations between 1990 and 2003 in both mathematics and reading.

NAEP scores indicate the following about achievement among California's public school students:

---

[27] A high-stakes test is one with immediate consequences for students, teachers, and schools. For discussions of the consequences and effects of high-stakes testing, see National Research Council, 1999; Le and Klein, 2002; and Stecher, 2002.

- California ranks 48th out of 50 states when the average NAEP score across all tests is used. California's fourth and eighth grade students consistently scored well below the national average, and California was the lowest scoring of the five most populous states in the nation.
- California ranks 47th out of 47 states when we compare scores for students from similar families—a better measure for comparing the education systems across states.
- Between 1992 and 2003, California made statistically significant gains in fourth grade mathematics scores. These gains were larger than the gains made in the nation and in the four other most populous states. While this is promising, California was still the lowest scoring of the five most populous states.
- California made gains of approximately 0.9 NAEP points per year from 1990 to 2003 in terms of reported test scores. When we control for family characteristics, California's gains were slightly larger—about 1.1 NAEP points per year for students from similar families.

CHAPTER SEVEN

Other Indicators of Student Progress

Society expects schools not only to enhance students' academic ability, but also to help foster behaviors that lead to students' eventual integration into society in a positive way. Accordingly, we explored California's experience with respect to five indicators of student performance that are known to affect the integration of youth into economically and civically productive adulthood. We then compared these outcomes for California's teenagers to those for teenagers in other states. The indicators we used are the following:

- Teenage pregnancy
- Substance abuse
- Juvenile delinquency
- High school completion
- College continuation

High school completion and college continuation directly relate to the efforts of the educational system. However, the links between the educational system and teenage pregnancies, substance abuse, and juvenile delinquency are not as direct. In fact, a variety of social and psychological factors, which are difficult to measure, likely play large roles in determining these outcomes. Still, schools attempt to directly influence these outcomes through programs aimed at the prevention of behaviors that can adversely affect the students themselves, their fellow students, and society in general. The schools also indirectly influence these outcomes by helping students develop career aspirations and become aware of the links between their current behaviors and the likelihood of achieving their aspirations.

Given the role of social influences, the measured differences across states in these outcomes are affected by a wide variety of factors other than the influence of schools. But these differences are also, to some degree, reflective of the influence of schools, especially when we consider within-state changes over time in the outcomes. In addition, the differences across states could reflect and influence the differences in the atmospheres of schools, which could contribute to the success or lack thereof of their students.

To account for the influences of the social, psychological, cultural, and other factors, we used regression models with controls for the percentage of teenagers in different racial/ethnic groups. The one exception is substance abuse, for which we do not have data across enough years to estimate regressions, although the fact that we have substance abuse rates for several racial/ethnic groups means we can still calculate an adjusted abuse rate. We present the unadjusted comparisons across states. In addition, after adjusting for racial/ethnic differences across states, we show how California compares with the nation as a whole, the four other most populous states—Texas, New York, Florida, and Illinois—and the aggregate of the rest of the United States.

It should be noted that these outcomes have many other determinants that are not captured by racial/ethnic divisions and that vary across states. Consider, as an example, parental substance abuse. If parental substance abuse affected children's substance abuse, and there were differences in parental substance abuse across states, then the effects of those differences on our estimated adolescent substance abuse rates across states would be reflective of factors unrelated to the school system. Accordingly, the results of the regression analyses reported here must be interpreted as upper-bound estimates of the effects of schooling on these indicators. The regression results indicate the extent to which the distribution of students across racial/ethnic groups explains differences across states in these indicators of student performance. The unexplained residual reflects the influence of both the schools and all other factors on these indicators.

The other outcomes that we discuss in this chapter—high school graduation and continuing on to college—affect older teens and are likely to be substantially influenced by pregnancy, substance abuse, and juvenile delinquency among younger teens. Accordingly, we examine California's performance with respect to each of these outcomes before turning to California's performance with respect to high school graduation and continuation to college.

Appendix B presents more detail about the methodology we used in analyzing each of the outcomes we discuss in this chapter.

Overall, the results of our analyses provide a mixed picture for how California's teenagers compare to those in other states on these nonachievement outcomes. Pregnancy rates are very high for California teenagers, but these rates, and the rates of teenage births, are decreasing in California relative to other states. California's teenage cigarette use and alcohol use are low, but the state's teenage use of illicit drugs is in the middle of the distribution. Juvenile delinquency rates are high in California for violent crimes, but not for property crimes. And, when we adjust for racial/ethnic composition, California's arrest rates are lower than those in other states for both violent and property crimes. Yet the trend for arrest rates is not as favorable in California as it is in other states. Finally, relative to those of other states, high school graduation rates in California have been high, but college continuation rates have been low.

Teenage Pregnancy

Background

In 1997, nearly 6 percent of 15–17 year old females became pregnant in the United States (Henshaw, 2001). The teenage birth rates in the United States far surpass the corresponding rates for the other G-7 countries,[1] which suggests that social factors contribute to the decisions teenagers make about sexual activity and the use of contracep-

[1] The G-7 countries are the United States, Canada, Japan, France, Germany, Italy, and the United Kingdom, which are the leading industrial nations in the world.

tion. Further evidence for social factors playing a major role is that there are large differences across racial/ethnic groups within the United States, as Table 7.1 shows.

Researchers have developed several types of models to determine what causes teenage pregnancies and the decisions leading to pregnancies. There have been psychological/social models as well as economic models. We describe a few of the models and then explain how an educational system could affect these decisions in the context of these models.

Hardy and Zabin (1991) developed a "life course model" that has biological/health and family/environmental factors interacting with each other to influence developmental outcomes, including teenage sexual activity. Among the major family/environmental factors are family background, schools, the community, peers, and the media. Hardy and Zabin argue that as family and school become less influential—due to, say, parents working long hours or schools not keeping teenagers interested—teenagers' behavior becomes more affected by the other influences.

Whereas the psychological and social models assume that decisions on whether to have sex and whether to use contraception are sometimes based on irrational, unplanned decisions that are made on the spur of the moment (Moore, Miller, Glei, and Morrison, 1995), economic models assume rationality—i.e., that a person will compare his or her perceptions of the benefits and costs of each decision.

Table 7.1
Annual Pregnancy Rates Across Racial/Ethnic Groups, United States (per 1,000 15–17 year old females)

	1990	1991	1992	1993	1994	1995	1996	1997
White	56	54	50	50	49	47	44	41
Black	165	165	160	158	150	137	128	120
Hispanic	101	107	111	110	114	110	105	99
All	80	80	77	77	76	72	68	64

SOURCE: Ventura et al., 2001.

O'Donoghue and Rabin (1999) argue within the context of this rational framework that teenagers can still act in ways that appear to be spontaneous even though they are weighing their perceived benefits and costs. The problem, they argue, is that the costs of sex are distant and uncertain, whereas the benefits are clear and present. Moreover, teenagers tend to think in terms of the present rather than the future, which means that the consequences of sex, which come in the future, would be significantly discounted in their sexual decisions.

These models from different disciplines explain to some extent the decisions teenagers make about sex and contraception. We use these models as a base in discussing some of the ways in which schools can affect teenagers' decisionmaking.

Schools could address the issue of whether to have sex and whether to take proper actions to prevent pregnancy directly through sex education or health education classes, reinforcing the idea that abstinence and/or careful contraception can significantly reduce the chances of getting pregnant. These efforts could help clarify the true costs of having sex and of not taking proper actions to prevent pregnancy. Oettinger (1999) found that sex education in the 1970s reduced the incidence of sex the most for teenagers who did not have many alternative sources for sexual information.

Schools can also affect outcomes indirectly. First and foremost, they can keep teenagers interested in school so that they do not drop out and get greater input into their decisionmaking from people on the "street" (Hardy and Zabin, 1991), where sexual encounters might be more prevalent and perhaps even expected. In addition, schools could provide resources for community activities (such as athletic programs) that may enhance confidence and responsibility among teenagers and keep them occupied at times when they would otherwise be unsupervised (Hardy and Zabin, 1991). Finally, in line with the stance of the economic models, schools could provide students with a sense of the future, helping them form aspirations for the pursuit of further education and for a career. This could reduce teenage pregnancies by raising the costs of getting pregnant.

Kirby (2002) reviewed several articles on how schools can influence the sexual practices of their students. He found that programs on sex education and HIV education reduce the amount of sex engaged in, increase contraception and condom use, and delay initiation of sex. In addition, he reports findings from a study, by Hawkins et al. (1999), indicating that a school program designed not to address sexual activity but, rather, to improve attachment to school and to reduce dropout rates actually reduced sexual activity and teenage pregnancy rates.

Teenage Pregnancy in California and Other States

We know that teenage pregnancy rates are high in the United States. Our objective with the data analyses was to determine how California's teenage pregnancy rates compare to those in other states. More detail about our data and methods is provided in Appendix B.

We examined the outcomes for 15–17 year old females because this is a common grouping used in the teenage pregnancy literature and because most of this age group should still be in school. We compared the following across states:

- Average pregnancy rates over the four most recent years for which teenage pregnancy data are available across states—1985, 1988, 1992, and 1996.
- 1996 actual pregnancy rates.
- 1996 adjusted pregnancy rates, adjusting for racial/ethnic differences (with the groups being black, Hispanic, Asian/Pacific Islander, and other). These were estimated with regressions analysis using all four years of data.
- Annual trend in unadjusted pregnancy rates.
- Annual trend in adjusted pregnancy rates, again adjusting for racial/ethnic differences.

Because pregnancy rate statistics across states are available only for these four years and because the latest of these years (1996) is not very recent, we supplemented the pregnancy rate data with birth rate data when examining the trends. While birth rates differ across states due to differences in abortion rates, within-state changes over time may be more reflective of changes in pregnancy rates than changes in abortion rates are. For the two years for which we have both pregnancy and birth data by states, the correlations across states between the pregnancy and birth rates are 0.86 in 1992 and 0.88 in 1996, and the correlation between the changes in pregnancies and births from 1992 to 1996 is 0.57. Thus, examining births as a supplement to examining pregnancies seems reasonable.

Table 7.2 shows the comparisons for the different pregnancy statistics. The average pregnancy rate for 15–17 year olds was higher in California than in any other state. For these four years of data (1985, 1988, 1992, and 1996), California averaged 95 pregnancies per 1,000 15–17 year old females (or 9.5 percent per year), which is much above the U.S. average of 70. In 1996, California's teenage pregnancy rate decreased to 80, still ranking it below most states. In fact, this rate was 25 pregnancies per 1,000 females above the average for the states other than the most populous ones. The four other most populous states all ranked in the bottom fifth among all states. The high pregnancy rates for California are likely partly attributable to the demographic composition of the state's population. In particular,

Table 7.2
Actual and Adjusted Pregnancies, Five Most Populous States (per 1,000 15–17 year old females)

	Average for 1985, 1988, 1992, and 1996		1996 Pregnancy Rate			Annual Pregnancy Trend		
			Unadjusted		Adjusted	Unadjusted		Adjusted
	Rate	Rank	Rate	Rank	Rate	Rate	Rank	Rate
California	95	50th	80	49th	66	–1.4	8th	–1.7
Texas	79	43rd	74	46th	54	+0.2	48th	–1.2
New York	76	39th	70	41st	60	–0.3	39th	–0.9
Florida	83	48th	71	43rd	67	–1.6	6th	–1.4
Illinois	69	34th	70	41st	58	–0.9	24th	–0.2
States other than 5 most populous	63		55		60	–0.8		–1.1
U.S.	70	–	62	–		–0.9		

SOURCES: Henshaw and Van Vort, 1989, for 1985 data; Henshaw, 1993, for 1988 data; Henshaw, 1997, for 1992 data; and http://www.agi-usa.org/pubs/teen_preg_stats.html for 1996 data.

California ranks second among all states in the fraction of its population that are female Hispanic teenagers, and Hispanics have much higher pregnancy rates than the general population does. After factoring out racial/ethnic differences, California still has a high number of pregnancies, but the rate is only six teenage pregnancies per 1,000 greater than the rates of the states other than the four most populous.

Despite California's having a high teenage pregnancy rate compared to other states, the decline of its pregnancy rate has been faster than the declines in most states. California's rate of decline for 1985–1996 ranked eighth among the states, with actual pregnancies per 1,000 15–17 year old females decreasing 1.4 per year, which is the second highest rate of decline among the most populous states. California has a high decreasing trend in adjusted pregnancies as well. When racial/ethnic differences are adjusted for, California has a decreasing trend of 1.7 per year, which is way above the 1.1 trend for states other than the five most populous.

The trends in teenage births are also favorable for California relative to other states, as seen in Table 7.3. Based on regressions using 1990 to 2000 data, California had the second fastest decline, at 1.7 fewer births per year per 1,000 15–17 year old females. Adjusted

Table 7.3
Annual Change in Actual and Adjusted Births, Five Most Populous States, 1990–2000 (per 1,000 15–17 year old females)

	Trend in Actual Births, 1990–2000		Trend in Adjusted (Actual – Predicted) Births, 1990–2000
	Rate	Rank	Rate
California	–1.7	2nd	–1.5
Texas	–0.7	40th	–0.6
New York	–0.9	28th	–0.8
Florida	–1.4	5th	–1.3
Illinois	–1.2	9th	–1.1
States other than 5 most populous	–1.0		–1.1
U.S.	–1.0	–	

SOURCES: Ventura et al., 2001; and Martin, Park, and Sutton, 2002.

for racial/ethnic differences, the trend was –1.5. Both of these trends were larger decreases than were seen in the four other most populous states and compare favorably to the –0.8 actual and –1.1 adjusted annual trends for the rest of the states.

In sum, California has a very high teenage pregnancy rate. Even when we controlled for the demographic composition of female teenagers, the rate remained one of the highest among the states. However, California also had one of the greatest rates of decline in teenage pregnancy rate from 1992 to 1996 and had the greatest decline in birth rates from 1990 to 2000.

Substance Abuse

Background

Teenage drug abuse in the United States soared in the 1990s. From 1992 to 1997, the percentage of teenagers who had used any illegal drug (e.g., marijuana, hallucinogens, hard drugs such as heroin) in the past year increased from 20.4 to 38.5 percent for tenth graders and from 27.1 to 42.4 percent for twelfth graders. Since 1997, teenage substance abuse has decreased slightly.[2]

There has been extensive research documenting a link between adolescent substance abuse and negative outcomes. Among the numerous negative outcomes associated with adolescent drug use are escalated drug use as an adult (Kandel, Davies, Karus, and Yamaguchi, 1986), labor market instability (Kandel, Davies, Karus, and Yamaguchi, 1986; Mijares, 1997), greater levels of juvenile delinquency (Kandel, Davies, Karus, and Yamaguchi, 1986), emotional problems (Kinnier, Metha, Okey, and Keim, 1994), and increasing chances of dropping out of high school (Yamada, Kendix, and Yamada 1996; Bray, Zarkin, Ringwalt, and Qi, 2000).

The question remains, however, whether these relationships represent the causal impact of substance abuse. For example, delinquent

---

[2] These data are from the Website for "Monitoring the Future," http://monitoringthefuture.org/data/01data/pr01t2.pdf (accessed September 2003).

behavior could reduce the inhibitions a person has to use drugs. In addition, one can imagine that emotional problems could lead to substance abuse. Despite these arguments, it is generally agreed that substance abuse, especially for a teenager, can be quite harmful.

Kandel (1985) suggests that the more important general determinants of teenage substance abuse are social factors—e.g., the influence of peers—and psychological factors—e.g., how a teenager's behavioral decision to use drugs is driven by pleasure rather than rational thought. Gaviria and Raphael (2001) consider influences of adolescent substance abuse that are more specific. They found that several aspects of parental behavior are related to teenage drug and alcohol use. Specifically, they found that parents' involvement in the teenager's homework, their attendance at school meetings, and their trying to keep track of how the teenager spends his or her money and where the teenager goes at night are all significantly negatively related to teenagers' use of drugs. Furthermore, living in a single parent household or having a parent with a drug problem, as expected, has a significant positive correlation with substance abuse.

Schools can influence teenage substance abuse decisions in many ways. Schools could, for example, provide educational programs on the effects of substance abuse. In addition, schools can strive to keep students enrolled in school to limit their exposure to influences from people on the street. Schools can also attempt to instill hope and aspirations for future economic success, thus raising the costs of substance abuse. And schools could provide resources for community activities that develop confidence and keep teenagers occupied when they would otherwise be unsupervised.

Caulkins, Pacula, Paddock, and Chiesa (2002) examined the results of several studies that evaluate the impact of school-based drug prevention programs. They report results from several studies that show how these different school-based prevention programs have reduced the use of cigarettes, alcohol, and marijuana.

Substance Abuse in California and Other States

To examine how California teenagers compare to teenagers in other states in terms of substance abuse rates, we used a sample of 12–17 year olds from the National Household Survey on Drug Abuse (NHSDA).[3] The NHSDA was originally designed to be a nationally representative study. However, starting with its 1999 wave, the NHSDA became the only survey on substance abuse designed to be representative at the state level.

Even though the data are now representative within a state, using a sample of just adolescents reduces the sample size in a given year to fewer than 300 in many states. This produces large standard errors for the estimated substance abuse rates. To improve the accuracy of the state estimates, we pooled the data for the two years for which data by state were available: 1999 and 2000. Due to the potential for sampling error, we provided a 95 percent confidence interval in addition to the sample means for the estimated substance abuse rates for California.[4] More details about our methods and the effects of sampling error are provided in Appendix B.

The results of our analyses, displayed in Table 7.4, show mixed evidence on how California teenagers compare to teenagers in other states in terms of substance abuse rates. California teenagers have significantly lower rates of cigarette use than teenagers in other states do; only 5.4 percent of California teenagers have smoked 100 cigarettes in their lifetime, which is the lowest use rate in the nation. The upper bound of the 95 percent confidence interval, which captures sampling error, would still place California teenagers fifth best in the nation. The cigarette use rate among California teenagers is 2.4 percentage points below what would be predicted based on the state's racial/ethnic composition, which ranks it 5th best (in terms of lowest use rates) among all states.

For heavy alcohol use (defined as five or more drinks at one sitting at least once within the past 30 days), California had the 14th lowest use rate, with the ranking increasing or decreasing by seven spots with the bounds of the confidence interval that represents un-

---

[3] Although the data pertain to 12–17 year olds, for simplicity we refer to this population as teenagers in discussing the results of the analysis.

[4] The 95 percent confidence interval indicates a range of use rates for which we can be 95 percent confident that the true use rate for the state is within that range.

Table 7.4
Teenage Substance Abuse in California, 1999–2000

	United States	California Abuse Rate		California at Lower Bound of Confidence Interval		California at Upper Bound of Confidence Interval		California Relative to Predicted Abuse Rate	
	Percent	Percent	Rank	Percent	Rank	Percent	Rank	Percentage Points	Rank
Smoked 100 cigarettes in lifetime	8.7	5.4	1st	4.7	1st	6.2	5th	–2.4	5th
Had 5+ drinks at least once in the past 30 days	9.7	8.5	14th	7.6	7th	9.4	21st	–0.8	19th
Smoked marijuana in the past year	12.9	13.2	25th	12.0	21st	14.5	33rd	0.8	25th
Used some illegal drug in the past year	19.1	19.7	24th	18.3	19th	21.2	34th	1.0	28th
Used an illegal drug other than marijuana in the past year	11.5	11.9	26th	10.9	20th	13.1	38th	0.7	29th

certainty due to sampling error. Relative to the predicted use rate, California's adolescents ranked 19th lowest.

With illegal substance use, California's teenagers were more in the middle of the distribution across states. They ranked 25th, 24th, and 26th for past-year marijuana use, use of any illegal drug, and use of any illegal drug other than marijuana. The rankings are about the same when we compare actual rates for California's teenagers with what we would otherwise predict based on the state's racial/ethnic composition. However, unlike the cases for cigarettes and alcohol, the actual abuse rates slightly exceed the predicted abuse rates for two of the measures of illegal drug use.

Table 7.5 shows the teenage substance abuse rates for the five most populous states. California had the lowest rate of cigarette use and the second lowest rate of heavy alcohol use, but had the second

Table 7.5
Substance Abuse Rates of 12–17 Year Olds, the Five Most Populous States and the United States

	Smoked 100 Cigarettes in Lifetime	Had 5+ Drinks at Least Once in Past 30 Days	Smoked Marijuana in the Past Year	Used Some Illegal Drug in the Past Year	Used an Illegal Drug Other Than Marijuana in the Past Year
California	5.4	8.5	13.2	19.7	11.9
Texas	8.0	10.6	11.3	18.0	12.1
New York	7.3	9.5	12.0	18.0	10.1
Florida	6.0	7.2	11.2	16.7	10.6
Illinois	10.2	11.3	13.9	20.1	10.3
U.S.	8.7	9.7	12.9	19.1	11.5

SOURCE: National Household Survey of Drug Abuse.

highest rate for each of the two measures of illegal drug use. Each of Florida's and New York's substance abuse rates is lower than the U.S. average, while Illinois's substance abuse rates are higher than the U.S. abuse rate for all but one measure, use of an illegal drug other than marijuana.

Juvenile Delinquency

Background

Of all the age groups, teenagers have the most arrests for violent crime and property crime in the United States. According to Levitt and Lochner (2002), violent crime arrests peak at age 18, at around six arrests per 1,000 individuals, while property crime arrests peak at age 16, at around 23 arrests per 1,000 individuals. Levitt and Lochner (2002) note that the literature indicates that being male, having low intelligence, having a high rate of preference for the present relative to the future (a high discount rate), lacking adequate supervision, having poor parenting, and rejection by the mother are some of the leading determinants of juvenile crime.

Schools can affect teenagers' decisionmaking about criminal behavior in some of the same ways that they can affect decisionmaking about pregnancy and substance abuse—e.g., by keeping adolescents interested in school (so that their influences come from schoolmates and not people on the street), instilling hope for the future, and providing community activities to keep teens occupied when they would otherwise be unsupervised. Of course, just as with rates of teenage pregnancy and substance abuse, juvenile delinquency rates across states are contributed to by many factors unrelated to schools.

While we are not aware of any studies that directly examine how schools could affect juvenile delinquency other than within the schools themselves, programs that improve teenagers' attachment to school are likely to reduce juvenile delinquency, just as they were found to reduce teenage pregnancy (Hawkins et al., 1999).

Juvenile Delinquency in California and Other States

To examine differences in juvenile delinquency, we turned to data on juvenile (10–17 year olds) delinquency across states, using data for 1994 to 2000 from the Uniform Crime Reporting (UCR) Program of the Federal Bureau of Investigation. The data are based on reports from precincts across the country on the age of the person arrested and the crime for which the person was arrested. The information from precincts within each county is summed up to the county level in data provided on the Web. The data from 2000 were the latest available at the time of the analysis; we provide more detail on the data and our methods in Appendix B.

Table 7.6 shows the results for California, Texas, New York, Pennsylvania, and Ohio. We show the results for Pennsylvania and Ohio because our two other most populous states, Florida and Illinois, were deleted from the sample due to missing data, and Pennsylvania and Ohio are the next two most populous states after our original five. The arrest rates we show are predictions for 2000 from the regression model. If we chose a separate year, the ranks of the predictions across states would be the same, even though the levels would be different.

Table 7.6
Juvenile Arrests for Property and Violent Crimes, 2000
(per 10,000 10–17 year olds)

	Property Crime Arrests			Violent Crime Arrests		
	Per 10,000 Juveniles	Rank of 46 States	Adjusted for Race/ Ethnicity	Per 10,000 Juveniles	Rank of 46 States	Adjusted for Race/ Ethnicity
California	141	14th	120	41	39th	25
Texas	153	21st	141	21	21st	14
New York	113	10th	106	62	45th	51
Ohio	144	17th	136	20	20th	28
Pennsylvania	147	16th	124	42	41st	42
States other than 5 most populous	155		161	26		28
U.S.	150		150	30		30

SOURCE: Uniform Crime Reports of the FBI.
NOTE: Both unadjusted and adjusted rates are based on regressions with 1994–2000 data. Ohio and Pennsylvania have been substituted for Florida and Illinois in this table for reasons discussed in the text.

California is in a little better than the middle of the distribution for its predicted (unadjusted) 2000 property crime arrest rate (141 property crimes per 10,000 juveniles). Still, California was second worst among the five states we examined. All five of these states had lower property crime arrest rates than the average rate for all the other states. After race/ethnicity is adjusted for, California has a relatively low number of juvenile property crime arrests—120, compared to a rate of 161 per 10,000 juveniles in the states other than the most populous.

The story is different for violent crime arrests. California ranked eighth worst (39th of 46 states) in violent crime arrests, with 41 per 10,000 juveniles. Once we adjust for race/ethnicity, however, the predicted 2000 violent crime arrest rate is 25 per 10,000 juveniles, making California second best among the most populous states and lower than the average for the other states. Of the four other states we examined, only Texas had a higher rate of property crime arrests, and only New York (which was the worst) had a higher rate of violent crime arrests.

In the period we examined, 1994 to 2000, youth arrests for both property crimes and violent crimes decreased slightly across most of the United States. As Table 7.7 shows, the annual percent changes in the actual and adjusted property crime arrests in California were, respectively, 8.7 and 9.0 percent, both of which are below (in magnitude) the corresponding annual percent changes for the states other than the five most populous, but still place California second among the five most populous states we examined. The story is similar for violent crime arrests, with actual and adjusted trends of –7.1 and –7.8 percent, both of which are below the rates for the other states and in about the middle of the rates for the other four states we examined and for all other states combined.

High School Graduation

Background

In this section, we examine how California compares to other states in high school graduation rates.[5] While most people would consider higher graduation rates to be unambiguously desirable, the net benefits to students and society are actually unclear. Graduation rates depend on the quality of the students (not attributable to schooling), the level of preparation the students are given in school, and the graduation standards. Changes over time in graduation rates would most likely be attributable to changes in the level of preparation or the graduation standards. In the former case, higher graduation rates would be beneficial for society. In the latter case, higher graduation rates would indicate that standards have been lowered. Although lower standards would produce more high school graduates, the costs would be that teachers and students would have less incentive to excel. Thus, the benefits of keeping graduation rates high are uncertain. This is something to keep in mind in this part of the analysis, but we

[5] One of the significant likely consequences of the nonachievement outcomes we have examined—teenage pregnancy, substance abuse, and juvenile delinquency—is hindered educational attainment.

Table 7.7
Annual Percent Change in Rates of Juvenile Arrests for Property and Violent Crimes, 1994–2000

	Annual Percent Change			
	Property Crime Arrests		Violent Crime Arrests	
	Actual	Adjusted	Actual	Adjusted
California	–8.7	–9.0	–7.1	–7.8
Texas	–9.2	–9.4	–11.8	–12.3
New York	–6.1	–6.3	–6.4	–6.5
Ohio	–6.6	–6.7	–9.8	–10.0
Pennsylvania	–5.2	–5.3	–3.2	–3.4
All other states combined	–11.0	–11.3	–8.3	–8.7
U.S.	–9.6		–8.1	

SOURCE: Uniform Crime Reports of the FBI.

will proceed under the assumption that higher graduation rates are desired.

Data on high school graduation rates are notoriously of poor quality, subject to both poor reporting and inconsistent definitions. As described in Appendix B, we used data compiled by NCES (Young, 2002), which measures the high school graduation rate as the number of individuals receiving a "regular high school diploma" at public schools, divided by the number of students that were enrolled in ninth grade in public schools three years earlier. This measure would be affected not only by poor reporting, but also by interstate moves and by movement into and out of private schools. These data problems for high school graduation also carry over to the data for college continuation.

High School Graduation Rates in California and Other States

Figure 7.1 shows the trends in graduation rates for the five most populous states. As can be seen, California's high school graduation rate in 2000 was close to the rates that existed in the state during most of the 1980s. The figure also shows that several of the five most populous states had large drops in graduation rates over this period,

Figure 7.1
High School Graduation Rates, Five Most Populous States, 1981–2000

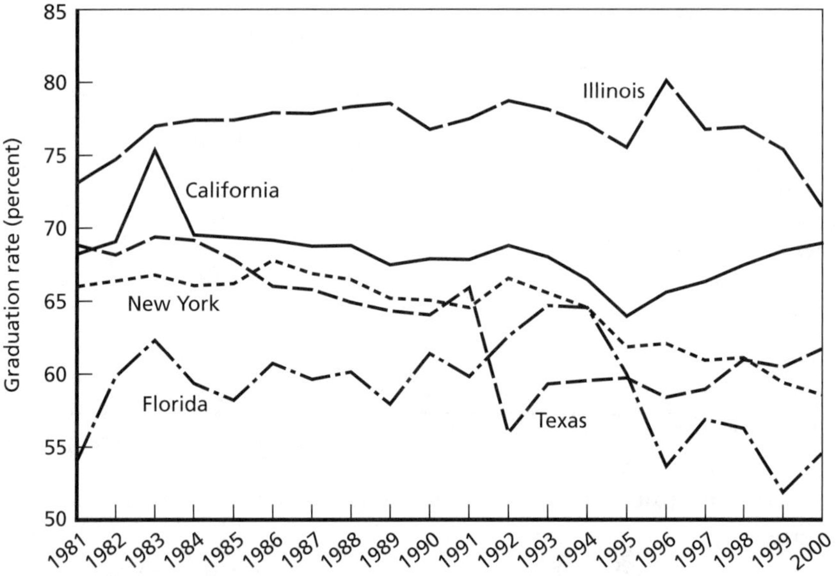

SOURCE: Postsecondary Education OPPORTUNITY, n.d., http://www.postsecondary.org/ti/ti_24.asp.
RAND *MG186-7.1*

and that in 2000, California was in second place for highest graduation rate among the five states.

Table 7.8 shows statistics on actual and adjusted rates for high school graduation. California ranked 31st among the states for its 2000 graduation rate of 69 percent. When the adjustment for race/ethnicity was made to this outcome, however, California's rank did not improve. Instead, it worsened, because the adjusted rate is based on a lower percentage of Asian/Pacific Islander students than California has, and the graduation rates of Asian/Pacific Islander students are higher than those of students in other racial/ethnic groups. After being adjusted, California's graduation rate thus decreased to 64 percent for 2000, putting it below the 69 percent adjusted rate for the states other than the five most populous.

Table 7.8
Actual and Adjusted High School Graduation Rates for 2000, and Annual Trends

	Graduation Rates, 2000			Annual Trend in Graduation Rates (percentage points)		
	Actual		Adjusted	Actual		Adjusted
	Rate	Rank	Rate	Rate	Rank	Rate
California	69	31st	64	–0.01	6th	+0.06
Texas	62	36th	63	–0.2	6th	–0.10
New York	59	44th	63	–0.7	35th	–0.61
Florida	55	47th	62	–0.8	37th	–0.54
Illinois	71	25th	75	–0.4	16th	–0.68
States other than 5 most populous	69		69	–0.6		–0.53
U.S.	68		68	–0.3		–0.3

SOURCE: Postsecondary Education OPPORTUNITY, n.d.

The trend in California looks more favorable than the trends in other states do. There has been a general decline in graduation rates, but California's decline was small, putting California at 6th highest—i.e., above 44 other states plus Washington, DC. When race/ethnicity was adjusted for, the four other most populous states had annual declines in high school graduation rate, the remaining states averaged a 0.5 percentage point annual decline in graduation rate, and California had a slight increase in graduation rate.

Differences among states in graduation rates and trends in graduation rates could be attributable to differences in the racial/ethnic compositions of their students. Using the data presented in Greene (2002), we were able to determine how each state did in terms of high school graduation within three racial/ethnic groups in 1998. Of course, the characteristics of members of a racial/ethnic group can differ across states—e.g., Hispanics in one state may have much higher per capita income than Hispanics in another state. However, comparing graduation rates for the specific racial/ethnic groups across states is a pure control for socioeconomic differences across states.

Table 7.9 presents the results. The table's top panel shows California's placement among all states in graduation rates, along with the rates for the four other most populous states. The 68 percent overall graduation rate places California 37th among the states. However, California's graduation rates for the three racial/ethnic groups—whites, blacks, and Hispanics—were more in the middle of the distribution for whites and Hispanics, and better than in the middle for blacks. This provides further evidence that the low ranking for overall graduation rate is probably attributable to California's high percentage of Hispanics, whose graduation rate tends to be lower than that of other groups. Relative to the four other most populous states, California is about average for white and Hispanic graduation rates and is high for black graduation rates.

Greene (2002) also examined high school graduation rates for the largest school districts in the country. The bottom panel of Table 7.9 lists California's six largest school districts, along with their 1998 graduation rates for all students and for the three racial/ethnic groups—whites, blacks, and Hispanics. Also listed is where these California school districts rank among the top 50 school districts in the United States, although data were not available for all 50 of the districts. For Oakland, which is the sixth largest school district in California but is not among the largest 50 school districts in the country, we indicate where it would place among the largest school districts if it were in that group. Except in the case of the Oakland district (which would be near the bottom of the distribution), the overall graduation rates tend to be in the high 50s and low 60s. This places three of the districts—Fresno, Long Beach, and San Diego—around the middle of the distribution. The Los Angeles and Orange districts, however, are ranked about two-thirds down from the top.

The primary reason for the relatively poor graduation rates in the Los Angeles school district appears to be its racial/ethnic composition. As Table 7.9 shows, the Los Angeles district is in the top half of the distribution for graduation rates within each racial/ethnic

Table 7.9
Graduation Rates and Rankings, Five Most Populous States and Six Largest California School Districts, 1998

		Graduation Rate							
		Overall		White		Black		Hispanic	
State	Population Rank	Rate	Rank (of 51)	Rate	Rank (of 42)	Rate	Rank (of 39)	Rate	Rank (of 39)
California	1	68	37th	78	21st	59	14th	55	22nd
Texas	2	67	40th	76	27th	59	13th	56	16th
New York	3	70	32nd	82	11th	51	32nd	53	23rd
Florida	4	59	49th	63	41st	51	31st	52	26th
Illinois	5	78	15th	89	4th	57	20th	55	20th

California School District	Population Rank	Rate	Rank (of 50)	Rate	Rank (of 46)	Rate	Rank (of 45)	Rate	Rank (of 36)
Fresno	36	58	29th	78	15th	51	28th	41	29th
Long Beach	34	64	21st	78	16th	62	8th	52	13th
Los Angeles	2	56	34th	81	10th	56	17th	48	17th
Orange	18	57	33rd	63	33rd	45	37th	51	15th
San Diego	14	62	23rd	79	13th	54	22nd	43	24th
Oakland	68	43	(48th)	34	(45th)	39	(43rd)	34	(33rd)

SOURCE: Greene, 2002.
NOTE: The states in the table are being compared to other states, not to the school districts. California's Oakland school district is not among the largest 50 school districts in the United States, so its rankings (shown in parentheses) indicate where it would rank in terms of graduation rate if it were among the largest 50.

group—in fact, the district ranks 10th out of 46 for whites. What brings down the Los Angeles school district's overall graduation rate is that the percentage of Hispanic students is high compared to that of other districts, and Hispanics generally have graduation rates that are low compared to those for other racial/ethnic groups.

Most of the other California school districts tend to fare much better in the rankings for the separate racial/ethnic groups than for the overall rate of high school graduation, with the Orange and San Diego districts being the exceptions. For white student graduation rates, four of the six districts are ranked in or near the top third. For black and Hispanic student graduation rates, three districts are in the top half of the distribution, and three are in the bottom half.

College Continuation

Background

We obtained data on college participation rates from Postsecondary Education OPPORTUNITY, a newsletter published on the Web by the Mortenson Research Seminar on Public Policy Analysis of Opportunity for Postsecondary Education (Postsecondary Education OPPORTUNITY, 2002). These data, which are compiled over time from the October supplement to the Current Population Survey, indicate what percentage of recent high school graduates in a state are now enrolled in college. One drawback to these data is that they are based on surveys of 50,000 households across the country, so some small states that are not well represented in the data have large sampling errors.

To prevent the measure of the college continuation rate from depending on the high school graduation rate, we measured the college participation rate as the product of the probability of graduating from high school and the probability of continuing on to college among the high school graduates. The college continuation rates were provided biennially from 1986 to 2000, except that there were no data in 1990. The first two years of data were quite volatile and, in some cases, clearly wrong. Thus, we limited our analysis to the data from 1992 to 2000.

The college continuation rate in a state depends on several factors, some of which are not reflective of the state's educational system. For example, a stronger economy would provide more opportunities in the civilian labor market, which could cause recent high school graduates to postpone or cancel college plans. Another potential factor is the educational attainment of parents—children of college-educated parents are more likely to attend college.

The determinants of college continuation rates that are related to the educational system include the availability and quality of public higher-education institutions, and the ability of schools to prepare students for college-level work, help students form aspirations for further educational attainment and their future, and prevent teenage pregnancy, substance abuse, juvenile delinquency, and other outcomes that could hinder their academic success.

College Continuation Rates in California and Other States

Table 7.10 compares California's success in sending its high school students to college with that of other states. In 2000, California had a college continuation rate of 32 percent, putting it at 43rd among all states (with Washington, DC, excluded in this case). After we adjusted for race/ethnicity, based on 1992 to 2000 data, California had a rate of 35 percent, which was in the middle of the distribution among the five most populous states but still well below the 40 percent adjusted rate for the rest of the states.

The trend for California is also not very favorable. California averaged an annual decline in college continuation rate of 0.6 percentage points. While this is also in the middle of the distribution among

Table 7.10
College Continuation Rates, 1992–2000 Biennial Data

	College Continuation Rate, 2000			Annual Trend in College Continuation Rate (percentage points)		
	Actual		Adjusted	Actual		Adjusted
	Rate	Rank	Rate	Rate	Rank	Rate
California	32	43rd	35	–0.6	41st	–0.62
Texas	32	42nd	31	0.4	11th	+0.39
New York	34	33rd	42	–1.1	47th	–1.02
Florida	32	44th	30	0.2	21st	+0.28
Illinois	42	14th	47	–0.7	42nd	–0.72
States other than 5 most populous	40		40	–0.1		–0.05
U.S.	38			–0.2		

SOURCE: Postsecondary Education OPPORTUNITY, 2002.

the five most populous states, it is a larger decline than that for the remaining states (with an annual 0.2 percentage point decline). And when we adjusted for race/ethnicity, the trend for California remained at 0.6.

Conclusions

Table 7.11 summarizes how California compares to other states in the various indicators examined in this chapter: teenage pregnancy, substance abuse, juvenile delinquency, high school completion, and college continuation. We compare California's actual rates and adjusted (for racial/ethnic composition) rates with those of the four other most populous states and to all the rest of the states. In addition, we compare California's trends with respect to the indicators with those of the four other most populous states and all the rest of the states. The relative positions of California in the adjusted and unadjusted trends were not that different, so we just summarize the actual trends here.

In terms of actual rates, California teenagers ranked favorably, with low rates, on cigarette and alcohol use and on property crime arrests; and they ranked average or below average for the other outcomes. After the racial/ethnic composition of the states was adjusted for, California ranked well, with low rates, for cigarette and alcohol use and property crime arrests, and for violent crime arrests as well. However, the racial/ethnic composition adjustment worsened California's relative position for high school graduation rates. A somewhat similar story emerged for the comparison of California with the four other most populous states. The adjustment improved or maintained California's strong rankings in cigarette and alcohol use and in property and violent crime arrests. Even with consideration of the adjusted rates, however, California still had a high teenage pregnancy rate and a low college participation rate relative to other states.

What appears to be a bright spot for California is that the state's trends in teenage pregnancies, teenage births, and high school graduation rates are favorable compared to those of other states. While Cali-

Table 7.11
Summary of Outcomes on Other Indicators of Progress for California Students

	How California's Rates Compare to the Rates of:				How California's Trend Compares to the Trend of:	
	States Other Than the 5 Most Populous		The Four Other Most Populous States			
	Actual	Adjusted	Actual	Adjusted	States Other Than the 5 Most Populous	The Four Other Most Populous States
Pregnancies	Poor	Poor	Poor	Poor	Good	Good
Births	–	–	–	–	Good	Good
Cigarette and alcohol use	Good	Good	Good	Good	–	–
Illegal drug use	Average	Average	Poor	–	–	–
Property crime arrests	Good	Good	Average	Good	Poor	Good
Violent crime arrests	Poor	Good	Poor	Good	Poor	Average
High school graduation rates	Average	Poor	Good	Average	Good	Good
College continuation rates	Poor	Poor	Poor	Average	Poor	Average

fornia's trends in property and violent crime arrests and in college continuation were poor relative to those of all states, California's arrest rates are decreasing and are average relative to those of the four other most populous states.

Of course, these outcomes depend on a variety of social and psychological factors, some of which are unrelated to schools. That does not mean, however, that a school system cannot influence these outcomes through several avenues, including

- Use sex education or health education to strongly reinforce the idea that abstinence and/or careful contraception can significantly reduce the chances of getting pregnant. Likewise, impart through educational programs the harmful effects of substance abuse.

- Keep teenagers in school. Doing so increases the influence that peers who are also in school have on the teen relative to the influence that people "on the street" have (Hardy and Zabin, 1991).

CHAPTER EIGHT

Summary and Conclusions

This study describes California's current K–12 public education system along a variety of dimensions. Our objective was to provide the information that those concerned with the system must have in order to appreciate its strengths and weaknesses. We examined the system in terms of

- Trends and patterns in the composition of the student population.
- The financial resources that the state has made available to meet the educational needs of the students in the system.
- The teaching force.
- The state's K–12 facilities and capital funding.
- Student academic achievement.
- Other important student outcomes that may be influenced by schools.

Our primary findings with respect to each of these dimensions are summarized below. Our conclusions then follow.

Summary

Student Population

California's distinctive demographics impose extraordinary demands on the state's public K–12 education system. This situation has evolved over recent decades and will persist into the foreseeable future. Several distinctive features of this demographic profile shape current and future statewide educational needs.

First, California has within its borders 12.8 percent of the nation's school-age population but only 11.8 percent of the nation's adult population (potential taxpayers). Consequently, California taxpayers shoulder disproportionate responsibility for persons of school age.

Second, California is among the most ethnically diverse states, with a "majority minority" population, and ethnic and racial diversity is much more advanced among California's youth, especially in the public schools. Furthermore, California is an immigrant "entry port." Nearly one in ten Californians is a recent immigrant—i.e., a foreign-born person who entered the United States within just the past ten years. By comparison, not even one in 20 persons nationally is a recent immigrant. Consequently, the state has an abundance of English learners and linguistically isolated households. Both of these disparities heighten educational costs for affected school districts: English learners by imposing specialized and/or higher per capita staffing needs, and linguistic isolation by hampering two-way communication between schools and parents.

Third, the continuing geographic redistribution of population within the state will amplify K–12 public school enrollment growth in particular clusters of counties. Inevitably, particular school districts will be strained by enrollment pressure, staffing needs, and the crowding of existing facilities.

Finally, California trails the nation and displays a worsening trend in the proportion of children living in poverty. Child poverty is costly for schools and limits educational attainment.

In many respects, California's school-age children pose more significant challenges to the schools than do their counterparts in other states and the nation as a whole. Further, within the state, the educational challenges and costs associated with California's distinctive population manifest themselves more intensely in some areas than others.

School Funding

When it comes to funding K–12 public education, the sheer numbers of students and the diversity of their needs present the people of California with a formidable challenge. A review of school finances over time in California as well as in other states points to several conclusions.

First, Proposition 13, passed by California voters in 1978 (combined with Proposition 98, which California voters approved in 1988), created a number of consequences for K-12 education, including instability in funding. Since Proposition 13 went into effect, education funding depends on the state's economy, and the local revenue options of school districts are limited. School districts, like the state as a whole, are challenged by extreme fluctuations in revenues, such as those experienced in recent years.

California's relative decline in per-pupil K–12 funding began in the late 1970s and early 1980s, following passage of Proposition 13. Prior to the late 1970s, the state's per-pupil funding was consistently above the national average; since then, it has been consistently at or below the national average. K–12 real revenues and expenditures per pupil grew fairly rapidly in California and the United States over the mid- to late 1980s, with California per-pupil spending largely tracking spending in the United States. But in the early to mid-1990s, California fell well behind other states. California then steadily added to education funding, as did other states, starting in the mid-1990s, putting real growth between 1994–1995 and 2001–2002 at an estimated 27 percent. Now, however, after several years of more positive finances, local schools in California are again confronting challenges associated with severe budget constraints.

A growing share of education dollars in California is being distributed as categorical, or restricted, aid, as opposed to "revenue limit," or general purpose, aid. This has raised concerns about a decline in local discretion and about equalization.

Compared to other states, California saw relatively large dollar growth in "other instructional" spending (which includes expenditures for supplies, materials, and contractual services) and school administration spending in its school districts over the 1990s. California per-pupil expenditures on pupil support and general administration have fallen by relatively large dollar amounts compared with those of other states and now represent a relatively small share of total spending.

Finally, California has a relatively high capacity to fund its schools (as measured by per capita personal income) compared with its effort to fund its schools.

Teachers

Education, particularly K–12 education, is labor intensive. In California, about 85 percent of all K–12 public school expenditures are devoted to personnel salary and benefits, and close to 40 percent of all expenditures are devoted to teacher salaries and benefits.

Real average annual teacher salaries in California in 2000–2001 were about the same as they were in 1969–1970 and have remained relatively flat over time.

California's average annual teacher salaries have consistently placed in the top ten across the nation over time in absolute terms. After the dollars are adjusted to reflect purchasing power, however, these teacher salaries are actually lower than the national average.

The dramatic growth in demand for new teachers seen in the 1990s is expected to continue, albeit at a slower pace.

Newly employed teachers make up about 15 percent of the teacher workforce. The majority of these new teachers, however, are not formally trained and state certified. In particular, the 1990s saw an increase in those coming into teaching through pre-intern, intern, and emergency permits. As a result, the gap between the demand for teachers and the supply of teachers with preliminary or professional clear credentials grew over the 1990s.

Teacher qualification requirements are generally lower in California than in other states. For example, 82 percent of school districts in the United States require full standard state certification in the field to be taught, compared with 46 percent of school districts in California.

Teachers in California who lack preliminary or professional clear credentials are concentrated in urban schools, the lowest performing schools, and schools with high percentages of low-income and minority students.

Despite the implementation of a large class size reduction program in the primary grades, California continues to have the second highest ratio of pupils to teachers of any state—about 20.9 students to one teacher, compared to the U.S. average of 16.1 students to one teacher. California pupil-teacher ratios largely tracked the national average until 1979–1980, when the state's schools were faced with leaner budgets, due in part to the switch to a state system of school finance.

School Facilities

Concerns about public elementary and secondary school facilities in California mirror those at the national level. A national study conducted in 1995 suggested that schools had reached the breaking point in terms of facilities, and California schools were experiencing some of the worst conditions. Over the past decade, California and the rest of the nation have made progress in addressing this problem, but the unmet facility needs remain sizable.

California's progress in addressing K–12 public school facility needs has largely been brought about by two factors: voter approval of several large state general obligation bond issues, and a variety of legislative changes that have enabled districts to approve local general obligation bond issues. In 2002 alone, voters approved the issuance of over $11 billion in state general obligation bonds and close to $10 billion in local general obligation bonds. While progress has been made, evidence on the condition of school building features and environmental factors, as well as per-pupil spending on construction, suggests that California still lags the nation as well as other large industrial states. In both the 1994–1995 General Accounting Office (GAO) survey and a 1999 follow-up survey by the National Center for Education Statistics (NCES), California school officials reported large percentages of schools—i.e., large compared with the national average and the percentages reported for the four other most populous states[1]—as having specific inadequate building features and specific inadequate environmental factors. The recent passage of Proposition 39 suggests that progress will continue to be made in addressing the state's facility needs.

However, as school facility funding becomes increasingly reliant on local funding, questions will likely be raised on how political and economic differences across communities affect the ability and willingness of districts to locally finance school facilities, and how state facility funding addresses these differences.

Student Achievement Outcomes

While California has developed and administered several student achievement tests over the years, California students' scores on these tests do not provide an accurate view of student achievement. A more accurate and representative view of student achievement is available from a national test, the National Assessment of Educational Progress (NAEP).

California placed 48th out of 50 states on the average NAEP score across all tests, just above Louisiana and Mississippi. California's fourth and eighth grade students consistently scored well below the national average on the average NAEP score across all tests, and California was the lowest scoring of the five most populous states in the nation.

California's low scores cannot be accounted for by the high percentage of minority students. California's scores for students from families with similar characteristics are the lowest in the nation: It ranks 47th out of 47 states when we compare scores for these students. California's black and non-Hispanic white students are the lowest performing in each category in the nation. California's Hispanic students outperform other Hispanic students in only four states—Arkansas, Louisiana, Alabama, and Mississippi—but these states generally have small Hispanic populations and would be ex-

---

[1] Here, as throughout this report, "most populous" means having the largest numbers of 5–18 year olds (K–12 students).

pected to provide less reliable estimates of the representative Hispanic populations.

California is making gains in NAEP scores: Its scores on the 2002 reading test and the 2003 mathematics and reading tests show some relative progress. California's rank using the average score across the 2002 and 2003 NAEP is 45th out of 50 states. This increase in relative standing can be attributed to the large gains made on the 2003 fourth grade mathematics NAEP—between 1996 and 2003, California's gains in these scores were larger than those made by the nation as a whole and by any of the four other most populous states. This progress is promising, but it has to be considered in light of the fact that California is still the lowest scoring of the five most populous states.

Other Indicators of Student Progress

California teenagers compare favorably to teenagers in other states with respect to such indicators of progress as cigarette and alcohol abuse and property crime arrests. However, relative to other states, California has a high teenage pregnancy rate and a low rate of students continuing on to college.

What appears to be a bright spot for California teenagers is that the trends in pregnancies, births, and high school graduation are favorable compared to those of teens in other states. And although the trends in rates of arrests for property and violent crimes and of college continuation are poor relative to those of most states, they are strong or average relative to the rates of the four other most populous states.

Conclusions

We found reason to be concerned about California's K–12 public schools. The results are not uniformly discouraging; K–12 public schools in California compare favorably to those in other states in some respects. However, overall, the comparisons are unfavorable to California more often than not. And in many instances, the results support the impression that California's relative standing in the nation has declined over the last three decades.

California's demography presents public education with extraordinary challenges. To effectively meet these challenges, the state's K–12 system is likely to require funding levels that are relatively high compared to funding in most other states. However, California school districts have experienced comparatively low levels of funding, and schools have been further stressed by extreme fluctuations in real spending per pupil. These relatively low funding levels for California's K–12 public schools reflect comparatively low "effort" relative to the state's capacity.

The comparatively low funding afforded K–12 public education in California can be seen in the resources that schools are able to make available to their students. A substantial portion of the state's teachers are not fully qualified and state certified. Further, despite having implemented a large-scale program to reduce class sizes, California continues to have the second highest pupil-teacher ratio of any state. Finally, the state has made substantial progress with respect to K–12 facility needs over the past 10 years, but it nonetheless continues to lag the nation in addressing those needs.

California's students have demonstrated comparatively low levels of academic achievement. California's NAEP scores are at the bottom of the distribution of participating states, and the scores of California's minority students are particularly low. There is, however, a bright spot in that California is making statistically significant annual gains in mathematics scores on the NAEP.

California students' nonacademic outcomes present a mixed picture. Teenage pregnancy rates are much higher in California than in most other states but are rapidly decreasing, and California is roughly similar to other states in teenage rates of substance abuse and crime arrests. Finally, in terms of high school graduation rates, California lags other states but is catching up. In terms of college continuation, however, California lags other states and is falling further behind.

APPENDIX A

Additional California Test Score Data and Analyses

California State Assessments

California Assessment Program (CAP)

California has administered standardized tests of student achievement since 1962. In 1972, the California Education Advisory Committee noted that the tests did not represent what California schools were teaching students (California Department of Education, 1985). For statewide testing to be used for program evaluation and to have real significance for California educators and policymakers, statewide testing needed to be aligned with California curricula.

In 1974, CAP, which was designed to test California curricula, began testing third, sixth, and twelfth graders in reading, written expression, and mathematics. In 1983, SB 813 added eighth graders to the testing program. CAP then added a history–social science test in 1985 and a science test in 1986. The program continued through 1992.

Generally, tests that are unique to a state cannot be used for state-to-state or national comparisons. The results of the CAP tests were aligned to national norm-referenced tests, but national norms are updated only every five to seven years, so the CAP results were frequently aligned to outdated norms, and they presented conflicting evidence on California's performance relative to the nation.

Data on early years of statewide testing in California are only available through published reports. A 1986 California Department of Education publication examined historical data on California student performance relative to student performance across the nation and concluded that the results for 1980 to 1986 generally showed California student performance improving in mathematics and reading both over time and compared with national norms (California Department of Education, 1986).[1] However, several caveats must be mentioned with respect to these historical results:

- Prior to 1980, results were reported as the percentage of correct responses, as was still the case for grade 12 test results through 1984. Trends in the percent correct are useful only if the test remains unchanged (California Department of Education, 1986).
- California began using item response theory and scaled scores[2] to report student achievement in grades 3 and 6 in math and reading in 1980 and in grade 8 in 1984.[3] California's scaled scores allow comparisons of achievement over time but do not allow comparisons of California students with other students in the nation. The California Department of Education equated the results of the CAP tests to nationally normed tests of student achievement suggesting the national percentile rank of the median California student. However, changes in the test used by the CAP over time and changes in the test used to norm the CAP results to the national results severely limit the validity of these comparisons.

---

[1] The estimated national percentile ranks of the median California student in grades 3, 6, and 12 in reading and mathematics were derived based on equating studies undertaken by California in the early years of statewide testing (California Department of Education, 1986, pp. A1–A4).

[2] The scale scores range from 100 to 400 with a statewide average of 250.

[3] Item response theory (IRT) is one method for calculating scaled scores from raw data collected from tests of student achievement. The scale scores estimated using IRT allow comparisons across tests (if the tests change) and across grades and subjects by reporting scores on a common scale (California Department of Education, 1985, p.2). IRT takes into account the difficulty and reliability of test questions based on the pattern of student responses; it is particularly useful when tests are conducted in a manner that reduces the time it takes students to complete testing by utilizing matrix sampling. Matrix sampling does not require each student to take the same test, but it ensures that each student receives a test of comparable difficulty.

Comparisons with students nationwide use outdated national norms, as shown below.

Scaled Scores. Figures A.1 and A.2 illustrate the scaled score results reported by the California Department of Education. They show, respectively, the average scaled scores of California students on CAP mathematics and reading tests in grades 3, 6, and 8.

National Percentile Ranks. To illustrate the pitfalls of using these data to draw any conclusions about the relative performance of California students, Table A.1 presents grade 3 reading data. The entry in each cell shows where the median California student would rank in comparison to students nationwide according to the test used as a norm. For example, in 1967, the median California student would have ranked in the 34th percentile nationwide according to the SAT 1963 results.

Figure A.1
CAP Mean Scaled Scores, Grades 3, 6, and 8, Mathematics

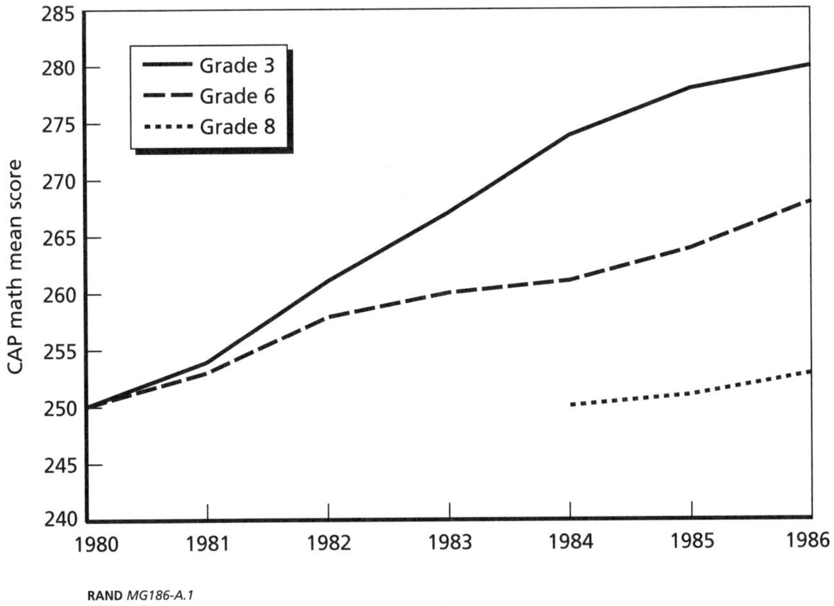

Figure A.2
CAP Mean Scaled Scores, Grades 3, 6, and 8, Reading

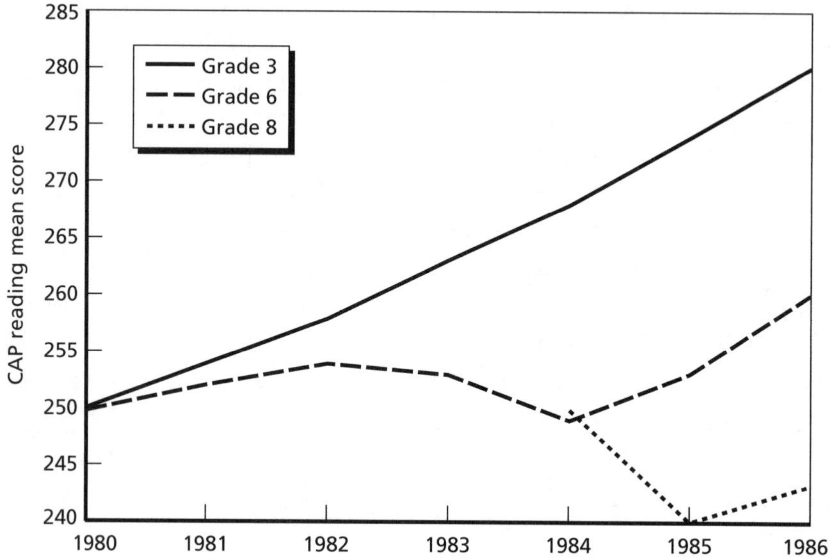

RAND *MG186-A.2*

The numbers in the first column of Table A.1 show that between 1967 and 1971, the median California student performed below the 40th national percentile. These tests were being compared to the SAT 1963 national norm. National norms are updated approximately every five to eight years, so using the SAT 1963 to norm the performance of California students in 1971 is equivalent to comparing California's third graders in 1971 to the nation's third graders in 1963. If student achievement were improving in both California and the nation, we would expect third graders in 1971 to outscore third graders in 1963.

California's performance relative to the nation seemed to improve dramatically beginning in 1972; however, the reading test administered to third graders, the national test used as a norm, and the norm year changed. So, while the national percentile rank of the median California student seemed to improve, when the test given to

Table A.1
Estimated National Percentile Rank of the Median California Third Grader, Reading, 1967–1986

	Test (Norm Test)				
Test Year	SAT (SAT 1963)	Cooperative Primary Reading Test (CPRT 1966)	Revised Reading Tests (CTBS 1973)	Survey of Basic Skills (CTBS 1981)	Survey of Basic Skills (SAT 1982)
1967	34				
1968	34				
1969	36				
1970	36				
1971	38				
1972		52			
1973		52			
1974		52[a]			
1975			55		
1976			55		
1977			56		
1978			57		
1979			58		
1980			58		
1981			59		
1982			60	41	45
1983			62	45	47
1984			64	46	49
1985			69	54	50
1986			71	55	51

SOURCE: California Department of Education, 1986.
[a]The first administration of the CAP reading test in 1973–1974 was equated to the Cooperative Primary Reading Test (CPRT) 1966 norm.

third graders changed again, this time to the Survey of Basic Skills in 1982, and the norm year changed as well, California students' standing fell below the 50th percentile. Given the number of times the tests administered prior to 1997 as part of the statewide program changed, the problems with outdated national norms from these tests, and the general unavailability of data (except for the data reported in publications) for further analyses, we cannot draw conclusions from these data. [4]

Standardized Testing and Reporting Program (STAR)

National Percentile Ranks. As noted in Chapter Six, California administered the nationally norm-referenced SAT/9 between 1998 and 2002.

Tables A.2 and A.3 present the percentages of California students scoring at or above the 50th national percentile rank on the SAT/9 in, respectively, mathematics and reading using the 1995 national norm. We would expect that if students in California were doing as well as their national counterparts, 50 percent of them would score at or above the 50th national percentile in both categories—i.e., the table entries would be 50 or higher. As can be seen, 43 percent of California's second graders scored at or above the 50th national percentile in mathematics, and 40 percent scored at or above the 50th percentile in reading.

Table A.2
Average Percentage of California Students Scoring At or Above the 50th National Percentile, Mathematics, 1998–2002

	Percentage of California Students Scoring at or Above 50th National Percentile Rank									
Year	Grade 2	Grade 3	Grade 4	Grade 5	Grade 6	Grade 7	Grade 8	Grade 9	Grade 10	Grade 11
1998	43	40	39	41	46	42	42	47	41	43
1999	49	48	44	45	50	45	45	48	44	45
2000	57	56	51	50	55	48	48	51	46	47
2001	58	59	54	54	57	50	49	51	45	46
2002	62	62	58	57	60	52	50	52	46	47

SOURCE: http://www.cde.ca.gov.

[4] No data are available for the later CAP years (1987–1992) or the years between CAP and STAR (1987–1997).

Table A.3
Average Percentage of California Students Scoring At or Above the 50th National Percentile, Reading, 1998–2002

	Percentage of California Students Scoring at or Above 50th National Percentile Rank									
Year	Grade 2	Grade 3	Grade 4	Grade 5	Grade 6	Grade 7	Grade 8	Grade 9	Grade 10	Grade 11
1998	40	38	40	41	42	44	46	34	32	36
1999	44	41	41	42	44	44	47	34	33	35
2000	49	44	45	44	46	46	49	35	34	36
2001	51	46	47	45	47	48	50	35	34	37
2002	53	47	49	46	48	48	49	34	34	37

SOURCE: http://www.cde.ca.gov.

The data in Tables A.2 and A.3 follow the same pattern of questionable gains in California student achievement relative to national student achievement that is present in Table A.1. The SAT/9 results show that between 1998 and 1999, less than 50 percent of California's students scored at or above the 50th national percentile in both mathematics and reading at every grade level. As the time between the norm year and the test year increases, the national norm becomes more outdated. Without further information, we cannot be sure that these "gains" in California's student performance relative to the national performance are real or a function of the norm year.

California NAEP

What we present here are average NAEP scores disaggregated by grade and subject. California's students consistently perform below the average across states and are the lowest scoring of the five most populous states. The average NAEP scores presented in Chapter Six do not hide significant variations in states' rankings by grade or subject.

Average NAEP Scores by Test Subject and Grade

Figures A.3 through A.6 display average NAEP scores by subject and grade. The pattern of performance across states when we average across subjects and grades is the same as the pattern when we average across all 17 NAEP test scores. We can summarize the results as follows:

- California's average mathematics score across the nine NAEP mathematic tests puts California at 44th out of 48 states and slightly below the national average. California has the lowest average mathematics score of the five most populous states.
- California ranks 48th out of 48 states in reading when we average across the eight reading NAEP tests.
- California's fourth grade students put California at 47th out of 48 states when we average across the mathematics and reading NAEP tests given to fourth graders. In this case, California is the lowest ranking of the five most populous states.
- California's student performance on the NAEP tests is slightly higher for eighth graders than for fourth graders. California ranks 43rd out of 48 states across the eight eighth grade NAEP tests in mathematics and reading. California has the lowest average eighth grade score of the five most populous states.

Average NAEP Scores for Students in Similar Families, by Test Subject and Grade

Figures A.7 through A.10 display the average NAEP scores, by subject and grade, for students from similar families. The estimates of state scores for students in similar families by subject and grade follow the same pattern followed for those presented in Chapter Six. To summarize:

- California remains the lowest ranking of the five most populous states in mathematics and reading for fourth and eighth grade. California's scores for students from similar families rank 43rd,

Figure A.3
Average State NAEP Scores, Grades 4 and 8, Mathematics, 1990–2003

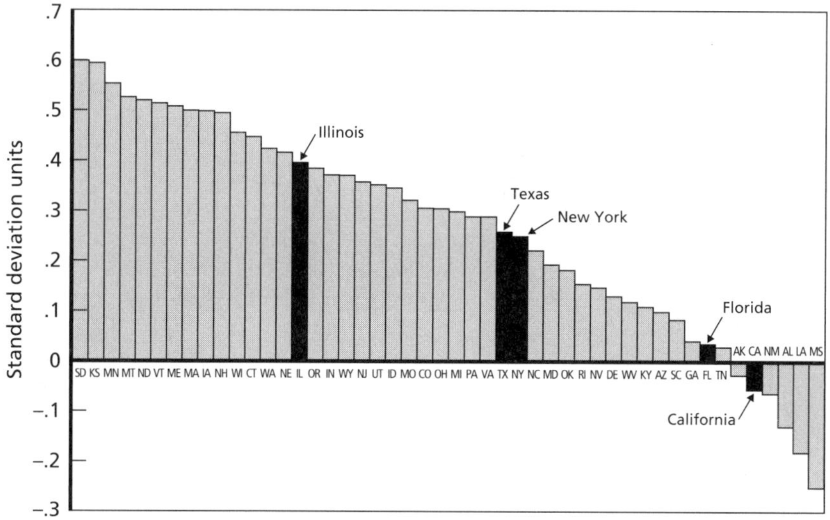

RAND *MG186-A.3*

Figure A.4
Average State NAEP Scores, Grades 4 and 8, Reading, 1992–2003

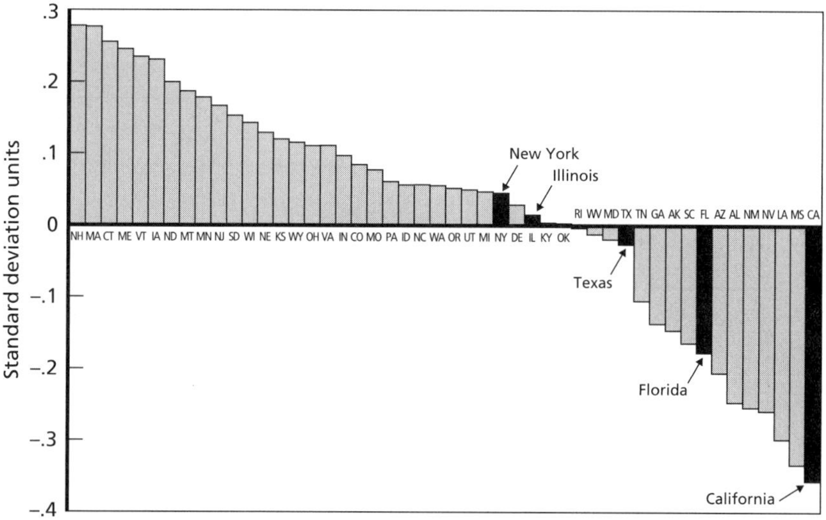

RAND *MG186-A.4*

Figure A.5
Average State NAEP Scores, Grade 4, Reading and Mathematics, 1992–2003

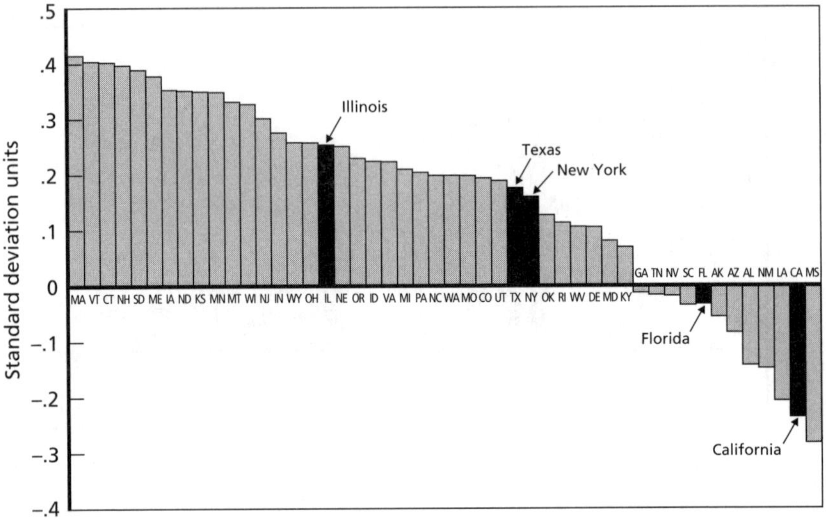

RAND *MG186-A.5*

Figure A.6
Average State NAEP Scores, Grade 8, Reading and Mathematics, 1990–2003

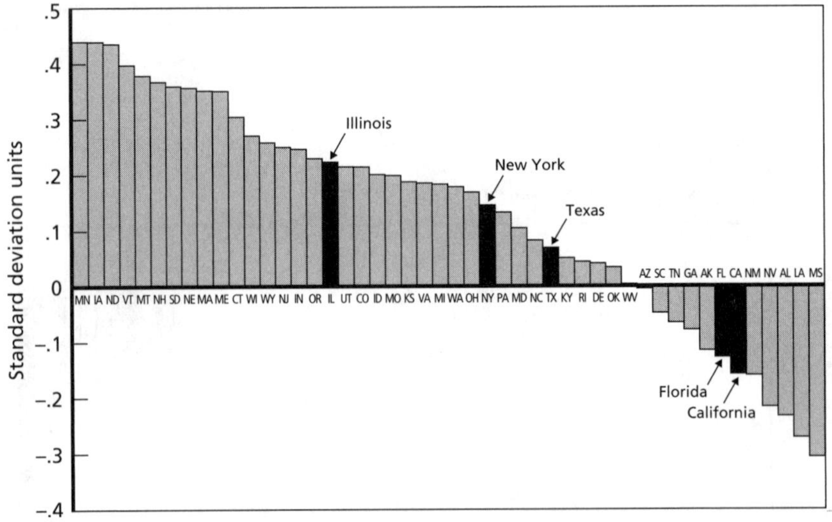

RAND *MG186-A.6*

Figure A.7
Estimated Average NAEP Scores for Students with Similar Families, Mathematics

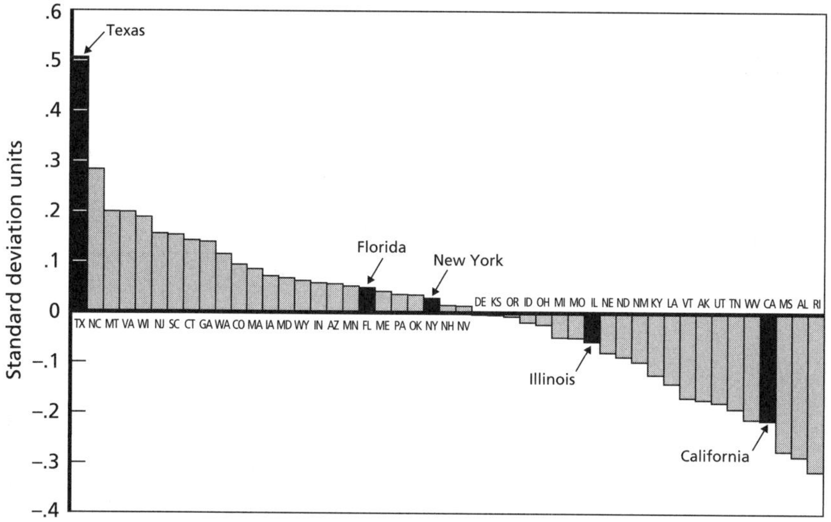

RAND *MG186-A.7*

Figure A.8
Estimated Average NAEP Scores for Students with Similar Families, Reading

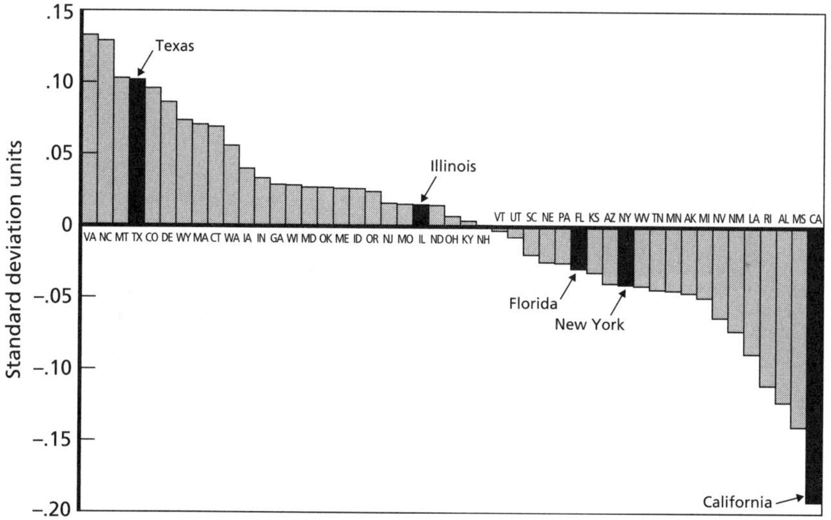

RAND *MG186-A.8*

Figure A.9
Estimated Average NAEP Scores for Students with Similar Families, Grade 4

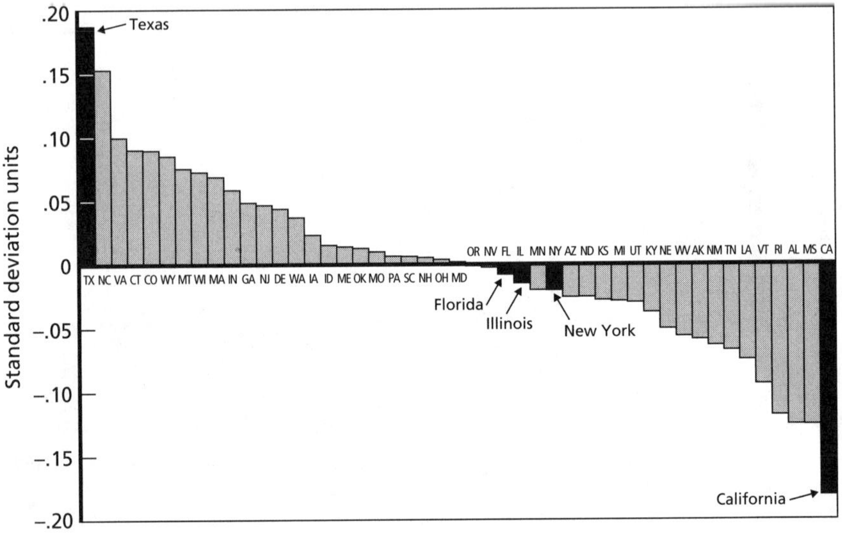

RAND *MG186-A.9*

Figure A.10
Estimated Average NAEP Scores for Students with Similar Families, Grade 8

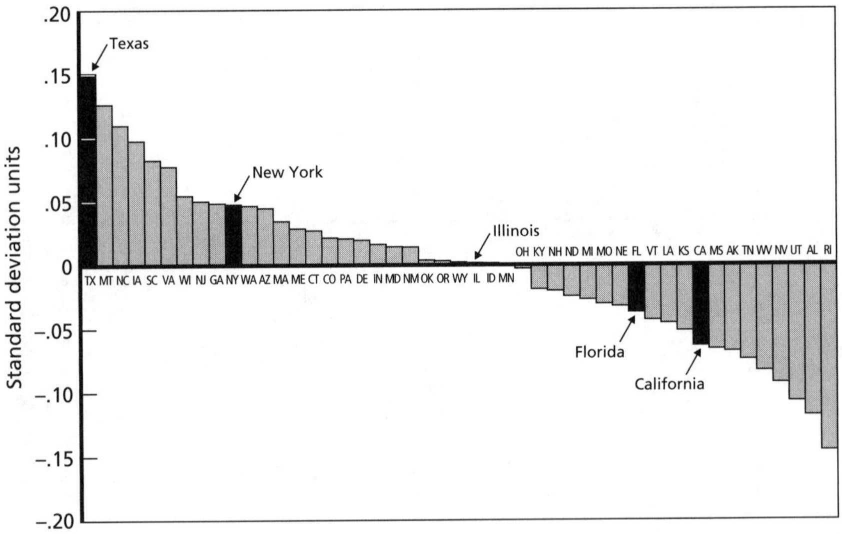

RAND *MG186-A.10*

47th, 47th, and 39th, respectively, on mathematics, reading, fourth grade NAEP tests, and eighth grade NAEP tests.

- Texas's scores for students from similar families are among the highest in the nation in fourth and eighth grade in both mathematics and reading. As noted in Chapter Six, in the discussion of average NAEP scores across all 17 tests, Texas's high scores are more likely related to school effects than to family effects.
- When students' family characteristics are controlled for, New York's, Florida's, and Illinois's students are performing better than expected, suggesting that the schools in these states are contributing to student performance.

APPENDIX B

Data and Methods Used to Describe Nonacademic Indicators

For outcomes with adequate years of information, we normally use regression models to control for the racial/ethnic composition of each state's relevant population. These models identify the outcome rates across states once differences in the racial/ethnic composition of the states are factored out. Unfortunately, the data for estimating the substance abuse models were inadequate, so we use an alternative approach, which we discuss below.

For the other outcomes, we design econometric models to measure both the differences in the outcome levels and the trends in the outcomes, once racial/ethnic composition is held constant. The first model, to measure differences in outcome levels, includes (1) year dummy variables; (2) state dummy variables for the five most populous states (i.e., those states with the largest populations of 5–18 year olds), which are, from largest down, California, Texas, New York, Florida, and Illinois; and (3) four variables indicating the percentage of the relevant population (e.g., 15–17 year old females, for pregnancies) that are of the black, Hispanic, Asian/Pacific Islander, and Other racial/ethnic categories. We obtain these population counts from the U.S. Census Website.[1] The coefficient estimates on the state dummy variables indicate how the state fared in the particular outcome relative to the 45 states other than the most populous states and Washington, DC.

[1] http://www.census.gov/population/estimates/state/sasrh/.

The second model, to capture differences in the outcome trends, includes the five state dummy variables and four racial/ethnic variables used in the first model. However, instead of using the first model's year dummy variables, we include interactions of a trend term and the state dummy variables. A trend term for the other 45 states plus Washington, DC, is also included. The coefficient estimates on these interaction terms are the estimates of interest. Once transformed, they indicate how the outcome changed for a given state relative to other states.

Each econometric model is estimated as a logistic model within a Generalized Linear Model framework to correct for heteroskedasticity and out-of-range predictions that could occur with proportions data.[2] In addition, we weight each regression by the total relevant population in the state. By including just five state dummy variables and six trend terms instead of 50 and 51, we lose the ability to calculate a specific "adjusted" ranking for California, but we obtain more-precise estimates on the racial/ethnic groups, which gives a more accurate relative position for California (and the four other most populous states). For the last year for which we have data, we show a comparison across states for that year of the actual outcome rates and an adjusted rate that comes from the regression and predicted values. The predicted values assume that the year is the latest year for which there are data (2000 for most outcomes, and 1996 for pregnancies) and that blacks, Hispanics, Asian/Pacific Islanders, and Other make up 15, 13, 4, and 1 percent of the relevant population, respectively. These are close to the numbers for 2000 for 17 year olds.

Teenage Pregnancy

The data on pregnancies come from reports from researchers at the Alan Guttmacher Institute (Henshaw and Van Vort, 1989; Henshaw,

[2] Heteroskedasticity occurs if the variance of the error term is different at different levels of the dependent variable. The existence of heteroskedasticity could bias the estimates of the variances.

1993; and Henshaw, 1999). The pregnancy rates are calculated by summing the actual birth rate in a state with the estimated abortion rate and a fixed miscarriage rate. To the extent that abortion data are of poor quality, the pregnancy rates will be as well. Because data on abortion rates were available only for four years (1985, 1988, 1992, and 1996), the pregnancy rate data were only available for four years for teenagers.

Data on birth rates are more accurate. They are based on birth records and compiled by the Centers for Disease Control and Prevention (CDC). All data for 1990 to 2000—for each state and national averages for racial/ethnic groups—are available in one report (Ventura, Mathews, and Hamilton, 2001).

Substance Abuse

We examine five different substance abuse measures—one each for the abuse of cigarettes, alcohol, marijuana, a drug other than marijuana, and any illicit drug. The measures are as follows:

- Cigarettes: whether the teenager smoked at least 100 cigarettes in his/her life.
- Alcohol: whether the teenager had at least five drinks at a time in the past 30 days.
- Marijuana: whether the teenager smoked marijuana in the past year.
- Other drugs: whether the teenager abused an illicit drug other than marijuana in the past year.
- Any drug: whether the teenager abused any illicit drug in the past year (marijuana or other drugs).

For each of these measures, we calculate the percentage of 12–17 year olds in a state for whom the measure applies. We weight the calculations with the sample weights provided by the National Household Survey on Drug Abuse (NHSDA). Next, we compare the abuse rates for California to those for the United States. We then rank California among the 50 states and the District of Columbia, with the lowest abuse rates having the highest ranks.

The estimated rankings may be off from the true rankings by some amount, not just because of California's sampling error, but also because of the sampling errors of other states. That is, some states whose substance abuse rates are close to California's may actually have abuse rates much higher or much lower than the abuse rates from the NHSDA sample because of sampling errors. In this case, California's true position in the rankings of substance abuse rates could be several spots higher or lower. On average, however, one would expect that sampling error would falsely move about the same number of states up the distribution as it moves down the distribution. That is, we would not expect the distribution of population abuse rates to be much different from the distribution of abuse rates based on the NHSDA sample.

The larger source of distortion in California's rankings would result from sampling error for California itself. To incorporate the effects of the sampling error, we calculate the lower and upper bounds of a 95 percent confidence interval of California's abuse rates. We then determine where California would rank in the two cases in which the upper and lower bounds were the true abuse rates. We hold the abuse rates of other states fixed. The validity of the rankings of the upper and lower bounds relative to other states does not rely on the assumption of no sampling error in other states. Rather, it relies on the assumption that the distribution of state substance abuse rates based on the NHSDA sample would be the same as the actual distribution of state substance abuse rates based on the population.

Finally, we determine how California's actual abuse rates compare to its predicted abuse rates and determine where California ranks relative to other states in actual relative to predicted. We predict substance abuse rates based on differences across racial/ethnic groups. We start by determining the percentage of teenagers (12–17 year olds, weighted by the abuse rates across age groups) in each of seven racial/ethnic groups as defined by both the NHSDA and the U.S. Census:[3]

- Non-Hispanic white
- Non-Hispanic black/African American
- Non-Hispanic native American/Alaska native
- Non-Hispanic native Hawaiian/other Pacific Islander
- Non-Hispanic Asian
- Non-Hispanic more than one race
- Hispanic.

We obtain the predicted substance abuse rates in a state by multiplying the percentage of teenagers in each state who are in each racial/ethnic group by the national substance abuse rates of each racial/ethnic group, as calculated with NHSDA data. These abuse rates are shown in Table B.1.

We then calculate how each state's actual abuse rates compare to its predicted abuse rates by subtracting the predicted abuse rates from the actual abuse rates based on the NHSDA sample. This adjusts for racial/ethnic differences.

Juvenile Delinquency

We use data from the Uniform Crime Reporting (UCR) program of the Federal Bureau of Investigation (FBI) to examine differences in juvenile (10–17 year old) delinquency across states. We use the variables on the total number of property-crime arrests and the total number of violent-crime arrests. The data are based on reports from precincts across the country on the age of the person arrested and the

[3] The weights across ages for 12–17 year olds are based on the national use rates for the variables 'SUMYR' in the NHSDA, which indicates whether the respondent used any illicit drug in the past year.

Table B.1
Adolescent Substance Abuse Rates Across Racial/Ethnic Groups, 1999–2000 (in percent)

Form of Abuse	All Groups	Non-Hispanic White	Non-Hispanic Black/African American	Non-Hispanic Native American/Alaska Native	Non-Hispanic Native Hawaiian/Other Pacific Islander	Non-Hispanic Asian	Non-Hispanic More Than One Race	Hispanic
Smoked 100 cigarettes in lifetime	8.7	10.5	3.5	17.8	7.2	5.4	8.8	6.6
Had 5+ drinks at least once in past 30 days	9.7	11.2	4.2	13.0	8.5	3.9	8.8	9.8
Smoked marijuana in the past year	12.9	13.9	9.7	28.3	10.8	6.5	16.1	12.5
Used some illegal drug in the past year	19.1	19.9	16.6	36.8	16.2	11.8	20.4	19.2
Used some illegal drug other than marijuana in the past year	11.5	12.4	7.8	18.5	10.6	7.0	12.0	11.7

crime for which the person was arrested. The information from precincts within each county is summed up to the county level in data provided on the Web.

Unfortunately, many precincts within counties did not report data in some months. The UCR program addresses this problem as follows:

- For precincts reporting between six and 11 months in a year, the number of arrests is increased by a weight of (12/number of months reported).
- Precincts reporting less than six months of the year are dropped from the county totals.
- A "coverage indicator" is included in the data to indicate what percentage of a county's population has nonimputed data. For example, if 80 percent of the county is in a precinct that has nine months of coverage for the year and 20 percent is in a pre-

cinct that has no coverage, then the coverage indicator would be 0.8*(9/12)+0.2*0, or 60 percent.

We use data from 1994 to 2000. The data prior to 1994 used a different imputation procedure, and although we could use a procedure to make the two imputation procedures match up a little closer, the analysis is cleaner if we use data only from 1994 to 2000. To maintain high quality in the data, we set 30 percent as the lower limit for the coverage indicator to use the county's data. If a county has less than 30 percent coverage, we impute the county's data based on the arrest information of other counties within that county's population stratum within the state.[4] If a state has more than one-half of its population in counties with less than 30 percent coverage, we delete that state-year observation from our analysis. Also, if the state is missing information on arrests (e.g., Florida, for 1995–2000), we delete those state-year observations from the analysis. Finally, if a state does not have at least four years of good data in the seven years of our analysis, we delete the state. Four states—Florida, Illinois, Kansas, and Kentucky—and Washington, DC, were deleted for this reason.

The final data set has 46 states and 312 observations, with five states missing between one and three years of data. If we were to make 50 percent the lower limit for the coverage indicator, we would have lost five additional states for the analysis. With these data, we run the set of regressions described in the introduction.

Because some states are missing data in some years, we calculate the unadjusted rates based on regressions rather than just calculating averages. The advantage of this over just taking the average is that some states may have good data only for years in which arrest rates across the country are higher (or lower) than average. Thus, the year effects may be captured in an unadjusted state average.[5] This regression factors out the year effects.

[4] We have seven population strata based on the following six cutoff population figures: 2,500, 10,000, 25,000, 50,000, 100,000, and 250,000.

[5] This would not be an issue if each state in the analysis had data for every year.

For the regressions to calculate the adjusted trends, we use the natural logarithms of the number of arrests as the dependent variables to capture the percent changes in arrests instead of the actual level of change in the arrest rates. We do this because a reduction in the arrest rate of 10 per 10,000 juveniles is more impressive for a state that has 100 arrests than for a state with 500 arrests per 10,000 people. The coefficient estimate on the trend term indicates what the average annual percent change in arrest rates from 1994 to 2000 is for each state.

High School Graduation and College Continuation

We obtained data on high school graduation rates from two sources. We use the time-series data on overall public high school graduation rates by state and time for 1981 to 2000 reported in Postsecondary Education OPPORTUNITY,[6] a newsletter published by the Mortenson Research Seminar on Public Policy Analysis of Opportunity for Postsecondary Education. This dataset is based on data collected by the U.S. Department of Education's National Center for Educational Statistics.[7] We use just the data from 1990 to 2000 in the regression analysis in order to keep the analysis based on current data. The second dataset on high school graduation rates comes from Greene (2002). This dataset has the high school graduation rates from each state and from the 50 largest school districts (plus a few others of interest) by three racial/ethnic groups—whites, blacks, and Hispanics.[8] However, the data are available only for 1998 graduations.

---

[6] These data are on the Internet at http://www.postsecondary.org/ti/ti_24.asp.

[7] The newsletter compiles the data from Young, 2002.

[8] The method of collection that Greene (2002) used was to divide the number of regular high school diplomas awarded in 1998 by the number of eighth grade students in fall 1993, adjusted for changes in student population in each district by the three racial/ethnic groups.

The data on college continuation rates also come from Postsecondary Education OPPORTUNITY.[9] These are compiled over time from the October supplement to the Current Population Survey. The data indicate what percentage of recent high school graduates from a state are now enrolled in college. One drawback to these data is that they are based on surveys of 50,000 households across the country, so some small states that are not well represented in the data have large sampling errors.

To prevent the measure of the college continuation rate from depending on the high school graduation rate, we measure the college continuation rate as the product of the probability of graduating from high school and the probability of continuing to college among the high school graduates. The college continuation rates are provided biennially from 1986 to 2000, except that there were no data in 1990. The first two years of data were quite volatile and, in some cases, clearly wrong. Thus, we limit our analysis to the data from 1992 to 2000.

---

[9] These data are at http://www.postsecondary.org/archives/Reports/SpreadsheetCollege19.htm.

Bibliography

Allen Guttmacher Institute, U.S. Teenage Pregnancy Statistics: Overall Trends, Trends by Race and Ethnicity and State-by-State, n.d. (available at http://www.guttmacher.org/pubs/teen_preg_stats.html).

Allen, Jeanne, and Christine Lynd, *Debunking the Class Size Myth: How to Really Improve Teacher Quality*, The Center for Education Reform, 2000 (available at http://edreform.com/pubs/class_size.htm).

American Federation of Teachers, calculation of the interstate cost of living index, http://www.aft.org/research/reports/col/colpape3.htm.

Augenblick, John, "The Status of School Finance Today," Denver, CO, Education Commission of the States, July 2001.

Ballator, Nada, and Laura Jerry, *NAEP 1998 Reading: State Report for California, NCES 1999-460-CA*, Washington, DC: National Center for Education Statistics, 1999.

Ballou, Dale, "Sizing Up Test Scores," *Education Next*, 2(2), 2002 (available at http://www.educationnext.org/20022/index.html).

Belfield, Clive, and Henry Levin, *The Effects of Competition on Educational Outcomes: A Review of the US Evidence*, National Center for the Study of Privatization in Education, Teachers College, Columbia University, 2002.

Betts, Julian R., and Ann Dannenberg, "School Accountability in California: An Early Evaluation," in Diane Ravitch (ed.), *Brookings Papers on Education Policy: 2002*, Washington, DC: Brookings Institution, 2003, pp. 123–184.

Betts, Julian R., Kim S. Rueben, and Anne Danenberg, *Equal Resources, Equal Outcomes? The Distribution of School Resources and Student*

Achievement in California, San Francisco, CA: Public Policy Institute of California, February 2000.

Bierlein, Louann, "The Charter School Movement," in Diane Ravitch and Joseph Viteritti (eds.), *New Schools for a New Century*, New Haven, CT: Yale University Press, 1997.

Bohrnstedt, G. W., and B. M. Stecher (eds.), *What We Have Learned About Class Size Reduction*, Sacramento, CA: California Department of Education, 2002a.

Bohrnstedt, G. W., and B. M. Stecher (eds.), *What We Have Learned About Class Size Reduction: Technical Appendix*, Sacramento, CA: California Department of Education, 2002b.

Braswell, J., M. Daane, and W. Grigg, *The Nation's Report Card: Mathematics Highlights 2003*, Washington, DC: National Center for Education Statistics, NCES 2004-451, 2003.

Braswell, J. S., A. D. Lutkus, W. W. Grigg, S. L. Santapau, B. Tay-Lim, and M. Johnson, *The Nation's Report Card: Mathematics 2000*, Washington, DC: National Center for Education Statistics, NCES 2001-517, 2001.

Bray, Jeremy, Gary Zarkin, Chris Ringwalt, and Junfeng Qi, "The Relationship Between Marijuana Initiation and Dropping Out of High School," *Health Economics*, 9(1):9–18, 2000.

Brunner, Eric J., and Kim Rueben, *Financing New School Construction and Modernization: Evidence from California*, Testimony, Finances and Facilities Working Group—K–12 Education, Joint Committee to Develop a Master Plan for Education, San Francisco, CA: Public Policy Institute of California, June 28, 2001a.

Brunner, Eric J., and Kim S. Rueben, "The Demand for Local School Facility Spending: Evidence from California School Districts," Working Paper, San Diego, CA: San Diego State University, 2001b.

Brunner, Eric, Jon Sonstelie, and Mark Thayer, "Capitalization and the Voucher: An Analysis of Precinct Returns from California's Proposition 174," *Journal of Urban Economics*, 50(3):517–36, November 2001.

California Department of Education, "California Assessment Program: Annual Report," Sacramento, CA, 1985.

California Department of Education, "California Assessment Program: Annual Report," Sacramento, CA, 1986.

California Department of Education, "Fact Book 2002," Sacramento, CA, 2003 (available at www.cde.ca.gov/facilities).

California Department of Education, "Fact Book 2004, Handbook of Education Information," 2004 (available at www.cde.ca.gov/re/pn/fb/documents/factbook2004.pdf).

California Employment Development Department, Labor Market Information, Income in 1989 for California and Counties, 1990 Census (available at http://www.calmis.cahwnet.gov/file/demoinc/inc90co.htm).

California Employment Development Department, Labor Market Information, Income and Poverty Level in 1999 for California and Counties, 2000 Census (available at http://www.calmis.cahwnet.gov/file/demoinc/inc2000co.htm).

"California Master Plan for Education," n.d., http://www.sen.ca.gov/ftp/sen/committee/joint/master_plan/_home/020909_final_master_plan_documents/020909_final_mp_intro.pdf (as of November 3, 2004).

Campbell, J. R., P. L. Donahue, C. M. Reese, and G. W. Phillips, *NAEP 1994 Reading Report Card for the Nation and the States: Findings from the National Assessment of Educational Progress and Trial State Assessments*, Washington, DC: National Center for Education Statistics, 1996.

Card, David, and A. Abigail Payne, "School Finance Reform, the Distribution of School Spending, and the Distribution of SAT Scores," National Bureau of Economic Research, NBER Working Paper 6766, 1998.

Caulkins, Jon, Rosalie Liccardo Pacula, Susan Paddock, and James Chiesa, *School-Based Drug Prevention: What Kind of Drug Use Does It Prevent?* Santa Monica, CA: RAND Corporation, MR-1459-RWJ, 2002.

Center for Education Reform, information on charter schools, including on a state-by-state basis, as of January 2004, http://www.edreform.com/index.cfm?fuseAction=stateStats&pSectionID=15&cSectionID=44.

Center for Education Reform, "Just the Facts—Charter Schools," http://edreform.com/school_reform_faq/charter_schools.htm (accessed November 4, 2004).

Center for the Future of Teaching and Learning , "California's Teaching Force: Key Issues and Trends 2002," Santa Cruz, CA: Center for the Future of Teaching and Learning, 2002.

Corcoran, T. B., L. J. Walker, and J. L. White, "Working in Urban Schools," Washington, DC: Institute for Educational Leadership, 1988.

Darling-Hammond, Linda, "The Quality of Teaching Matters Most," *Journal of Staff Development* 18(1):38–41, 1997.

Darling-Hammond, Linda, Barnett Berry, and Amy Thoreson, "Does Teacher Certification Matter? Evaluating the Evidence," *Educational Evaluation and Policy Analysis*, 23(1):57–77, 2001.

Donahue, P., M. Daane, and W. Grigg, *The Nation's Report Card: Reading Highlights 2003*, Washington, DC: National Center for Education Statistics, NCES 2004-452, 2003.

Donahue, Patricia L., Kristen E. Voelkl, Jay R. Campbell, and John Mazzeo, *NAEP 1998 Reading Report Card for the Nation*, Washington, DC: National Center for Education Statistics, NCES 1999-459, 1999.

Downes, Thomas, and David Figlio, "School Finance Reforms, Tax Limits, and Student Performance: Do Reforms Level Up or Dumb Down?" Washington, DC: Institute for Research on Poverty, Discussion Paper No. 1142-97, 1997.

EdSource, "California's School Facilities Predicament," Palo Alto, CA, April 1998.

EdSource, "Understanding School Finance: California's Complex K–12 System," Palo Alto, CA, February 2000.

EdSource, "How California Ranks," Palo Alto, CA, October 2001a.

EdSource, "School Finance 2001–02: Holding Steady in an Uncertain Economy," Palo Alto, CA, November 2001b.

EdSource, "Resource Cards on California Schools," Palo Alto, CA, 2002a.

EdSource, "Teacher Pay in California: Is it Fair? Is it Competitive? Is It Enough?" Palo Alto, CA, April 2002b.

EdSource, "School Finance 2002–03," Palo Alto, CA, November 2002c.

EdSource, "School Finance 2003–04: State Budget Woes Reverberate Through K–12 Education," Palo Alto, CA: November 2003.

EdSource Online, "Basic Aid," February 20, 2003, http://www.edsource.org/edu_fin_basicaid.cfm.

edweek.org, http://www.edweek.org/ew/ewstory.cfm?slug=05mcas.h22.

edweek.org, "Standards and Accountability," http://www.edweek.org/sreports/qc02/reports/standacct-t1g.htm.

edweek.org, "State of the States, School Climate," http://www.edweek.org/sreports/qc02/tables/climate-t1.pdf.

Elmore, R. F., C. H. Abelmann, and S. H. Fuhrman, "The New Accountability in State Education Reform: From Process to Performance," in H. F. Ladd (ed.), *Holding Schools Accountable: Performance-Based Reform in Education*, Washington, DC: Brookings Institution, 1996, pp. 65–98.

Esch, Camille E., and Patrick M. Shields, "Who Is Teaching California's Children?" Santa Cruz, CA: Center for the Future of Teaching and Learning (CFTL), 2002.

Evans, William N., Sheila E. Murray, and Robert M. Schwab, "School Houses, Court Houses and State Houses After Serrano," *Journal of Policy Analysis and Management*, 16(1), Winter 1997.

Evans, William N., Sheila E. Murray, and Robert M. Schwab, "The Property Tax and Education Finance: Uneasy Compromises," Wallace Oates (ed.), *Property Taxation and Local Government Finance*, Boston, MA: Lincoln Institute of Land Policy, 2001.

Finn, Jeremy, and Charles Achilles, "Tennessee's Class Size Study: Findings, Implications, Misconceptions," *Educational Evaluation and Policy Analysis*, 21(2):97–109, Summer 1999.

Friedman, Milton, *Capitalism and Freedom*, Chicago, IL: University of Chicago Press, 1962.

Gaviria, Alejandro, and Steven Raphael, "School-Based Peer Effects and Juvenile Behavior," *Review of Economics and Statistics*, 83(2):257–268, 2001.

Geronimus, Arline T., and Sanders Korenman, "The Socioeconomic Consequences of Teen Childbearing Reconsidered," *Quarterly Journal of Economics*, 107:1187–1214, 1992.

Gill, Brian, P. Michael Timpane, Karen Ross, and Dominic Brewer, "Rhetoric Versus Reality: What We Know and What We Need to Know

About Vouchers and Charter Schools," Santa Monica, CA: RAND Corporation, MR-1118-EDU, 2001.

Goldfinger, Paul M., "Revenues and Limits," Sacramento, CA: School Services of California, 1994.

Goldhaber, Dan, "How Has Teacher Compensation Changed?" in *Selected Papers in School Finance, 2000–01*, Washington, DC: National Center for Education Statistics, 2000.

Goldhaber, Dan, and Dominic Brewer, "Does Teacher Certification Matter? High School Teacher Certification Status and Student Achievement," *Educational Evaluation and Policy Analysis*, 22(2):129–145, 2000.

Goldhaber, Dan, and Dominic Brewer, "Evaluating the Evidence on Teacher Certification: A Rejoinder," *Educational Evaluation and Policy Analysis*, 23(1):79–86, 2001.

Greene, Jay, "High School Graduation Rates in the United States," Manhattan Institute, 2002 (available at http://www.manhattan-institute.org/html/cr_baeo.htm).

Grigg, W. S., M. C. Daane, Y. Jin, and J. R. Campbell, *The Nation's Report Card: Reading 2002*, Washington, DC: National Center for Education Statistics, NCES 2003-521, 2003.

Grissmer, David, and Ann Flanagan, "Exploring Rapid Score Gains in Texas and North Carolina," Commissioned Paper, National Education Goals Panel, Washington, DC, 1998.

Grissmer, D. W., S. N. Kirby, M. Berends, and S. Williamson, *Student Achievement and the Changing American Family*, Santa Monica, CA: RAND Corporation, 1994.

Hamilton, Laura S., and Daniel M. Koretz, "Tests and Their Use in Test-Based Accountability Systems," in Laura S. Hamilton, Brian M. Stecher, and Stephen P. Klein, *Making Sense of Test-Based Accountability in Education*, Santa Monica, CA: RAND Corporation, MR-1554-EDU, 2002, pp. 13–49.

Hanushek, Eric, "Conclusions and Controversies About the Effectiveness of School Resources," *Economic Policy Review*, 4(1):11–27, 1998.

Hanushek, Eric, John Kain, and Steven Rivkin, "Teachers, Schools, and Academic Achievement," National Bureau of Economic Research, Working Paper No. 6691, 1998.

Hardy, Janet B., and Laurie Schwab Zabin, "Adolescent Pregnancy in an Urban Environment," Baltimore, MD, and Washington, DC: Urban and Schwarzenberg, and The Urban Institute, 1991.

Harvey, Lynn R., "1994 Michigan School Finance and Property Tax Reform," in *Increasing Understanding of Public Problems and Policies*, National Public Policy Education Conference, ERIC No. ED386341, 1995.

Hawkins, J. D., R. F. Catalano, R. Kosternman, R. Abbot, and K. G. Hill, "Preventing Adolescent Health-Risk Behaviors by Strengthening Protection During Childhood," *Archives of Pediatrics and Adolescent Medicine*, 153:226–334, 1999.

Henderson, Richard, "An Analysis of Selected School Finance Litigation and Its Impact upon State Education Legislation," *Journal of Education Finance*, 17(2):193–214, Fall 1991.

Henshaw, Stanley K., "Teenage Abortion, Birth, and Pregnancy Statistics by State, 1988," *Family Planning Perspectives*, 25(3):122–126, 1993.

Henshaw, Stanley K., "Teenage Abortion and Pregnancy Statistics by State, 1992," *Family Planning Perspectives*, 29(3):115–122, 1997.

Henshaw, Stanley K., "Special Report: U.S. Teen Pregnancy Statistics: With Comparative Statistics for Women Aged 20–24," 1999 (available at http://www.agi-usa.org/pubs/teen_preg_sr_0699.html; accessed August 20, 1999).

Henshaw, Stanley K., "U.S. Teenage Pregnancy Statistics with Comparative Statistics for Women Aged 20–24," The Alan Guttmacher Institute, 2001 (available at http://www.agi-usa.org/pubs/teen_preg_sr_0699.html).

Henshaw, Stanley K., and Dina J. Feivelson, "Teenage Abortion and Pregnancy Statistics by State, 1996," *Family Planning Perspectives*, 32(6):272–280, 2000.

Henshaw, Stanley K., and Jennifer Van Vort, "Teenage Abortion, Birth and Pregnancy Statistics: An Update," *Family Planning Perspectives*, 21(2):85–88, 1989.

Hofferth, Sandra L., "Social and Economic Consequences of Teenage Childbearing," in Cheryl D. Hayes (ed.), *Risking the Futures: Adolescent*

Sexuality, Pregnancy, and Childbearing, Washington, DC: National Academy Press, 1987.

Hotz, Joseph, S. McElroy, and S. Sanders, "The Impacts of Teenage Childbearing on the Mothers and the Consequences of Those Impacts for Government," in Rebecca A. Maynard (ed.), *Kids Having Kids: The Economic Costs and Social Consequences of Teen Pregnancy*, Washington, DC: Urban Institute Press, 1996, pp. 55–94.

Jennings, Wayne, Eric Premack, Andrew Adelmann, and Debra Solomon, *A Comparison of Charter School Legislation: Thirty-Three States and the District of Columbia Incorporating Legislative Changes Through October, 1998*, RPP International Report, 1998.

Jepsen, Christopher, and Steven Rivkin, *Class Size Reduction, Teacher Quality, and Academic Achievement in California Public Elementary Schools*, San Francisco, CA: Public Policy Institute of California, 2002.

Jerry, L., and A. Lutkus, *The Nation's Report Card: State Reading 2002, Report for California*, Washington, DC: National Center for Education Statistics, NCES 2003-526-CA, 2003.

Joint Committee to Develop a Master Plan for Education (Senator Dede Alpert, Chair; Assemblywomen Elaine Alquist and Virginia Strom-Martin, Co-Vice Chairs), http://www.sen.ca.gov/masterplan.

Kandel, Denise B., "On Processes of Peer Influences in Adolescent Drug Use: A Developmental Perspective," *Advances in Alcohol & Substance Abuse*, 4(3-4):139–163, 1985.

Kandel, Denise, Mark Davies, Daniel Karus, and Kazuo Yamaguchi, "The Consequences in Young Adulthood of Adolescent Drug Involvement," *Archives of General Psychiatry*, 43(8):746–754, 1986.

Kane, T. J., and D. O. Staiger, "Volatility in School Test Scores: Implications for Test-Based Accountability Systems," in D. Ravitch (ed.), *Brookings Papers on Education Policy 2002*, Washington, DC: Brookings Institution Press, 2002, pp. 235–283.

Kinnier, Richard, Arlene Metha, Jeffrey Okey, and Jeanmarie Keim, "Adolescent Substance Abuse and Psychological Health," *Journal of Alcohol and Drug Education*, 40(1):51–56, 1994.

Kirby, Douglas, "The Impact of Schools and School Programs upon Adolescent Sexual Behavior," *The Journal of Sex Research*, 39(1):27–33, February 2002.

Klein, Stephen, Laura S. Hamilton, Daniel McCaffrey, and Brian M. Stecher, "What Do Test Scores in Texas Tell Us?" Santa Monica, CA: RAND Corporation, Issue Paper IP-202, 2000.

Koretz, Daniel, and Sheila Barron, *The Validity of Gains in Scores on the Kentucky Instructional Results Information System (KIRIS)*, Santa Monica, CA: RAND Corporation, MR-1014-EDU, 1998.

Kozol, J., *Savage Inequalities: Children in America's Schools*, New York, NY: HarperCollins Publishers, 1991.

Krop, Cathy S., *The Finances of Education Governance Reforms in California*, Santa Monica, CA: RAND Corporation, RGSD-131, 1996.

Krueger, Alan, and Diane Whitmore, "The Effect of Attending a Small Class in the Early Grades on College-Test Taking and Middle School Test Results: Evidence from Project STAR," *The Economic Journal*, 111(468):1–28, 2001.

Le, Vi-Nhuan, and Stephen P. Klein, "Technical Criteria for Evaluating Tests," in L. S. Hamilton, B. M. Stecher, and S. P. Klein (eds.), *Making Sense of Test-Based Accountability in Education*, Santa Monica, CA: RAND Corporation, 2002, pp. 51–77.

Legislative Analyst's Office, "Source and Uses of K–12 Education Funding Growth: 1982–83 Through 1991–92," Sacramento, CA, August 1991.

Legislative Analyst's Office, "Analysis of the 2001–02 Budget Bill, Education Chapter," Sacramento, CA, February 2001a.

Legislative Analyst's Office, "A New Blueprint for California School Facility Finance," Sacramento, CA, May 1, 2001b.

Legislative Analyst's Office, "School Finance 2002–03," Sacramento, CA, November 2002 (available at http://www.lao.ca.gov).

Legislative Analyst's Office, "2003–04: Overview of the Governor's Budget," Sacramento, CA, January 15, 2003.

Levitt, Steven, and Lance Lochner, "The Determinants of Juvenile Crime," in Jon Gruber (ed.), *Risky Behavior by Youths: An Economic Analysis*, Chicago, IL: University of Chicago Press, 2002.

Lewis, A., et.al., *Wolves at the Schoolhouse Door: An Investigation of the Condition of Public School Buildings*, Washington, DC: Education Writers Association, 1989.

Livingston, Andrea, and John Wirt, "The Condition of Education in Brief 2003," Washington, DC: U.S. Department of Education, National Center for Education Statistics, NCES 2003-068, 2003.

Loewenstein, George, "Out of Control: Visceral Influences on Behavior," *Organizational Behavior and Human Decision Processes*, 65(3):272–292, 1996.

Martin, Joyce A., Melissa M. Park, and Paul D. Sutton, "Births: Preliminary Data for 2001," *National Vital Statistics Reports*, 50(10), 2002 (available at http://www.cdc.gov/nchs/products/pubs/pubd/nvsr/nvsr.htm; accessed October 17, 2004).

Mazzeo, John, J. E. Carlson, K. E. Voelkl, and A. D. Lutkus, *Increasing the Participation of Students with Special Needs in the NAEP: A Report on 1996 NAEP Research Activities*, Washington, DC: National Center for Education Statistics, 2000.

McLaughlin, Donald H., "Protecting State NAEP Trends from Changes in SD/LEP Inclusion Rates," Paper presented at the National Institute of Statistical Sciences Workshop on NAEP Inclusion Strategies, Research Triangle Park, NC, July 2000.

McLaughlin, Donald H., "Exclusions and Accommodations Affect State NAEP Gain Statistics: Mathematics, 1996 to 2000," Report to the NAEP Validity Studies Panel, American Institutes for Research, Palo Alto, CA, November 2001.

Meyer, Lori, Greg F. Orlofsky, Ronald A. Skinner, and Scott Spicer, "The State of the States," *Education Week*, 21(17):68–70, 2002.

Meyer, R. H., "Comments on Chapters Two, Three, and Four," in H. F. Ladd (ed.), *Holding Schools Accountable: Performance-Based Reform in Education*, Washington, DC: Brookings Institution, 1996, pp. 137–145.

Mijares, John, "Early Drug Use and Quits and Discharges Among Adolescent Males," *Journal of Socio-Economics*, 26(4):439–458, 1997.

Miller, Karen E., Jennifer E. Nelson, and Mary Naifeh, *Cross-State Data Compendium for the NAEP 1994 Grade 4 Reading Assessment*, Washington, DC: National Center for Education Statistics, 1995.

Moore, Kristin A., Brent C. Miller, Dana Glei, and Donna Ruane Morrison, *Adolescent Sex, Contraception, and Childbearing: A Review of Recent Research*, Washington, DC: Child Trends, June 1995.

Mullis, I. V. S., J. A. Dossey, E. H. Owen, and G. W. Phillips, *1992 Mathematics Report Card for the Nation and the States: Data from the National and Trial State Assessments*, Washington, DC: National Center for Education Statistics, 1993.

Murray, Sheila E., William N. Evans, and Robert M. Schwab, "Education Finance Reform and the Distribution of Education Resources," *American Economic Review*, 88(4):789–812, September 1998.

National Education Association, "Rankings and Estimates," various years.

National Research Council, *High Stakes: Testing for Tracking, Promotion and Graduation*, Washington, DC: National Academy Press, 1999.

National Telecommunications and Information Administration, "A Nation Online: How Americans Are Expanding Their Use of the Internet," Washington, DC, February 2002 (available at http://www.ntia.doc.gov/ntiahome/dn/index.html).

Nelson, Beryl, Paul Berman, John Ericson, Nancy Kamprath, Rebecca Perry, Debi Silverman, and Debra Solomon, *The State of Charter Schools 2000: Fourth-Year Report*, RPP International, 2000.

Nelson, F. Howard, "An Interstate Cost-of-Living Index," *Educational Evaluation and Policy Analysis*, 13:103–111, Spring 1991.

Nelson, F. Howard, Rachel Drown, and Jewell C. Gould, *Survey and Analysis of Teacher Salary Trends 2000*, Washington, DC: American Federation of Teachers, AFL-CIO, 2000.

O'Day, Jennifer, and Catherine Bitter, *Evaluation Study of the Immediate Intervention/Underperforming Schools Program and the High Achieving/Improving Schools Program of the Public Schools Accountability Act of 1999*, Washington, DC: American Institutes for Research, 2003.

Odden, Allan, "Class Size and Student Achievement: Research-Based Policy Alternatives," *Educational Evaluation and Policy Analysis*, 12 (2):213–227, 1990.

Odden, Allan R. (ed.), *Rethinking School Finance: An Agenda for the 1990s*, San Francisco, CA: Jossey-Bass Publishers, 1992.

O'Donoghue, Ted, and Matthew Rabin, "Doing It Now or Later," *American Economic Review*, 89(1):103–124, 1999.

Oettinger, Gerald S., "The Effects of Sex Education on Teen Sexual Activity and Teen Pregnancy," *Journal of Political Economy*, 107(3):606–644, 1999.

Picus, Lawrence, "Educational Governance in California: Defining State and Local Roles," in Jon Sostelie and Peter Richardson (eds.), *School Finance and California's Master Plan for Education*, San Francisco, CA: Public Policy Institute of California, 2001.

Postsecondary Education OPPORTUNITY, "Chance for College by Age 19 by State," September 18, 2002 (available at http:// www.postsecondary.org/archives/Reports/Spreadsheets/College19.htm; accessed November 17, 2004).

Postsecondary Education OPPORTUNITY, Topical Index, High School Graduation, n.d. (available at http://www.postsecondary.org/ti/ti_24.asp; accessed November 17, 2004).

Public Policy Institute of California, "Relationships Between Class Size Reduction, New Teachers, and Student Achievement," Research Brief, Issue 60, 2002.

Reese, Clyde M., L. Jerry, and N. Ballator, *NAEP 1996 Mathematics Report for California*, Washington, DC: National Center for Education Statistics, NCES 1997-974-CA, 1997.

Rouse, Cecilia, "School Reform in the 21st Century: A Look at the Effect of Class Size and School Vouchers on the Academic Achievement of Minority Students," Princeton University Industrial Relations Section, Working Paper 440, 2000.

Schnaiberg, Lynn, *A National Study of Charter Schools: Second-Year Report, 1998*, Washington, DC: Office of Educational Research and Improvement, U.S. Department of Education, 1998.

Schnaiberg, Lynn, *Charter Schools Struggle with Accountability: An Evaluation*, Washington, DC: Office of Educational Research and Improvement, U.S. Department of Education, 1998.

Senate Concurrent Resolution No. 29, Statutes and Amendments to the Codes, Chapter 43, filed with Secretary of State, May 27, 1999.

Shaughnessy, C.A., J. Nelson, and N. Norris, *NAEP 1996 Mathematics Cross State Data Compendium for the Grade 4 and Grade 8 Assessment*, Washington, DC: U.S. Department of Education, NCES-98-481, 1998.

Shields, Patrick M., Camille E. Esch, Daniel C. Humphrey, Marjorie E. Wechsler, Christopher M. Chang-Ross, Alix H. Gallagher, Roneeta Guha, Juliet D. Tiffany-Morales, and Katrina R. Woodworth, *The Status of the Teaching Profession 2003*, Santa Cruz, CA: Center for the Future of Teaching and Learning, 2003.

Silva, Fabio, and Jon Sonstelie, "Did Serrano Cause a Decline in School Spending?" *National Tax Journal*, 48(2):199–215, 1995.

Sims, David, "How Flexible Is Educational Production? Combination Classes and Class Size Reduction in California," Working Paper, 2003.

Slovacek, Simeon, Antony J. Kunnan, and Hae-Jin Kim, "California Charter Schools Serving Low-SES Students: An Analysis of the Academic Performance Index," Program Evaluation and Research Collaborative, 2002 (available at http://www.calstatela.edu/academic/ccoe/c_perc/rpt1.pdf).

Snyder, Thomas D., and Charlene M. Hoffman, *State Comparisons of Education Statistics: 1969–70 to 1993–94*, U.S. Department of Education, National Center for Education Statistics, Washington, DC, NCES 95-122, 1995.

Solomon, C., L. Jerry, and A. Lutkus, *The Nation's Report Card: State Mathematics 2000, Report for California*, Washington, DC: National Center for Education Statistics, NCES 2001-519-CA, 2001.

Sonstelie, Jon, Eric Brunner, and Kenneth Ardon, *For Better or For Worse? School Finance Reform in California*, San Francisco, CA: Public Policy Institute of California, February 2000.

Sonstelie, Jon, and Peter Richardson (eds.), *School Finance and California's Master Plan for Education*, San Francisco, CA: Public Policy Institute of California, June 2001.

State of California, Department of Finance, "California Public K–12 Enrollment and High School Graduate Projections by County, 2003 Series," Sacramento, CA, October 2003a.

State of California, Department of Finance, "California Public K–12 Enrollment Projections by Ethnicity, 2003 Series," Sacramento, CA, October 2003b.

State of California, Department of Finance, "Population Projections by Race/Ethnicity, Gender and Age for California and Its Counties 2000–2050," Sacramento, CA, May 2004.

Stecher, Brian M., "Consequences of Large-Scale, High-Stakes Testing on School and Classroom Practice," in Laura S. Hamilton, Brian M. Stecher, and Stephen P. Klein, *Making Sense of Test-Based Accountability in Education*, Santa Monica, CA: RAND Corporation, MR-1554-EDU, 2002.

Stecher, Brian M., and Jeremy Arkes, "Rewarding Schools Based on Gains: It's All in How You Calculate the Index and Set the Target," Santa Monica, CA: RAND Corporation, DRU-2532, 2001.

Stecher, Brian M., Sheila I. Barron, Tammi Chun, and Karen Ross, "The Effects of the Washington State Education Reform on Schools and Classrooms," Santa Monica, CA: RAND Corporation, DRU-2263-EDU, 2000.

Stecher, Brian M., and George Bohrnstedt (eds.), *Class Size Reduction in California: The 1998–99 Evaluation Findings*, Sacramento, CA: CSR Research Consortium, California Department of Education, 2000.

Stecher, Brian M., and George W. Bohrnstedt (eds.), *Class Size Reduction in California: Findings from 1999–2000 and 2000–2001*, Sacramento, CA: CSR Research Consortium, California Department of Education, 2002.

Stecher, Brian M., Laura S. Hamilton, and Gabriella Gonzalez, "Working Smarter to Leave No Child Behind: Practical Insights for School Leaders," Santa Monica, CA: RAND Corporation, WP-138-EDU, 2003.

Stecher, Brian M., Daniel F. McCaffrey, and Delia Bugliari, "The Relationship Between CSR Exposure and Achievement at the School-Level," Appendix B in George Borhnstedt and Brian M. Stecher (eds.), *What We Have Learned About Class Size Reduction in California*, Sacramento, CA: CSR Research Consortium, September 2002.

Towne, George, et al., "Michigan School Finance Reform, Analysis of the Enacted School Finance/Education Reform Package," Issue paper, ERIC No. ED394166, 1994.

2003 California Standardized Testing and Reporting (STAR) Program, http://star.cde.ca.gov/star2003/.

U.S. Census Bureau, Index of Population Estimates for States, http://www.census.gov/population/estimates/state/sasrh/.

U.S. Census Bureau, *Public Education Finances*, Washington, DC: Government Printing Office, various years.

U.S. Department of Education, *Goals 2000: A Progress Report*, Fall 1996.

U.S. Department of Education, National Center for Education Statistics, *Cross-State Data Compendium for the NAEP 1994 Grade 4 Reading Assessment: Findings from the Trial State Assessment in Reading of the National Assessment of Educational Progress*, Washington, DC: U.S. Government Printing Office, 1995a.

U.S. Department of Education, National Center for Education Statistics, *Private Schools in the United States: A Statistical Profile 1990–91*, Washington, DC: U.S. Government Printing Office, NCES 95-330, 1995b.

U.S. Department of Education, National Center for Education Statistics, *Conditions of America's Public School Facilities: 1999*, Washington, DC, NCES-2000-032, June 2000.

U.S. Department of Education, National Center for Education Statistics, *The Condition of Education 2003*, 2003 (available at http://nces.ed.gov/pubsearch/pubsinfo.asp?pubid=2003067, accessed January 2, 2004).

U.S. Department of Education, National Center for Education Statistics, *Digest of Education Statistics*, various years (available at http://nces.ed.gov/edstats/index.asp?gLevel=0&reqEdition=Prev, accessed October 14, 2004).

U.S. Department of Education, National Center for Education Statistics, National Assessment of Educational Progress Data, Results from NAEP's National and State Assessments, n.d. (available at http://www.nces.ed.gov/nationsreportcard/naepdata/, last updated October 31, 2003).

U.S. Department of Health and Human Services, Centers for Disease Control and Prevention, National Center for Health Statistics, National Vital Statistics System, n.d. (available at http://www.cdc.gov/nchs/data/nvsr/nvsr47/nvs47_26.pdf).

U.S. Department of Health and Human Services, Substance Abuse and Mental Health Services Administration, Office of Applied Studies, "National Household Survey on Drug Abuse, 1999," computer file (ICPSR version), Research Triangle Park, NC: Research Triangle Institute, 2001.

U.S. General Accounting Office, *School Facilities: Condition of America's Schools*, Washington, DC, GAO/HEHS-95-61, February 1995a.

U.S. General Accounting Office, *School Finance: Trends in U.S. Education Spending*, Washington, DC, GAO/HEHS-95-235, September 1995b.

U.S. General Accounting Office, *School Facilities: States' Financial and Technical Support Varies*, Washington, DC, GAO/HEHS-96-27, November 1995c.

U.S. General Accounting Office, *School Facilities: America's Schools Report Differing Conditions*, Washington, DC, GAO/HEHS-96-103, June 1996.

U.S. General Accounting Office, *School Facilities: Construction Expenditures Have Grown Significantly in Recent Years*, Washington, DC, GAO/HEHS-00-41, March 2002.

Ventura, Stephanie, T. J. Mathews, and Brady Hamilton, "Births to Teenagers in the United States, 1940–2000," *National Vital Statistics Reports*, 49(10), 2001 (available at http://www.cdc.gov/nchs/products/pubs/pubd/nvsr/nvsr.htm; accessed October 17, 2004).

Ventura, S. J., W. D. Mosher, S. C. Curtin, J. C. Abma, and S. Henshaw, "Trends in Pregnancy Rates for The United States, 1976–97: An Update," *National Vital Statistics Reports*, 49(4):Table 1, 2001 (available at http://www.cdc.gov/nchs/products/pubs/pubd/nvsr/nvsr.htm; accessed October 17, 2004).

Wilhelm, Tony, Delia Carmen, and Megan Reynolds, "Connecting Kids to Technology: Challenges and Opportunities," Kids Count Snapshot, Annie E. Casey Foundation, 2002 (available at http://www.aecf.org/publications/data/snapshot_ june2002.pdf).

Yamada, Tetsuji, Michael Kendix, and Tadashi Yamada, "The Impact of Alcohol Consumption and Marijuana Use on High School Graduation," *Health Economics*, 5:77–92, 1996.

Young, B. A., "Public School Student, Staff, and Graduate Counts by State: School Year 2000–01," Washington, DC: National Center for Education Statistics, NCES 2002-348, April 2002.